REFUGEE LIFEWORLDS

In the series *Asian American History and Culture*, edited by Cathy Schlund-Vials, Shelley Sang-Hee Lee, and Rick Bonus. Founding editor, Sucheng Chan; editors emeriti, David Palumbo-Liu, Michael Omi, K. Scott Wong, and Linda Trinh Võ

ALSO IN THIS SERIES:

A list of additional titles in this series appears at the back of this book.

REFUGEE
LIFEWORLDS

The Afterlife of the Cold War in Cambodia

Y-Dang Troeung

TEMPLE UNIVERSITY PRESS
Philadelphia • Rome • Tokyo

TEMPLE UNIVERSITY PRESS
Philadelphia, Pennsylvania 19122
tupress.temple.edu

The research and publication of this book was supported by the following: the UBC
Scholarly Publication Fund, the Peter Wall Institute for Advanced Research Wall Scholar
Grant, the Hong Kong RGC Early Career Scheme Grant, and the Social Sciences and
Humanities Research Council Postdoctoral Fellowship.

Library of Congress Cataloging-in-Publication Data

Names: Troeung, Y-Dang, 1980– author.
Title: Refugee lifeworlds : the afterlife of the Cold War in Cambodia /
  Y-Dang Troeung.
Other titles: Asian American history and culture.
Description: Philadelphia : Temple University Press, 2022. | Series: Asian
  american history and culture | Includes bibliographical references and
  index. | Summary: "Utilizing the concept of aphasia, this book
  demonstrates how Cambodian refugee narratives resist state violence and
  take head-on hegemonic discourses across popular and scholarly spaces
  that prop up colonial, imperial, capitalist, heteropatriarchal, and
  ableist formations of the Cold War in Cambodia"— Provided by publisher.
Identifiers: LCCN 2022006677 (print) | LCCN 2022006678 (ebook) | ISBN
  9781439921760 (cloth) | ISBN 9781439921777 (paperback) | ISBN
  9781439921784 (pdf)
Subjects: LCSH: Refugees—Cambodia—Social conditions. |
  Refugees—Cambodia—Psychology. | People with
  disabilities—Cambodia—Social conditions. | People with
  disabilities—Cambodia—Psychology. | Genocide—Cambodia—Psychological
  aspects. | Political atrocities—Cambodia—Psychological aspects. |
  Cambodia—History—Civil War, 1970–1975. | Cambodia—History—1975–1979.
Classification: LCC HV640.5.C35 T76 2022 (print) | LCC HV640.5.C35
  (ebook) | DDC 362.8709596—dc23/eng/20220608
LC record available at https://lccn.loc.gov/2022006677
LC ebook record available at https://lccn.loc.gov/2022006678

Printed in the United States of America

9 8 7 6 5 4 3 2 1

This book is dedicated to my family: Yok Troeung, Heung Troeung,

Meng Troeung, Pheng Troeung, Sophia Troeung, Christopher Patterson,

and Kai Basilio Troeung. And to all Cambodian people, with love.

Contents

Preface

A Genealogy of the Cold War in Cambodia

If the Cold War was a world-shaping experiment in global confrontation without direct military engagement, it was "cold" only in some parts of the world; in the "hot" battlegrounds of this war, such as Cambodia, the fires raged, the earth burned, and the people fled. In Cambodia, the U.S. military secretly dropped over 2.7 million tons of bombs on a neutral country that it was not officially at war with, bombing beyond officially declared boundaries, irrespective of the cost to life and the social consequences of institutional collapse. What happened in Cambodia, then (during the U.S. bombings) and afterward (during the Cambodian Genocide), was indeed a *collapse* in the most literal sense of a falling down or giving way of something—in this case, a complete break with, and reformation of, the existing societal structure and political order (see Fig. P.1).

Refugee Lifeworlds maps out a genealogy of the Cold War in Cambodia in response to my discomfort with scholarly approaches that often treat the refugee as a figure who comes into being only through arrival in the asylum state.[1] In the imaginaries of the Global North, the refugee becomes legible only when whiteness enters the frame as an adjudicator of the refugee's humanity. I have often observed my parents' puzzled faces when they were asked about the hardships of living in a *refugee camp*, as if their lives were blank slates before then. What they consider to be the most formative experiences of their lives took place well before their arrival in a refugee camp. Their lives in Canada today, over forty years since they left Cambodia, remain irrevocably shaped

Figure P.1 Aerial view of craters made by U.S. bombs, Kandal Province, Cambodia, November 14, 2014. (Kimlong Meng, CC BY-SA 4.0, via Wikimedia Commons.)

by experiences that took place long before, and well after, their entry into the frame of whiteness.

Refugee Lifeworlds begins by contending with what we might describe as Cambodia's problem of nomination. What do we call what happened in Cambodia in the twentieth century? The term "Cold War," Lisa Yoneyama explains in her book *Cold War Ruins*, generally refers to the "U.S.-Soviet confrontation, its globality, and the term's universalistic imaginary, as well as the Western hemispheric periodization of history" from 1945 to 1990.[2] Bracketed by the end of World War II and the fall of the Berlin Wall, the Cold War is typically remembered as a war defined by the absence of direct military fighting between the global superpowers. This normative western hemispheric periodization reflects, however, what Yoneyama has described as a "post–World War II, Cold War knowledge formation" that has relegated the account of the Cold War's regional manifestations to the space of silence and illegibility.[3] Cambodia was one such regional manifestation, yet there is little understanding of how Cambodian history is Cold War history, part of the memory of the world. In her book *A Violent Peace*, Christine Hong writes that "the political economy of Cold War U.S. military imperialism in Asia and the Pacific has demanded critical analysis—and an explanatory language—beyond that of existing paradigms."[4]

Rithy Panh, a key figure in this book whose voice has been at the center of Cambodia's artistic renaissance, has called for new paradigms in how we critically approach the afterlife of war and genocide in Cambodia. In his memoir, *The Elimination*, Panh writes: "No one can consider those crimes [in Cambodia] as a geographical peculiarity or historical oddity; on the contrary, the twentieth century reached its fulfilment in that place."[5] Fixating on the peculiarity or anomaly of Cambodia's tragedy implies, in Panh's words, "a license to disregard intellectual mistakes, moral mistakes, strategic mistakes," to "pass over the French protectorate; the American commitment to Lon Nol's regime; the implacable bombing."[6] To reckon with these mistakes, we need new analytics that illuminate how the Cold War transformed Cambodia into a "laboratory of ideology."[7] By insisting on the Cold War calculations that brought this laboratory into being, *Refugee Lifeworlds* aims to construct and animate a genealogy of the afterlife of the Cold War in Cambodia in the service of decolonial, antiwar, and abolitionist futures. There is no denying that a genocide took place in Cambodia from 1975 to 1979, despite the legal wrangling that continues to insist otherwise. There is also no denying that the Cambodian Genocide was a part of the Cold War in Cambodia.[8] But to speak of the genocide as an event separate from the calculations of empire that came before and after it enables an eclipsing of the *longue durée* of imperial violence.[9] To name Cambodia's tragedy as "the Killing Fields" or the "Cambodia self-genocide" enables a comforting myth for the West.[10] It is the myth that Cambodia's trauma was culturally endemic, foreseeable, and anomalous—a cultural dystopia apart from the world's making in the twentieth century. Repositioning Cambodia within the broader formation of the Cold War, however, reframes questions of international complicity and responsibility in ways that implicate us all.

This book thus engages the historical formation that I refer to as the "Cold War in Cambodia" and tracks how it continues to circulate with vivid intensity in the lifeworlds of Cambodian people decades later. As a study of the historical present, this book is a "genealogy" in Michel Foucault's sense of a transhistorical excavation of the relations of power that condition the contemporary moment. As Foucault reminds us, genealogy is less about restoring a "true" or complete history of *what actually happened* in the past and more about constructing a counterhistory that is necessarily partial and incomplete. A genealogy draws on an eclectic, vernacular, and anecdotal range of sources, what Foucault termed "subjugated knowledges," culled from the fragments of research, conversations, and other archival scraps that have traditionally been disqualified as unscientific and unauthoritative.[11] To construct a genealogy, as opposed to an "objective" history that appeals to "some arbitrary idea of what constitutes a true science and its objects," is to "emancipate historical knowledges from that subjection, to render them . . . capable of opposition and struggle against the coercion of a theoretical, unitary, formal and scientific discourse."[12] A genealogy of the Cold War in Cambodia must necessarily counter the standard systems of knowledge that strive to delimit the parameters of what can be said about this history and who is seen as a credible speaker. This genealogy seeks to excavate and animate the subjugated knowledges of Cambodian people and Cambodian refugees, a community that has scarcely been afforded the opportunity to claim ownership and authority over our own stories, even as we have so intimately lived them in our bodies, minds, nerves, and hearts.

Scholars may disagree on the exact dating of the Cold War in Cambodia from roughly 1970 to 1998, but I take my cue from the curation of the War Museum Cambodia that "offers visitors a unique and insightful view of the perils that Cambodia faced during the last 3 decades of the 20th century."[13] This museum tells a story of thirty years of "hot war" in Cambodia, not simply the genocide that took place over the period of four years.[14] I also take my cue from my parents' stories of the war that always begin in 1970. Cambodian people remember this period as "Lon Nol time," named after the Cambodian general who came to power through a U.S.-backed military coup that deposed Prince Norodom Sihanouk. Though frequently eclipsed in historical accounts by the violence of the genocide that came afterward, "Lon Nol time" (1970–1975) was a period marked by civil war, arbitrary disappearances, extrajudicial executions, U.S. economic warfare, and intense U.S. bombings.[15]

What the U.S. military euphemistically called "Operation Menu" (1969–1970) and "Operation Freedom Deal" (1970–1973) authorized the use of long-range B-52 aircraft to carpet-bomb the Cambodian border regions of the so-called Ho Chi Minh Trail. As a part of the "Vietnamization" strategy of U.S. president Richard Nixon—in partnership with his National Security Advisor Henry Kissinger—it was "believed, for reasons that remain obscure, that Cambodia was in some sense the 'key' to America's future strategy in Indo-China."[16] As the perceived key to the American military's triumph in the Vietnam War, the U.S. bombing of Cambodia was rationalized by Nixon and Kissinger as a means of rooting out North Vietnamese military supply lines in Cambodia. By dropping more bombs on Cambodia between 1965 and 1973 than the Allies dropped in *all* of World War II combined,[17] the U.S. military turned Cambodia into what historians Taylor Owen and Ben Kiernan describe as "one of the most heavily bombed countries in history—perhaps *the* most heavily bombed."[18]

My parents recall the daily sight of the military planes scanning, surveying, and photographing the Cambodian landscape from the skies above. They remember the deafening sound of U.S. fighter jets roaring across the skies. Fear and anticipation of the bombings became a part of their everyday lives for over five years. One day, my mother and father packed up their two children (my two brothers) and fled for shelter to a Buddhist temple complex, where they believed the bombs would not fall. When they were not running from the bombs, they were shielding themselves from the military cross fire between the Khmer Rouge army and the Lon Nol regime. Eventually, my family fled to Phnom Penh as refugees, along with hundreds of thousands of other internally displaced refugees. As Ros Kosal, narrator of the audio guide to Cambodia's Tuol Sleng Genocide Museum, explains, in the early 1970s, Phnom Penh swelled to a city of over three million refugees as people fled the U.S. bombings in the countryside: "More than half were refugees from battles between Khmer Rouge and Lon Nol forces, and also from the 8 years of American bombing of Cambodia. It was part of their war with Vietnam. In the U.S., bombing Cambodia was called the secret war. It was no secret here."[19] Like Ros Kosal and many other Cambodian people, I do not subscribe to the Euro-American legal-bureaucratic taxonomies that define the refugee category through an absolute inside/outside binary: that is, through the maintenance of a distinction between those who have been displaced by war within the borders of their own nation (internally displaced people) and those who have been forced across transnational borders to find legal asylum in a host nation (legitimate refugees). Those who ran from the U.S. bombs within the borders of Cambodia did not necessarily suffer more or less than those who fled across the Cambodian border. Ros Kosal draws attention not only to the disavowed history of refugee displacement *within* Cambodia but also to how this historical formation emerged in relation to the U.S. secret war. As Ma Vang writes about the secret war in Laos in her book *History on the Run*, "State secrets are not secret to refugees or those who survived the material violence enacted by policies of secrecy."[20] This lived refugee embodiment of the "open secret" of the U.S. war in Cambodia was evidenced in the entrepreneurial spirit of the Cambodian people who established the B-52 Café in the town of Pailin in 1973, cognizant of the catchy sound of "B-52" (ប៊ី-៥២) in Khmer (*be-har-pee*, which would sound like "be happy!"). Today, in Pailin, local people have reconstructed a new B-52 Café in homage to the original establishment, a satirical nod to the painful realities of the bombings as well as the missing legacies that the bombings left unresolved (see Fig. P.2).

The secret war in Cambodia afforded U.S. planners an opportunity to test the limits of a massive reliance on airpower, marking an early instance of

Figure P.2 B-52 Café, Pailin, Cambodia, 1973. (Courtesy of Colin Grafton. Photograph by Colin Grafton.)

what has been called the "new American way of bombing."[21] Like in neighboring Laos, where war was waged in secrecy, Cambodia's land and skies provided the foreign terrain wherein crucial elements of today's U.S. aerial military wars were tested and trialed.[22] As news of the secret bombing broke around the world, students at Kent State University in Ohio protested against the invasion of Cambodia, digging a shallow "grave" to bury a copy of the U.S. Constitution in symbolic defiance of Nixon's violation of the founding laws of the country.[23] Those who protested were labeled by the government as "unpatriotic communist sympathizers"—even as hundreds of these protesters were military veterans themselves.[24] In an unprecedented act of campus militarization, the Ohio National Guard entered Kent State University on May 4, 1970, and opened fire on unarmed student protesters, killing four. It was a day that "nearly broke America," and the shootings at Kent State marked a turning point in the antiwar movement.[25] "It is vitally important," however, as James A. Tyner and Mindy Farmer write in their book *Cambodia and Kent State*, "that future generations understand that alongside four deaths in Ohio, there were many hundreds of thousands of deaths in Cambodia."[26] The Kent State shootings should not serve as the necessary marker to make the U.S. killings of Cambodian people legible and meaningful to Western publics.

What would be the collateral aftermath of being one of the most heavily bombed countries in modern history? Who would pay the price of this damage for decades to come in catastrophic ways that perhaps even the U.S. military could not have foreseen in giving that flippant order to mobilize "Anything that flys [*sic*] on anything that moves"?[27] As the Cambodian Civil War wore on, the Khmer Rouge was able to rise in power by using the destruction and loss of life to recruit new followers to the regime's cause. Gathering up survivors of the U.S. bombings, Khmer Rouge leaders were known "to point to the skies to the American planes that were bombing, and say: there's your enemy."[28] From fewer than ten thousand cadres in 1969, the regime grew to over two hundred thousand cadres in 1973.[29] Though most of these recruits were young men, many Cambodian girls and women also voluntarily enlisted in the regime, propelled by the rumors that "the Khmer Rouge were fighting against the United States."[30] On April 17, 1975, Khmer Rouge troops stormed into the capital city of Phnom Penh and began to evacuate the entire city of nearly two million people, using the pretext of an impending U.S. bombing attack on the capital to convince citizens to leave their homes. Having already been made refugees multiple times over by years of U.S. bombing and civil war, Cambodian people were receptive to the rumor that evacuation was necessary. On this day, my parents packed up their belongings and set out with my two young brothers, not knowing that they would never return to their home again. What happened afterward is something that has haunted my mother her whole life, a jumble of hazy memories that she has mostly repressed but still blames herself for, believing that she, as the mother of two young children, should have taken the opportunity to evacuate her family from Cambodia in the last days of the civil war. As Cambodian people often say, "We had no idea what was about to happen, we could *never* have imagined." Seemingly overnight, Cambodian society was plunged into a dystopia that, in terms of the scale and intensity of violence inflicted by the state, rivals any work of dystopian fiction and by comparison might seem exaggerated or unrealistic to contemporary audiences.

Clad in black clothes and signature red-checkered scarfs (*krama*), the Khmer Rouge began rounding up and executing targeted groups of people. These groups included anyone affiliated with the monarchy, former government officials, members of the bourgeois class, artists, intellectuals, doctors, ethnic minorities, and any other suspected "enemies of the state." As Phnom Penh fell to the new regime, Western nations with a diplomatic presence in Cambodia, such as the United States, Britain, and France, barred the doors of their embassies from local people seeking asylum and orchestrated the evacuation of the foreign expatriate population. Scenes of white expatriates evacuating from the airport at the last minute, sometimes with a Cambodian child in tow, proliferated. Mixed-race Cambodian children watched helplessly, such as the

French Cambodian artist Séra (Ing Phousera), whose Cambodian father was forced out of the French embassy, never to be seen by his family again, while Séra, his siblings, and his French mother were granted asylum and evacuated to France.[31] Others like Sam Nakatsu, a mixed-race infant, were abandoned, alongside dozens of other Cambodian children, in an orphanage in Phnom Penh. Nakatsu and the orphans were taken to Canada House, a former hotel converted into a safe house by Canadian sisters Eloise and Anna Charet, who worked with the Canadian government to orchestrate an airlift of Cambodian children from Phnom Penh to Canada as refugees.[32]

For the Cambodian people, this period following Lon Nol time is referred to in Khmer as the time of *"a-Pot,"* a grammatical construction that translates to "Pol Pot time." Unfolding over three years, eight months, and twenty days,[33] Pol Pot time saw the death of over two million people, a quarter of the nation's population.[34] Metaphorically resetting the nation's clock to "Year Zero" to symbolize the dawn of a new deindustrialized era, Pol Pot became the official leader of the Communist Party of Kampuchea and the new nation of Democratic Kampuchea. The son of a farmer, Pol Pot (a nom de guerre that was short for "Political Potential") was a former teacher and a part of a small elite group of Cambodians educated in France in the 1950s. Pol Pot drew on Marxism-Leninism and Maoism to form his own brand of communist ideology—the ideology of Democratic Kampuchea—that was symbolized by the metaphor of the "wheel of history."[35] That life was expendable in the name of revolutionary progress was reflected in one of the regime's party slogans, which warned, "He who does not move forward fast enough will be crushed by the wheel of history."[36] Under the rule of Pol Pot, Cambodian people were subjected to repeated relocation, societal dissection, mass executions, torture, and forced labor. After walking for days from their homes, Cambodians, like my family, arrived in the countryside to work in labor communes from dusk until dawn, sustained by as little as two bowls of watered-down rice gruel a day. Taking inspiration from Mao Zedong's "Great Leap Forward," Pol Pot's "Super Great Leap Forward" was to become a massive experiment in human labor extraction as people worked to the point of exhaustion, illness, and death. The disposability of human life alongside the chronic hunger and illness that stunted the population functioned as the primary means through which the regime was able to suppress people's capacity for physical resistance or revolt. But as I later discuss, Cambodian people found other ways to resist—through emotional resistance and other undercurrents of rebellion.

Adding to the Khmer Rouge regime's efforts to eliminate all traces of the old prerevolutionary society, Democratic Kampuchea saw the destruction and ransacking of libraries, banks, schools, and hospitals. Western medicine was banned as the Khmer Rouge established its own "revolutionary" labs and hospitals. Eventually, as the regime became desperate to reproduce a population of cadres it could draw on for the front lines of the war against Vietnam, Cambodian women's reproductive capacities became a focal point of the regime's biopolitical tactics. Conscripted into marriages with Khmer Rouge cadres, many Cambodian women during Pol Pot time were compelled to participate in group wedding ceremonies orchestrated by the regime.[37] Some women, like one of my aunts, chose to commit suicide rather than submit to the transformation of her body into a vessel for biological reproduction.

Along with reordering Cambodia into a nationwide network of carceral labor, the Khmer Rouge established over three hundred sites of direct execution. The most infamous site was known as Tuol Sleng S-21 Security Center, run by Khmer Rouge leader Kaing Guek Eav (also known as "Duch").[38] At S-21, prisoners were subjected to a wide array of brutal interrogation methods designed to uncover their perceived ties to those deemed enemies of the regime: the monarchy, the previous government, the CIA, the Vietnamese government, and the KGB, among others. The activities at Tuol Sleng involved the compilation of thousands of prisoner dossiers, including mug shots, prisoner biographies, autobiographical confessions, and interrogation notes.

The file of Hout Bophana, sometimes referred to today as the "Anne Frank of Cambodia," continues to stand as one of the most complete of these dossiers. Hout Bophana's S-21 archive has drawn the attention of scholars such as Elizabeth Becker for its detailed portrait of this Cambodian woman who wrote love letters to her husband from S-21 alongside thousands of pages of false confessions.[39] The defiant gaze that emanates from Hout Bophana's S-21 mug shot has been a source of inspiration for many Cambodian films and artistic works. It is an image that has become emblematic of Cambodian people's quiet forms of rebellion and resistance during Pol Pot time. It is an image that inspired the creation of the Bophana Audiovisual Resource Center in Phnom Penh, established by Rithy Panh to document and preserve Cambodian history.[40] Including Hout Bophana, an estimated fourteen thousand to twenty thousand people were murdered at Tuol Sleng, with only a small number of inmates surviving their incarceration. Illustrating the regime's extreme paranoia, the majority of the people killed at Tuol Sleng in the later part of the revolution consisted of former Khmer Rouge cadres themselves, blurring the distinction between victims and perpetrators.[41] My mother's brother, Ching Kok Huor, a Cambodian foreign exchange student who had been studying engineering in the Soviet Union and who was a former chargé d'affaires at the Cambodian embassy in France, was rounded up at the Pochentong airport one day in 1976. Part of an infamous roundup of all the intellectuals and diplomats who had been studying abroad and tricked into coming back to Cambodia to help "rebuild the country" after decades of colonial and imperial destruction, my uncle, along with dozens of others, were secretly transferred directly from the airport tarmac to either S-21 or K-15 (a reeducation prison for returnees, intellectuals, and their families, located within the compound of the Khmer-Soviet Poly Technic Institute).

The archival records of my uncle's file, the subject of a CBC Radio Canada documentary I made in 2009, contain his prison mug shot and a description of his torture and death at the prison.[42] As the archives at Tuol Sleng have recently been fully digitized, it is likely that more details of my uncle's case will come to light in the future. At Tuol Sleng Genocide Museum, a team of researchers, including my dear friends Colin Grafton and Keiko Kitamura, continue to investigate my uncle's case file, uncovering new information about this enigmatic story with each passing month. In April 2021, the Tuol Sleng mug shots ignited controversy once again when U.S. media group *VICE* published an article featuring mug shots that had been colorized and digitally altered to show victims at Tuol Sleng smiling. While the artist claimed to be wanting to "humanize" the victims with this tactic, Cambodian people decried the indignity and *VICE* later apologized and removed the article.[43]

Initially, those executed at Tuol Sleng were taken to urban areas adjacent to the prison for burial in mass graves. As this practice became unsustainable for the regime, prisoners were transferred to an area about seventeen kilometers south of Phnom Penh known as "Choeung Ek." Here, at Choeung Ek, people were beaten to death by blunt force trauma to the head, and their bodies thrown into mass graves of up to 450 people and dissolved by the chemical DDT. At Choeung Ek, as many as three hundred prisoners, including some children, were killed in a day, and, after 1979, it was revealed that the site's 2.4 hectares of land consisted of 129 mass graves containing the remains of twenty thousand victims. Today, many of these skeletal remains are housed in a large Buddhist memorial stupa and cared for by local "keepers" at the site. What to do with the bones of the dead continues to be a source of tension among various interested parties, with some calling for the preservation of forensic evidence and others arguing for the cremation of the bones according to traditional rites.[44] In the words of tour guide Ros Kosal, the Choeung Ek Genocide memorial today stands as a "documentation for all of mankind" of the "dreadful things that happened from 75 to 79,"[45] yet, for many people, myself included, the shocking makeshift aesthetic of the site is a highly unsettling experience. Choeung Ek serves as a painful reminder of the global economic asymmetries of the post–Cold War "recovery" period wherein countries like Cambodia have little access to the "wealthy memory" required to erect elaborate and awe-inspiring memorials made of concrete and stone.[46] With every tourist who visits this site and leaves with nothing more than an interesting travel anecdote about having visited Cambodia's barbaric "Killing Fields" or about having "stood before the Killing Tree" (to quote from Maggie Nelson's memoir *The Argonauts* in reference to her mother's travel anecdote about Cambodia), our community's pain is subject to the indignity of violent spectacle over and over again.[47] Almost any time "Khmer Rouge," "Pol Pot," or just "Cambodia" is even slightly mentioned in popular media, our community's suffering is again enlisted as the ethical currency for the shoring up of white liberal personhood.

This suffering has also been politicized and instrumentalized by both the Left and Right alike, discounted either as a necessary loss in the name of realizing utopia or as an example of a self-made and culturally and racially derived dystopia in need of humanization. During the era of Democratic Kampuchea, many scholars and intellectuals, particularly in the United States and Europe, heard about what was happening in Cambodia and chose to champion the cause of the Khmer Rouge from afar.[48] The romanticization of Pol Pot's communist experiment by Western intellectuals came to be known as the "Standard Total Academic View on Cambodia" (STAV), which, as Cambodian political scientist Sophal Ear explains, "hoped for, more than anything, a socialist success story with all the romantic ingredients of peasants, fighting, imperialism, and revolution."[49] Proponents of the STAV aligned themselves with the Khmer Rouge, only to later disown their past alliances by claiming to be mistaken or uninformed. Tour groups such as the Sweden-Kampuchea Friendship Association, for instance, traveled to Cambodia, drawn by their previous sympathy "towards the Chinese Revolution and Mao Zedong."[50] Like those who marched in the streets of Paris waving Mao's *Little Red Book* in 1968, this delegation arrived in Democratic Kampuchea thinking they "had found something even better; a real egalitarian state, with no oppression, free of slavery."[51] Here, these Western tour groups encountered a staged reality, projections that met their illusions of a communist utopia. Adhering to the popular dictum, "you have to break some eggs to make an omelet,"[52] STAV supporters discounted Cambodian refugee testimonies as "unreliable tales told by refugees."[53] In hindsight, decades later, after millions of Cambodian deaths and irrefutable evidence of atrocities, many of those who once refused to see beyond Pol Pot's facade expressed regret at rushing to defend Democratic Kampuchea as the realization of an idealized communism. They lamented that they had once looked on Cambodia with a distorted orientalist gaze, seeing only what they wanted to see. "For my part in this," writes one member of the Swedish tour group who visited Cambodia in 1978,

"I am deeply sorry. But I can't turn back history."[54] While not necessarily stemming from malicious intent, the Cold War complicities of these intellectuals were not simply accidental, uninformed, or retrospectively justifiable; the STAV reflected the rigid commitment to unyielding ideological visions and agendas, at the expense of Cambodian lives. To this day, I regularly enter into disagreements with my Marxist-informed colleagues and friends, often white and male, about both the nature of leftist sympathy with the Khmer Rouge during the Cold War and the degree of forgiveness that should be accorded to someone like Noam Chomsky, in particular. My position these days is that I am no longer interested in centering figures like Chomsky in this conversation, whether he was or was not justified in his sympathy for the Khmer Rouge, a circular discourse that merely displaces the injury done to Cambodian lives once again.

When the borders of Cambodia closed from 1975 to 1979, the only other foreigners besides the tour groups allowed to travel to Democratic Kampuchea were Chinese engineers, sent over by Mao's regime to consult on Pol Pot's agricultural dam projects.[55] My father witnessed the betrayal felt by the ethnic Chinese in Cambodia, mostly Teochew people, who had once committed themselves to Mao's revolution, but who were not spared the cruelty of the Khmer Rouge. This picture of Cold War fraternity between Cambodia and China, the narrator of Rithy Panh's Oscar-nominated film *The Missing Picture* comments, "is not missing."[56] This comradeship left its traces in the grainy archive of Pol Pot's meeting with the Maoist regime's Gang of Four.[57] China's inspiration of the ideology of Democratic Kampuchea contributed to the loss of innumerable lives, both Cambodian and Chinese, yet tour groups who travel to Tuol Sleng from China today have little interest in learning about this history. Cambodian tour guides at Tuol Sleng adjust their historical scripts in order not to anger Chinese tourists: "They say, 'We [Cambodia and China] are friends now. Do not talk about the past.'"[58] In the dual State interests of forging ahead with renewed economic and military partnerships, the suffering of the past has remained unspeakable.

In January 1979, the army of the Socialist Republic of Vietnam invaded Cambodia and ousted the Khmer Rouge regime from power, marking the official end of the period of the Cambodian Genocide. The end of the genocide was far from the end of conflict and insecurity for those who had managed to survive, however. Writing about this period of the Vietnamese occupation, Michel Foucault, in one of his 1979 lectures, wrote that the Cambodian government had "massacred its people on a scale never before witnessed."[59] He continued, "The remaining population that survived was saved, of course, but finds itself under the domination of an army which has used a destructive and violent power."[60] The international community had an obligation, Foucault asserted, to oppose the state's biopolitical exercising of the "unconditional right of life and death," whether this took place during the U.S. intervention or the ensuing Communist takeovers.[61] The 1980s chapter of the Cold War in Cambodia thus saw Cambodian people struggling to process the suffering and loss they had just lived through while seeking asylum across national borders. In an interview about the history of Cambodian border camps, Rithy Panh articulates the emotional pain of Cambodian refugees during this period as a condition of suffering tied to the dispossession of land and spiritual essence. As Panh explains, "If we live in our land, no matter what our problems are, we have relatives and friends who can help us. We still have hope. But when it comes to living in a refugee camp, the only hope is to go to a third country, and it is still difficult after that. When they have children, they don't know their own identities."[62] To live as a Cambodian refugee in the border camps was to be stripped of what Cambodian people call *tuek-dey* (ទឹកដី), which literally translates to "water-land." *Tuek-dey*, however, is also expressive of a Khmer cosmology at the heart of Cambodian lifeworlds, an elemental essence that Cambodian people believe gives us life on Earth. "For Cambodians," Panh explains, "*tuek-dey* is not a simple word. . . . If we have no land, we will wander. Like [Cambodian refugees say], 'I'm like a floating weed carried off by the current. With no roots.'"[63] Forced out of their homeland by war, genocide, famine, and ongoing insecurity, Cambodian refugees were left with no other choice but to confront the reality of a future without *tuek-dey*.

Many of those refugees who were deemed the "lucky ones" made it to the refugee camp known as Khao-I-Dang (KID), the place of my birth and my namesake (see Fig. P.3). Expanding to a population of over one hundred thirty thousand people in 1980, KID, by comparison to other border refugee camps, was known for being relatively better resourced, less susceptible to militia attacks, and less overrun by infectious disease epidemics such as outbreaks of dengue fever, cholera, and malaria. Designed for semipermanent settlement, KID is remembered by Cambodian refugees and humanitarian workers as a place marked by intervals of both joy and excruciating loss.[64] My mother and father recall the prisonlike enclosure of the camp, the lack of water, the interminable boredom of camp life, and the stories about the rape of Cambodian women and girls by Thai soldiers. They also remember the anguish and guilt they felt at "abandoning" the family and friends they had left behind in Cambodia, loved ones left to fend for themselves in postwar conditions of utter insufficiency and foreign occupation by the Vietnamese military. Ten years after the camp was established, the atmosphere at KID

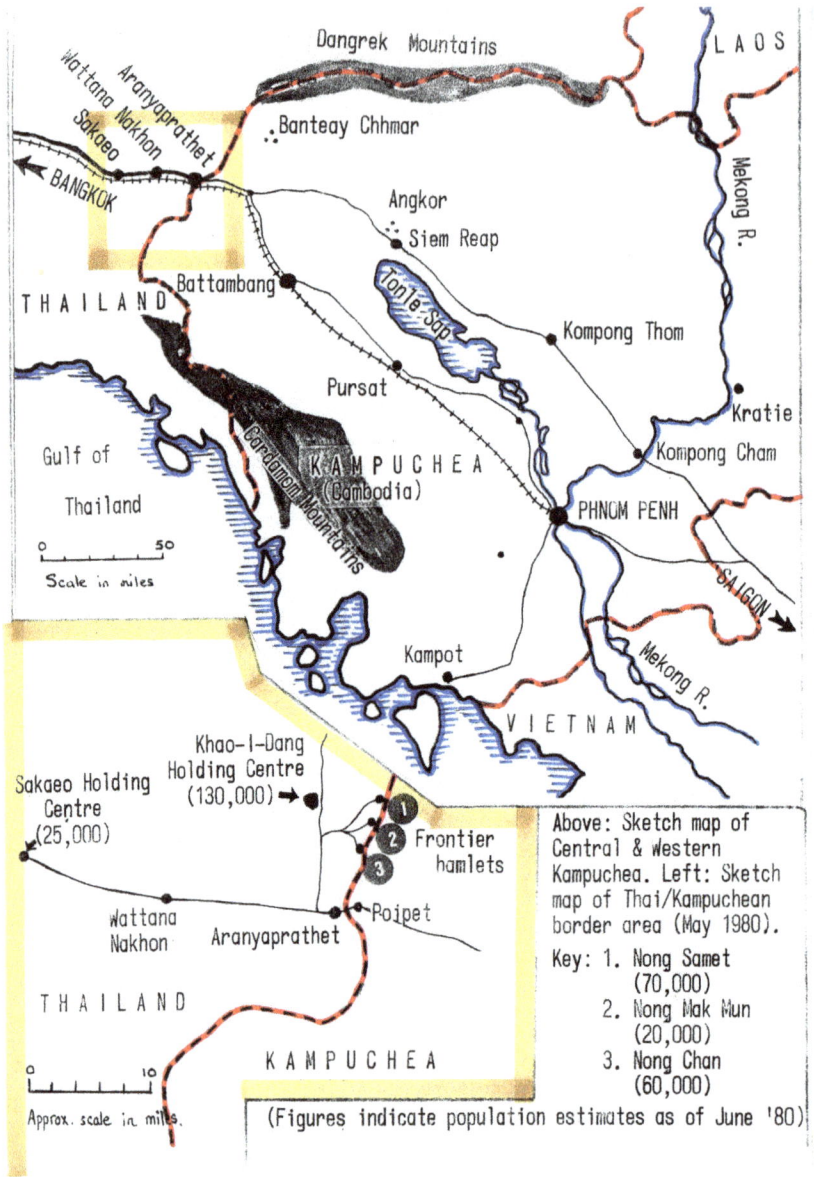

Figure P.3 Map of Cambodian border camps, population of KID is 130,000 in June 1980. (Courtesy of Colin Grafton. Hand-drawn by Colin Grafton.)

worsened considerably as refugees who had been lingering in limbo for over a decade became hopeless and desperate. Like in other Cambodian border refugee camps such as Site 2 and Sa Kaeo, Cambodian refugees "were desperate and felt helpless to do anything. After waking up, they sat, waited until night, and went back to sleep. They did this repeatedly every day. Their lives seemed meaningless. Thus gradual despair prompted them to commit suicide."[65] Life in a refugee camp was a structurally debilitating and dehumanizing experience—not a "free ride" to the West or a "lucky," enviable position.

Meanwhile, in Cambodia, the war raged on and the country entered into a stage of widespread famine resulting in part from Western sanctions that prevented foreign aid from reaching Cambodia's interior. Propelled by the rumors of humanitarian aid at the Thai border camps, thousands of Cambodian people walked or traveled by oxcarts to pick up the stockpiles of rations that could not reach the interior. By 1979, these movements materialized in what came to be called the "Cambodian land bridge," a human network of refugee rice and seed distribution[66] (see Fig. P.4). Women, some with babies and small children in tow, carried bags of rice on their head while walking across miles and miles of dangerous terrain. They brought this food back to Cambodia to feed their starving families and to avert more famine. While the land bridge saw a two-way human flow of refugees, over six hundred thousand Cambodian refugees, like my family, fled overland to the Thai border camps in search of resettlement in an asylum country. Along the way, many refugees were stopped and prevented from going any further at Vietnamese military checkpoints, captured as hostages by the Khmer Rouge, or fired on by Thai soldiers guarding the border. Other refugees, like my aunt's family, trekked through the dangerous Dangarek Mountains path. My aunt, who lives in Australia today, has vivid memories of her younger brother carrying their frail and elderly mother on his back at various points during this excruciating journey. She remembers the severe dehydration they endured, and how refugees warned each other to stay away from the ponds and lakes lined with landmine traps. Forced to turn back from the Thai border, my aunt's family found another escape route out of Cambodia via Vietnam and then eventually on to Australia.

Cambodian people commonly associate the 1990s chapter of the Cold War in Cambodia as a time of transition, but one that was fragile at best. The 1990s were characterized by the presence of the United Nations Transitional Authority in Cambodia (UNTAC) and the first conversations about the establishment of an official tribunal to prosecute Khmer Rouge leaders. While these mechanisms have been hailed by the West as institutions of humanitarian rescue, others remark that the peace process in Cambodia unraveled in the late 1990s, and, correspondingly, "UNTAC dropped out of sight from the

Figure P.4 The Cambodian land bridge. Cambodian women carry bags of rice from the border camps back to Cambodia. (Commissioned art by Ulrike Zöllner, 2021.)

UN inventory of success stories."[67] Before he could be brought to trial in any official way, Pol Pot died in 1998, reportedly from heart failure at his home in Anlong Veng Province. The Cold War in Cambodia is typically seen as coming to an official end in 1998, with Pol Pot's death and the conclusion of three decades of war that involved the cessation of military fighting, the first general election in Cambodia, and the dissolution of the Khmer Rouge. This same year, Hun Sen, a former low-level Khmer Rouge cadre himself, came to power. He began his role as prime minister asserting that Cambodian people "should dig a hole and bury the past," that they should "look ahead to the 21st century with a clean slate."[68] Set against the U.S. government's ongoing disavowal of its own war crimes during the U.S. bombing of Cambodia, Hun Sen's call to erase the memory of the Khmer Rouge regime's genocidal past reflects what Cathy J. Schlund-Vials has called the "Cambodian syndrome"—"a transnational set of amnesiac politics revealed through hegemonic modes of public policy and memory."[69] The Cambodian syndrome, Schlund-Vials argues, inflects the post–Cold War politics of both the U.S. imperial state and the Cambodian authoritarian state—two regimes that engage in selective processes of remembering and forgetting aspects of the Cold War in Cambodia in order to obfuscate their own culpabilities.

The mechanisms of transitional justice in Cambodia have not been exempt from the politics of the Cambodian syndrome. On July 26, 2010, the Extraordinary Chambers in the Courts of Cambodia (ECCC) convicted the first Khmer Rouge leader, Kaing Guek Eav for crimes against humanity. From its inception to its conclusion in 2018, scholars have importantly questioned the value of the tribunal within the broader paradigm of transitional justice in the Global South. Some have argued that the trials were a necessary step in countering decades of impunity and finally bringing the Khmer Rouge to justice;[70] others have argued the trials benefited ordinary Cambodian people *the least* and that justice provided in a purely legalistic, state-sanctioned framework denied the "culturally-specific models, rooted in the desires of the Cambodian people."[71] Surveys of public opinion showed that the majority of Cambodians were in favor of the tribunal, motivated out of a desire not necessarily for retributive justice but rather for answers to difficult existential questions about what had happened.[72] Kaing Guek Eav's conviction in 2010 was followed by the guilty verdict against Nuon Chea and Khieu Samphan in June 2014, a combined case described as the "largest and most complicated prosecution since Nuremberg in 1945."[73] I recall the experience of sitting in the ECCC court auditorium on this day of the verdict. I clutched my partner's hand tightly, tears streaming down my face uncontrollably, as the historical account was read out loud. Despite my mixed feelings about the tribunal (how could the conviction of a handful of Khmer Rouge leaders possibly make amends for the past?), there was a palpable weight in the air about what this day represented for survivors. The significance of this day for Cambodian people gathered inside and outside the auditorium was undeniable. The verdict meant something affective and intangible for Cambodian people. It meant something for my mother, who was following the news from her home in Canada, to see if her brother's S-21 executioner would finally be held accountable for his crimes. It meant something for me to hear the crimes that had been committed set down in words.

The battle for the legal designation of the term "genocide" continues to be fought by both Cambodian people and the international community. On November 16, 2018, the ECCC recognized for the first time that the crime of "genocide" had taken place in Cambodia from 1975 to 1979. This verdict, however, did *not* acknowledge that the Khmer people, the vast majority of the victims of the Khmer Rouge, had suffered a genocide. As Cambodian people have pointed out, there is a perverse absurdity in declaring the crime of genocide for some victims but not for others, as ethnic minorities such as the Cham and the Vietnamese did not necessarily suffer more or less than the ethnic Khmers.[74] According to Gayatri Spivak, "Evidentiary detail [must] be accumulated to decide if a situation, past and present, qualifies as 'genocide.' Such decisions are important. The law demands that 'cases' be constructed before action can be taken. But they do not bring closure. Because the effort to establish a name becomes all-consuming, the fact of what remains after naming is ignored."[75] While the ECCC verdicts have been meaningful for Cambodian people at individual and personal levels, the tribunal has illustrated what Lisa Yoneyama calls the "predicament of transitional justice"— the requirement of a subject to avail herself to "juridical, legislative, and other processes to be reckoned as a legitimate speaking subject."[76] In the end, the ECCC cost over $300 million dollars and "took longer to convict three defendants than it did for the United States, England, and France to try nearly 5,000 war criminals after World War II."[77] In this way, the case of Cambodia's redress movement reveals more than just the *predicament* of transitional justice: It highlights a spectacular failure of post-1990s redress culture that continues to be underwritten by universalist assumptions and uninterrogated questions about who ultimately benefits from transitional justice. In Cambodia, this process has bolstered an entire legal-humanitarian-academic industry (NGOs, tribunal lawyers, judges, interns, volunteers, expatriates), while Cambodian people are still left grieving with open wounds. As the United States remains one of the ECCC's biggest supporters, contributing millions of dollars to the tribunal with the aim of prosecuting the perpetrators responsible for the Cambodian Genocide, America's own complicity endures as a site of impermissible reckoning and unredressed injury.

For all that Cambodia's Cold War history (and my own familial story within it) has taught me about life and death at the end of the world—materially, existentially, spiritually, and philosophically—Cambodia has, for the most part, been irrelevant as a site of meaning and theory in the "great" scholarly treatises of the twentieth and twenty-first century. In his book *Asia as Method*, Taiwan-based cultural studies scholar Kuan-Hsing Chen asks why theory and philosophy have never been seen as emanating *from* Asia but are always framed as originating from the West *for* Asia. According to Chen, the Cold War relegated many countries in Asia to the status of U.S. subempires (garrison states for U.S. military buildup in the Asia Pacific) and established America as the dominant cultural and intellectual reference point for these nations. As a result, Chen argues, "useful ways of understanding our own societies have lain dormant."[78] Chen's metaphor of dormancy is intriguing here, given the themes of Cambodian people's vernacular articulation of resistance to the Khmer Rouge through idioms of planting, rooting, and regeneration that I discuss later in the Introduction. Calling for a rethinking of Cold War frameworks that privilege the West, Chen asserts a mode of strategic regionalism that he calls "Asia as method": the use of "Asia as an imaginary anchoring point [that] can allow societies in Asia to become one another's reference points, so that the understanding of the self can be transformed, and subjectivity rebuilt."[79] On the other side of the Pacific, in the United States, Jodi Kim, in her book *Ends of Empire*, argues that the Cold War persists as a structure of feeling and an unfinished knowledge project that "exceeds and outlives its historical eventness."[80] This unfinished knowledge formation— what Lisa Yoneyama describes as a set of "transwar, interimperial, and transnational entanglements"—continues to exert its force and its influence through intertwined modes of economic relations, transitional justice mechanisms, military interventions, everyday speech acts, and cultural and popular imaginaries.[81] These foundational studies have informed my understanding of the transpacific Cold War formation and its continued presence in the lives of Cambodian people today.

And yet, I have noticed the repeated absence of Cambodia in these discussions of the Cold War.[82] Among the scholarly works that adopt a comparative transpacific approach, a pattern emerges.[83] Without seeming to promote a simplistic call for demographic expansion, it is important to ask why Cambodia has so consistently been passed over as a site of analysis, despite the view among many historians that the hot fighting in Cambodia represented "the Cold War era's darkest chapter."[84] As Cambodian American scholar Khatharya Um explains in her book *From the Land of Shadows,* "Even in a century of mass atrocities, the Cambodian experience under the Khmer Rouge (1975–1979) stands out as one of the most extreme and traumatic instances in human history."[85] The recognition of the scale and intensity of this violence, however, has not translated into a critical mass of knowledge production by and for Cambodian people.

This Preface has mapped out a genealogy of the Cold War in Cambodia to highlight Cambodia's specificity as a site of unredressed violence in broader narratives of the Cold War, but this genealogy is one that expressly seeks to resist what Alexander Weheliye describes as the "idiom of exception."[86] In his book *Habeas Viscus,* Weheliye cautions scholars against designating some categories of suffering as more exceptional than others. Instead, he affirms the need to see political violence as a part of a long genealogy of racial assemblages that adjudicate "who is deserving of personhood and who is not (habeas)."[87] Like Weheliye, I am inclined toward a critical method that attends to the everyday forms of subjection and ongoing crises that mark the bodies of racialized people in ways that cannot be relegated to a distant or recent past.

Today, it is not uncommon to hear references to the "Cambodian precedent" in discussions about the nature of the contemporary conflicts in the

Greater Middle East. To what extent do past wars become legible and griev-able only insofar as they offer "lessons" for the contemporary moment? And to what degree is it even possible to cite Cambodia as a meaningful lesson for the present when we have yet to look seriously at the example itself, on its own terms? Such logics of naming precedents and the unprecedented forecloses an understanding, in Denise Ferreira da Silva's words, of how the assemblage of global capital that produces the global displaced is sustained by the "racial figure of the human" that "allows the demarcation of who falls on either side of the law, namely the protective and the punitive."[88] The "refugee lessons of the past" reasoning also relies on liberal positivist assumptions of enlighten-ment progress—what Weheliye calls a "liberal notion of wounding"—which assumes that "suffering must always follow the path of wounded attachments in search of recognition from the liberal state."[89] Some wars that we think are over are merely on hold, in a lull. The afterlife of one war bleeds into and merges with the afterlife of another, forming an entangled web of death, injury, loss, and heartbreak for victims and perpetrators alike, albeit asym-metrically.[90]

Acknowledgments

With deepest gratitude to all those who have helped me carry the weight of this book for so long. I hold your names in my heart, always. អរគុណច្រើន. Thank you, especially to Christopher, my soulmate and lifeline, without whom this book would never have been published.

REFUGEE LIFEWORLDS

Introduction

On War, Disability, and Refugee Life

Throughout my life, I have heard my mother tell and retell the story of my birth. In 1979, my mother, father, and two young brothers escaped from Cambodia, barely surviving after living through four years of deprivation under the rule of the Khmer Rouge. They made it to a refugee camp called Chumrum Thmei (New Camp), located on the Cambodian side of the border. The genocide was over, but the war continued among political factions. Every day, a Red Cross bus arrived in the morning to transport a caravan of people across the border. When the bus arrived on one particular morning, my parents were determined to get on it. They sensed an imminent danger and knew the time had come to pick up and leave, yet again. In a crowd of refugees pushing forward, they jostled in front of the bus in hopes of being selected. Knowing the sick and the pregnant were being given priority, my mother showed her eight-months-pregnant belly to the Red Cross workers and managed to secure a spot for our family.

After a sixteen-hour journey, the bus arrived at Khao-I-Dang Holding Center, a sprawling camp inhabited by over one hundred thirty thousand people. Soon after they got off the bus, my mother and father heard the news about the attack on Chumrum Thmei: The night before, just after my family had boarded the Red Cross bus, Khmer Rouge soldiers arrived at the camp without warning. They burned the camp to the ground, turning it to nothing but rubble and ash. Everyone my mother and father knew at that camp was killed, captured, or subjected to worse horrors. It shamed them to marvel at their luck in making it out yet again, but they felt as though they had crossed into a new life in reaching Khao-I-Dang.

When my mother would tell this story to people when I was growing up, she liked to emphasize the part about my presence in her womb. "I think it is because of Y-Dang, because I was pregnant with her. That's why we got lucky." In Khmer, giving birth is referred to as chlong tonle (ឆ្លង ទន្លេ) meaning to "cross a river."

My mother gave birth to me in Khao-I-Dang (เขาอีไล) about one month after our arrival there. With no real doctors, hospitals, or medicine, my mother labored for hours to bring me into this world. She remembers how my aunt was the person who cut my umbilical cord, the severed tether that meant I had passed through the difficult journey into life. In Thai, Khao (เขา) means mountain. I-Dang (อีไล) is the name of the mountain near the camp. The camp takes the name of the mountain. Khao-I-Dang. Nickname: KID. My mother and father chose the name I-Dang for me. On the refugee papers, my name was transliterated from Thai to English as Y-Dang. Y-Dang Troeung. In English, my name is pronounced e-dang trung. Y-Dang Troeung. How heavy it has been to carry this with me. And yet, this name (張依蘭; ប្រទ្បងអ៊ីជាង; Y-Dang Troeung), mom and dad always remind me, carries the memory of our multiple crossings.

*R*efugee Lifeworlds is a book about refugee life in the aftermath of the Cold War in Cambodia; it scrutinizes this topic from a specific angle. As in Figure I.1, taken in the refugee camp where I was born, this angle extends up from the ground of Cambodian refugee history. In the background, the mountains of Khao-I-Dang loom, forming a picturesque backdrop for six refugees (my mother, me, an unknown girl, and three other members of my extended family). A story of pain subtends and saturates this image—death, illness, disappearance, starvation, forced marriage, child loss, and so much more. But what is pictured here is not a portrait of suffering. It is an image of serendipitous reencounter and reconstituted, ephemeral family—of a mother's fleeting instance of joy born out of a chance encounter with another Cambodian refugee wielding a Polaroid camera. What mother would not want a photo—at least one photo—of her new baby in that fragile first year? From this vantage point of fragmented family history, I set out in this book to explore how the Cambodian refugee archive offers alternative ways of knowing, sensing, and imagining the refugee afterlives of war.

In places such as Cambodia, where the archive has been shattered and is still in the process of being restored and rebuilt, conventional scholarly methods do not suffice. For refugee-scholars, such as myself, it is important

Figure I.1 My mother holding me at nine months of age with cousins at Khao-I-Dang (KID) Holding Centre, Thailand, September 1, 1980 (person second-to-left unknown). (Courtesy of the Troeung family. Photo credit unknown.)

to honor and respect the knowledge that has been passed down to us by our families and community. Some of these stories that we carry are never meant to be heard outside of the family or the community, while some others, if curated with care, might begin to genuinely move and circulate in the world with the force of transformation. It is a delicate ground that we must carefully navigate. Those of us in the 1.5 or second generation of the Cambodia diaspora, like myself, hold the knowledge that just a few decades ago, our families lived through a war and genocide that the world scarcely remembers. Cambodian American author Monica Sok has written about the kind of struggles with language that we grapple with as the children of Cambodian survivors: "As a poet," Sok writes, "I'm afraid of misrepresenting my family's stories, the general history as well—though I believe the risk of going there is greater than fear. A big part of me is afraid of perpetuating the brutality through language."[1] Channeling Audre Lorde's assertion that "we can learn to work and speak when we are afraid in the same way we have learned to work and speak when we are tired," Sok affirms, in the end, the importance of "going toward that silence" as a means of transforming what terrifies and immobilizes her.[2] Like Lorde and Sok, I also believe in the risk of going toward that space of fear and silence. But I have also struggled with the process of writing and rewriting draft after draft of my book in a cycle of fury, depression, exhaustion, illness, self-doubt, inspiration, depression, and inspiration again. We labor tirelessly in the hope and fear of getting it "right," realizing only in hindsight that this goal is impossible. We supposedly live with the imprint of epigenetic trauma in our genes. We fear passing it on to our children. We know intimately what it is like to live our lives with a kind of debilitating silence, an aphasia, coupled with an ever-present knowledge that carrying our silence for too long will shatter us or, to use Lorde's metaphor, "choke us" from within. But we also know something else: that what we carry cannot be reduced to a defective history, psychology, or genetic profile; that it is possible to speak through silence, to use the pieces of our fragmented past to remake new worlds.

To this end, *Refugee Lifeworlds* interrupts the conventional expectations of scholarly writing and experiments with a method of autotheory that melds critical theory, autobiography, and textual analysis. A term popularized with the publication of Maggie Nelson's *The Argonauts*, "autotheory," according to Lauren Fournier, is the integration of the autobiographical self "with philosophy or theory, often in ways that are direct, performative, or self-aware."[3] Autotheory is the inscription of the self into one's scholarship and theoretical pursuits, a mode of writing that intentionally disrupts the expectations of the "distanced" and "objective" scholar via their object of study. It entails turning toward, not away from, our own lived experiences of colonialism, race, gender, refuge-seeking, survival, and family inheritance as sources of knowledge. As Barbara Christian influentially stated in 1988, people of color have always theorized, "but in forms quite different from the Western form of abstract logic."[4] What constitutes "theory" must always be responsive and responsible to the shifting material and geopolitical conditions and crises of any given time and place, since, for too long, "theory" has operated as "a commodity that helps determine whether we are hired or promoted in academic institutions—worse, whether we are heard at all."[5] As Ocean Vuong, author of the critically acclaimed novel *On Earth We're Briefly Gorgeous*, asserts, "A writer of color does not arrive at the literary table, as is often believed, *in spite* their geographical and cultural roots, but *because* of them."[6] Viewing his "origins" as a rich and creative foundation to his artistic praxis, Vuong gives value to the (queer) refugee's epistemic standpoint as a creative force. While not something to be seen as exceptional or privileged in any way, this refugee lens on the world is an opening rather than a shackling of the imagination.[7]

The racialized gendered self's experience as a foundation rather than a barrier to theory marks a long genealogy of autotheory by Indigenous and feminist writers and writers of color.[8] For writers of color, autotheory often emerges out of the need to write the self in response to the emotions of rage, anger, and madness that percolate within but that are made from without.

Autotheory offers a lifeline toward other people of color and other allies with whom we can safely share the space of negation, forging alternative futures together, without hurtling toward self-annihilation. As Cathy Park Hong asserts in her book of autotheory, *Minor Feelings*, we write because we "don't want to be left stranded in [the] rage" that accrues from living in a system of pervasive racial violence.[9] In order to write so that we do not lose ourselves in what Frantz Fanon called the "infernal circle" in our minds,[10] every chapter of this book, including this Introduction, is bookended by autotheoretical and curated family stories—fragments, anecdotes, sketches, vignettes—as a way of approaching that space of silence, where historical, theoretical, and scholarly languages have failed to reach.

Refugee Lifeworlds

The anecdotes that help me knit together the complex fabric of this book emerge from the texture and temporalities of refugee life as embodied and inherited experience. The category of the "refugee" is undoubtedly a flawed and limited term, one that emerges from liberal imperial technologies of governance designed to police the boundaries of when, how, and who is granted asylum and thus accorded legibility by the settler-colonial nation-state. As I have already alluded to in the Preface, in these legal-bureaucratic lexicons, the refugee is defined as a person who is outside of his or her country of origin owing to a "well-founded fear of being persecuted because of his or her race, religion, nationality, membership of a particular social group or political opinion."[11] As an idiom of administrative power, a refugee is situated within a continuum of displaced positionalities, such as an internally displaced person, an asylum seeker, a migrant, and an undocumented person, all of which depend on the upholding of the illegitimate nation-state border itself. Moreover, the descriptor of "refugee" rarely emerges from the lives and vocabularies of displaced peoples themselves. It does not describe the refugee's own ontology but rather names their function within a universalized idiom of human rights. The question of "who is a refugee" has been discussed at length by scholars, and so it is not my goal to rehearse those debates of taxonomy here.[12]

Instead, I explore in this book the conditions of possibility that the category of the refugee enables for those of us who have been named and disciplined by this label and thus by the state. We are not refugees because we ever wanted to be. Rather, we carry this label because it has been foisted on us over and over again, shaping and directing our routes and trajectories, our legibility within the settler-colonial nation-state, and the parameters of what is permissible or impermissible for us to speak about. In Canada, the

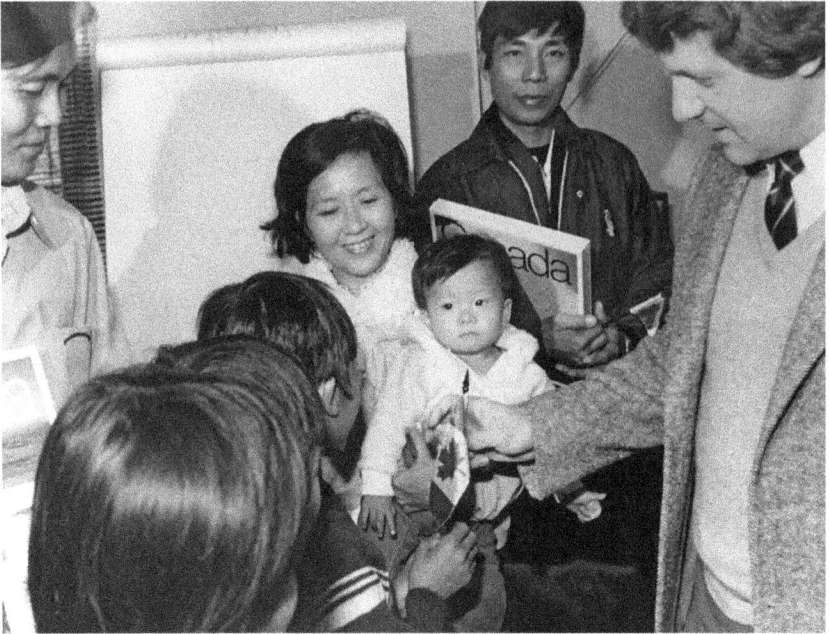

Figure I.2 Y-Dang (eleven months old) waves a Canadian flag for the camera as Canadian Minister of Citizenship and Immigration Lloyd Axworthy welcomes Cambodian refugees to Canada in 1980 in a government arranged photo op. (Courtesy of the Troeung family. Photo credit unknown.)

figure of the refugee has played a particularly important role in the nation's structure of exaltation, deployed to the detriment of other minority groups in Canada, including Black and Indigenous peoples, who are persistently cast as "the undeserving poor" in opposition to the "poor deserving Asian refugee." I have witnessed firsthand the Canadian state's exaltation of my own "refugee image" for the consolidation and shoring up of white liberal multiculturalism. Arriving in Canada as the designated "last" refugee of the Canadian government's Special Indochinese Refugee Program in the 1980s, I became a poster child for this program[13] (see Fig. I.2). Of course, anyone in my position would rather be "saved" than left behind to die in a genocide or refugee camp, but the question of my gratitude or ingratitude is not the point. Such images of the rescued refugee cast the refugee as an inspiration, a model of determination, a "minor anecdote" in the story of Canadian exceptionalism. Like the long history of the media and the medical industry's parading of disabled children as poster children for medical and scientific fundraising, what critical disability studies scholar and activist Eli Clare calls the iconography of "hope in motion," the refugee poster child also embodies the nation's

Figure I.3 Troeung family, in 1980, the "last" group of refugees to be sponsored from Cambodia as a part of the Canadian government's Indochinese refugee resettlement program, being greeted by Canadian prime minister Pierre Trudeau who gestures with the Khmer *sampeah*. (Courtesy of the Troeung family. Photo credit unknown.)

investment in settler innocence and hope.[14] This is a settler subjectivity that deploys the image of one exalted racialized group (i.e., the refugee child) to sanitize and deflect from its systemic structure of ongoing settler-colonial violence. I have photos of myself as a baby staring into the camera as then Canadian prime minister Pierre Trudeau greets my family for a government-arranged photo op at Parliament Hill in Ottawa, just days after we arrived in Canada. I have watched the CBC news footage of this officious event in 1980: my mother and father bowing in gratitude with the Cambodian gesture of the *sampeah* to the prime minister, the embodiment of national magnificence.[15] In December 2019, I watched the CBC's fortieth anniversary commemoration of this event on television again, the same image of me as a baby waving the Canadian flag flashing across the screen[16] (see Fig. I.3). In 2021, I wrote to the CBC asking them to take down the photos of me and my family published in their 2019 human interest story, "'The wounds never go away': Baby Y-Dang Named after Cambodian Refugee Camp Remembers Canadian Arrival." I explained that I had supplied the CBC with some family photos and archival documents while in a state of mental distress, and that the final article replicated a colonial practice of putting refugee images and information on public display in an exploitive way. The CBC journalist said she saw no evidence that I was experiencing a mental health crisis at the time of the interview. My request was denied. The commemoration lives on.

Heralded as a model for the world, the refugee program that brought my family to Canada incentivized ordinary Canadian citizens to become refugee sponsors by pledging matching government funds. The Special Indochinese Refugee Program was celebrated as such a success that, in 1986, the "people of Canada" were awarded the United Nations High Commissioner for Refugees (UNHCR) Nansen Refugee Award. Established in 1954 to honor "individuals, groups and organizations who go above and beyond the call of duty to protect refugees, displaced, and stateless people," the 1986 Nansen Award remains the sole instance of the award being given to an *entire country*.[17] Even as the majority of the Canadian population polled in the early 1980s were against the government's granting of asylum to Southeast Asian refugees, this period continues to be remembered by the liberal Canadian media as "an inspiring chapter in Canada's immigration story, a testament to what citizen altruism can achieve when met with government goodwill."[18] Feminist scholar of Canadian multiculturalism Sunera Thobani describes "the exalted subject" of whiteness as a figure included in the state to help delineate Canada's "unique nationality."[19] As Thobani explains, "Canadians routinely describe their citizenship, immigration, and refugee policies as the most humanitarian and compassionate in the world. These claims shape their sense of collective pride and national identity."[20] This sentiment is evidenced in liberal establishment publications such as *The Walrus*, in which political commentator Simon Lewsen notes: "Canada prides itself on being a haven for the downtrodden."[21] Within this national imaginary, the refugees themselves are remembered as little more than objects of charity, evacuated of personhood, to fit a familiar repertoire of Canadian exceptionalism.

From the images of Southeast Asian refugees in the 1970s to those of Syrian refugees after 2015, this refugee charity aesthetic has changed very little. In 2015, the media aired images of recently elected Canadian prime minister Justin Trudeau welcoming a planeload of Syrian refugees to Canada. These refugees were being commemorated as the "first flight in a government program to resettle Syrians in Canada."[22] In the video, Trudeau explains that the welcome ceremony is an attempt "to show the world how to open our hearts and welcome in people who are fleeing extraordinarily difficult situations. . . . They step off the plane as refugees, but they walk out of this terminal as permanent residents of Canada."[23] Trudeau shakes hands with Syrian men and women as they disembark from the plane; he presents a young Syrian child with a new winter coat; he reaches out to touch the arm of a Syrian infant held in her father's arms. For me, the gesture of welcome echoes across time and space. I am reminded of the CBC video footage of my family's arrival in 1980 and the welcome ceremony at Parliament Hill where Pierre Trudeau reaches out to pat my infant head.[24] There is an uncanny reflection between the Syrian girl and the Cambodian girl, the First and the Last, of the thousands of other charity "showpieces" in the nation's reiterating master narrative of benevolence. There is also a mirroring of Justin Trudeau and his father, the *good men* welcoming the *good refugees* to the *good refuge.* In the invisibilized background of both these images is the settler-colonial state's pattern of "quiet complicity" in the *longue durée* of war from Cambodia to Syria.[25] Finally, there are also echoes of war below the "welcome" videos in the online comments, which are full of vitriol and hate directed at both groups of refugees. Forty years apart, the Syrian girl and the Cambodian girl belong to the same image repertoire. Such repertoires have worked to shape a pervasive kind of silence for the refugee, delineating the boundaries of what can and cannot be said. What is permissible is the story of luck, gratitude, and goodness; what is impermissible is the recounting of the state's war making, abandonment, apathy, and racism. This is the violence of benevolence.

It is thus from this inescapable space of being made a refugee—by the infrastructures of permanent war, genocide, and forced displacement as well as by the repertoires of settler subjectivity—that the concept of refugee lifeworlds emerges. As an analytic, refugee lifeworlds builds on theories of biopolitics by Michel Foucault as well as Achille Mbembe's concepts of deathworlds and lifeworlds. As Foucault influentially argued, power disciplines the body and the mind in ways that are not merely destructive but also rehabilitative, corrective, or capacitating. Moreover, power-knowledge is never entirely monolithic: it domesticates subjectivity and renders the body docile just as it opens unforeseeable spaces of resistance. According to Foucault, biopower is characterized by an emphasis on the protection of life rather than destruction of life by a sovereign power. Focused on the regulation of bodies and the production of sexuality, biopower, Foucault argues, is "an explosion of numerous and diverse techniques for achieving the subjugations of bodies and the control of populations."[26] In his book *Necropolitics*, Mbembe argues, however, that notions of biopower inadequately account for modes of subjugation in our modern era that exceed the use of disciplinary technologies of the body to exercise sovereignty. Biopolitics only gives us half of the story of how warfare operates in the contemporary era. We need an understanding of how death, bare life, and the state of exception continue to saturate the zones of abandonment in vast swaths of the world. Mbembe thus asserts that "contemporary forms of subjugating life to the power of death (necropolitics) are deeply reconfiguring the relations between resistance, sacrifice, and terror."[27] Necropolitics and necropower involve the transformation of spaces into "death-worlds" in which vast populations become the "living dead."[28] Deathworlds consist of entire spaces that are reduced to the temporalities of ensuing and impending death, wherein disposable populations are targeted for elimination with statistical perfection and minimal local resistance. If the deathworld is the zone of the living dead from which the refugee emerges (the ground zero upon which the refugee's world is shattered and destroyed), then the lifeworld can perhaps be thought of as the space of regeneration wherein the refugee's world might begin to be rebuilt. In *On the Postcolony*, Mbembe defines the "life world" as the dynamic zone of existence that arises from the fissures in the apparatus of colonial power. The lifeworld is where people "live their lives out and confront the very forms of their death."[29] It is the space of everyday material life and death, an arena of existence marked by "its character of urgency, its distinctive mark, its eccentricities, its vocabularies, and its magic."[30] In dialectical tension with the production of deathworlds, lifeworlds index the postcolony's "languages of life."[31] Capturing the material realities of "distress" and "terrible movements" of the postcolony, lifeworlds also asserts the postcolony's unseen beauty and state of becoming.[32] Mbembe's definition of lifeworlds reminds us of the need to find registers of meaning in the wake of colonialism, war, and genocide that can account for duress without flattening out states of existence that can attend to pleasure, creativity, and the heterogeneity of life in blocked passages without idealizing or romanticizing the site of the subaltern.

In this book, the lifeworld strives to reactivate and reanimate refugee ways of knowing and being that have been destroyed, depoliticized, and evacuated of meaning in the service of maintaining the liberal imperial status quo. Never wholly outside of, nor fully disciplined by, the infrastructures of legalistic, bureaucratic, and diagnostic power, refugee lifeworlds are the continually negotiated space of loss and survival, injury and joy, accommodation and refusal. As a concept, refugee lifeworlds explores and experiments with what the category of the refugee *can do* rather than what *it is*, especially when this term is brought to bear on, and critically juxtaposed with, other sites of knowledge: the Cold War in Cambodia, the Cambodian diaspora, critical disability studies, and transpacific studies.

From Trauma to Disability

In an analytic sense, refugee lifeworlds intervenes at the limits of trauma theory. Trauma-based paradigms, such as theories of postmemory, haunting, and intergenerational trauma, tend to reiterate a particular account of violence and disablement that locates the wounding "traumatic" moment in a discrete and distant past.[33] This is seen in trauma theory's frequent recourse to tropes of haunting, spectrality, and the "return of the repressed."[34] As feminist philosopher Veena Das writes, in trauma studies, it is "as if the processes that constitute the way everyday life is engaged in the present have little to say on how violence is produced or lived with."[35] The end point of trauma theory, Lauren Berlant asserts, is too often "defining a group of individuals merely as afflicted with the same ailment."[36] There also tends to be a universalization of trauma and an uncritical transposition of concepts and terms from one context to another. Such methods tend to obfuscate the particularities of specific conflicts and locations, lending priority to some genocides of the twentieth century as paradigmatic while "anecdoting" others as minor or peripheral. Moreover, theories of trauma can sometimes result in the imposition of a stigmatizing, deterministic lens on an entire community, wherein the community is seen as permanently and inescapably impaired and damaged, even at the molecular and genetic level.

Since the end of the Cold War, Cambodian people have been described and studied as one of the most "traumatized" populations in the world, with studies frequently emerging about the "appalling mental health crisis" said to be enveloping the Cambodian community.[37] Cambodian people are persistently described as having "psychological scars," "psychological fallout," and "major depression," while Cambodia as a nation is characterized as a place defined by "decades of conflict," "chronic poverty," and "miserable conditions."[38] Diagnostic rates of post-traumatic stress disorder have varied over time from as high as 86 percent of the Cambodian population in 1991 to roughly 40 percent of the population today.[39] The country's "traumatic history" has been so determinant of the Cambodian narrative that "even those who did not live through genocide or civil war are often assumed to have inherited this suffering."[40] In the United States in the early 1980s, Cambodians came to be associated with trauma and post-traumatic stress disorder to such an extent that the term "Depressed Cambodian Refugees" became a public cliché and synonymous with the diasporic population writ large.[41] In popular discourse, Cambodian people have been stigmatized as "cursed" with an irreparable and irreversible trauma that permeates their psyches and genetics.[42]

It cannot be denied that Cambodian people have lived through a history of trauma. The U.S. bombing of Cambodia left a legacy of body counts, maiming, and belated injury; the Cambodian Genocide that came afterward subjected Cambodian people to death and injury on a completely different order of magnitude. The Cambodian Genocide enveloped an *entire* population of over six million people, killing a quarter of this population and debilitating the rest in physical and cognitive ways that are not yet fully understood. In other words, a quarter of Cambodia's population died during the genocide, and the remaining three-quarters of the population were physically and mentally debilitated. As critical disability studies scholar Jasbir Puar recounts about her fieldwork in four refugee camps in the West Bank, "There was not a single family or group of people among those we conversed with in the refugee camps that did not have close proximity to family and community with histories of disability."[43] In Cambodia and in the diaspora, I, likewise, have yet to meet a Cambodian family that was untouched by the violence of the war and genocide. As Cambodian Canadian graffiti artist FONKi Yav explains in the biopic documentary film *The Roots Remain*, "I always say, each family in Cambodia, and every person you meet here is directly linked to the genocide. It really wasn't that long ago."[44] FONKi's articulation of the rawness of the past emphasizes the visceral materiality of suffering that persists in Cambodian communities. It is necessary to affirm the trauma of Cambodian people as *real* without locking the community into an overdetermined narrative of traumatic damage.

Today, Cambodian refugees continue to live with "substantial health disparities," including a disproportionate vulnerability to stroke and cardiovascular disease—two of the leading causes of death and disability in the United States.[45] These disparities have occurred not by happenstance but through exposure to interwoven systems of imperial and racial capitalism—U.S. bombings, the Khmer Rouge genocide, toxic and carcinogenic exposures, carceral humanitarianism, incarceration, urban and rural divestment, and deportation. In the words of Aihwa Ong, the author of the ethnographic study *Buddha Is Hiding*, Cambodian refugees who sought asylum in the United States moved "from a regime of power over death [in Cambodia] to a regime of power over life [in the United States]."[46] This "power over life" includes the preparation of refugee bodies for low-wage, precarious labor sectors such as factory line work, agricultural processing, farmwork, domestic labor, or sewing piecework.[47] Many refugees, such as my own parents, worked all day on the factory lines and then, at night, turned to picking worms in the fields to make ends meet.[48] Unable to access childcare, they took me with them to the cemeteries where they picked worms at night, letting me sleep in the car until dawn. I offer this anecdote about our family's nightly worm picking work to suggest how the "overrepresentation" of Cambodian people with mental illness and disabilities highlights the structural and systemic divestment of this population, who, like my parents, could scarcely access a fraction of the psychological, disability, and health support services they actually needed as refugees during those early years and resettlement. Rather, the persistent screams in their minds, the unhealed scars on their bodies, and the pain and sadness in their hearts not only went unaddressed but was intensified by new forms of physical and psychological incapacitation stemming from their new lives in Canada. This breaking down of the racialized body's capacity reflects Ruth Wilson Gilmore's definition of racism—"the state-sanctioned or extralegal production and exploitation of group-differentiated vulnerability to premature death."[49] Undeniably, my mother and father lived with unaddressed trauma carried over from the war, but, more importantly, they lived with multiple forms of incapacity, debilitation, impairment, madness, and disability that dwell uneasily within the paradigm of "trauma studies" as it has developed with the Euro-American academy.

In this book, I seek to enact a shift in the way that we approach the question of trauma in the afterlife of the Cold War in Cambodia. This is a shift, I argue, from the language of trauma as an individual, knowable impairment to that of disability, understood as both a lived embodiment and a system of differential impairment of racialized and gendered bodies. Specifically, I turn in this book to the language, terminologies, and theoretical lexicons of *debility*, *cripistemology*, and *aphasia*, three key terms taken up in this book in ways that become clearer as this book unfolds. These terms offer necessary insights into the ways in which refugee bodies are marked by pain and suffering in ways that have yet to be adequately addressed in the existing scholarship. As critical disability studies scholars have argued, there is a need to attend to the production of disability (and, by extension, of refugee disablement) in the Global South, where 80 percent of the world's people with disabilities are located. Nirmala Erevelles, for instance, argues that the "violence of imperialism is instrumental not only in the creation of disability but also in the absence of public recognition of the impact of disability in the third world."[50] Helen Meekosha likewise proposes a "southern theory of disability" that "specifically incorporates the role of the global North in 'disabling' the global South."[51] The field of "southern disability," Jasbir Puar clarifies, is not simply an epistemological corrective of what is "left out" of the Eurocentric paradigm of disability studies: "It is, rather, a constitutive and capacitating absence" of this field.[52] That is, to conduct southern disability studies in places such as Cambodia, where paradigms of "refugee trauma" have generally displaced attention away from any kind of meaningful analyses of the geopolitics of disability, we must understand how Cambodia has been imbricated within the assemblages of what Puar, borrowing from Lauren Berlant, calls "slow death."[53] The concept of refugee lifeworlds move us into the realm of slow death in order to grasp not just how Cambodian refugee disability occurs "within the time scale of the crisis" but how it "starts and stops, redoubles and leaps ahead" across time and space.[54]

Refugee Gain

In turning to critical disability studies within the afterlife of the Cold War, I hope to avoid the common rhetorical conflation of disabled peoples "with the remnants of wartime trauma."[55] As Natalia Duong suggests, it is important to see war and colonial violence as a primary cause for unfathomable amounts of death and debility, while also understanding how the consistent rhetorical conflation of war and disability can result in disabled bodies being represented as monstrous or horrific war remnants, rather than allowing "for disability to be valued."[56] *Refugee Lifeworlds* attempts to avoid both the devaluing of disabled bodies as mere war remnants and the discursive occlusions of war and its afterlives as they have conditioned and continue to condition the lives of Cambodian refugees. I attempt this through the concept of "refugee gain."

When I first began thinking about the concept of refugee lifeworlds, I was intrigued by the conversations about "disability gain" emerging in the field of critical disability studies. If disability gain was a concept being increasingly mobilized by the disability community, I wondered, might it also be possible to theorize a politically robust notion of "refugee gain"? Surely, I thought, it should be the goal of a refugee-scholar to develop a theory of refugee gain—to prove how refugees are positive and valuable assets to the economy and to society at large.

To be sure, "gain" is a loaded term. Gain conjures an association with the accumulation of wealth, money, and resources, but gain simply means an increase or an addition of something: for instance, the acquisition of a new worldview, political consciousness, or set of kinship relations. In the disability community, the word gain has been associated with the creativity and universal benefit of reorienting our societies toward disabled people's needs. The term "deaf gain" was first coined by the performance artist Aaron Williamson in 2005 to describe how the accessibility accommodations developed to assist deaf people could also benefit society at large. Moreover, the politics of "deaf-gain" shifts the meanings of deafness away "from sensory lack to a form of sensory and cognitive diversity that offers vital contributions to human diversity."[57] Picking up on this discourse emerging from the deaf community, disability studies scholar Rosemarie Garland-Thomson began using the term "disability gain" around 2016 to posit disability as a creative force rather than something to be corrected or eliminated. Not to be mistaken for meaning that the disabled body is somehow the product of a "fortunate" disabling accident, the notion of disability gain stresses the need to divest from ableist logics of normalcy that posit disabled peoples as aberrant and, therefore, in need of correction or rehabilitation through, for instance, invasive technological interventions. In her *New York Times* op-ed essay titled "Becoming Disabled," Garland-Thomson cites examples of disability gain such as: "learning to be disabled . . . by bonding with other young people new to disability"; "gaining blindness rather than losing sight"; and the collective gain of building accessibility, such as ramps and elevators, that originate from the history of ADA (Americans with Disabilities Act) legislation and disability activism.[58]

I remain compelled by the concept of disability gain, yet scholars have rightly pointed out the pitfalls of conceptualizing disability gain as an extension of liberal disability rights frameworks that situate the question of disability liberation as simply a matter of recognition, individual pride, and empowerment. This sentiment is expressed, for instance, in Garland-Thomson's assertion that "disability is a resource, rather than a restriction."[59] This limited understanding of disability gain tends to divert attention away from the structural causes of impairment to highlight instead the "creativity" or empowering aspects of disability. As Jasbir Puar points out, this perspective reinforces the "neoliberal transit of disability rights," promoting a "highly privileged conversation about Western philosophical bioethics that remains uninterrogated in terms of distinctions between disability and debilitation."[60] What Garland-Thomson's work misses, Puar asserts, is "the politics of debilitation that render some populations as definitively unworthy of health and targeted for injury."[61] While seeing disability as a condition of possibility is a laudable goal, this needs to be counterbalanced with a robust structural critique of how disability operates within the assemblage of racial, gendered, sexual, and settler-colonial violence. Instead of simply posing the question of how disability can be seen as a creative gain, we should be asking, in the words of Liat Ben-Moshe, "what can be gained from the presence of disability, or from disability justice or crip critiques of the carceral emanating from disability/ mad movements?"[62] Put differently, what would an abolitionist notion of disability gain look like? Both Puar and Ben-Moshe move away from individual or identarian models of disability gain toward the potentiality of disability critique as a collective project of decolonial and disability liberation. As Puar asserts, a disability justice approach "is unequivocally antiwar, pro-labor, antiracist, prison abolitionist, and anti-imperialist. This approach is resolutely vigilant about critiquing U.S. imperialism both within the United States— as a settler colonial state—and internationally."[63] In conjunction with these scholars, I posit here a theory that is less about (neoliberal models of) refugee gain and more about refugee and disability justice for all. It is vital that we aim to dislodge the refugee from neoliberal identarian politics enmeshed within the assumptions and logics of global capitalism.

Both disabled peoples and refugees are also all too familiar with the binary of defect/cure that structures neoliberal discourses of refugee/disability gain. As Eli Clare writes, "Charity has long organized itself around the twin notions that disability is tragic and disabled people are pitiful."[64] This logic, Clare argues, "frames disability yet again as damage located entirely within individual body-minds while disregarding the damage caused by ableism. It ignores the brilliant imperfection of our lives."[65] The charity model also tends to remain invested in the exalted subject of the "disabled poster child" or what Clare calls the "supercrip" figure—the inspirational disabled person who has acquired success at all odds, *despite* their disability.[66] What is suppressed in the believe-it-or-not narrative of the poster child supercrip is the reckoning with ableism and with the conditions that make it so difficult for disabled peoples to access systemic liberation. As Robert McRuer argues, refugees are either "targeted in dominant discourses, alongside disabled people, as unwelcome welfare scroungers" and are "left out in the cold" by austerity measures and cuts to social services, or they are exalted by the state as exceptional symbols of inspiration.[67] Some refugees, as I have already discussed with reference to my own story, get singled out as "refugee poster children," or "supercrip refugees," if you will. As Gada Mahrouse has pointed out, the rhetorical figure of the "supercrip" figure in critical disability studies has the counterpart in refugee studies of a "super refugee" figure, whose "inspirational stories . . . similarly entrench a notion of responsibility at the level of the individual and not on society."[68]

If we, as scholars, strive to abandon our commitments to any kind of neoliberal rationalities of refugee gain (that refugees are "good for the economy" or "models of resilience," for example), then where does the refugee go from there? Ushered in by the foundational work of Yến Lê Espiritu, the field of critical refugee studies has sought to challenge these logics. Instead of the rooted citizen, Lê Espiritu argues, it is the refugee "that provides the *clue* to a new politics and model of international relations [emphasis mine]."[69] In his book *Unsettled: Cambodian Refugees in the New York City Hyperghetto*, Eric Tang argues that this clue resides in the refugee's attuned sensitivity to the temporal reiterations of state power that sustain the refugee's captivity—that is, in "the refugee's knowledge that, with each crossing, resettlement, and displacement, an old and familiar form of power is being reinscribed."[70] Vinh Nguyen describes this refugee knowledge as a mode of "refugeetude"—"a condition of possibility, a method of knowing and affecting the world."[71] The refugee's embodiment of an emergent world is linked to her possession of a critical consciousness that has the potential to disrupt the taken-for-granted order of power.

The refugee intimates *a world to come*—a world increasingly straining under the pressures of empire, global capitalism, and climate insecurity. Like Hannah Arendt's assertion of the epistemic power of the Jewish refugee as a "conscious pariah,"[72] my parents have always affirmed the view that Cambodian people's experience of surviving Pol Pot time represents knowledge of *value*—for the society at large but especially for our own community. They believed that this knowledge could fortify us (in the second generation and beyond) for the inevitably difficult future to come. As Cambodian American writer Anthony Veasna So explains, his father's favorite joke was about how the Khmer Rouge years were good preparation to be a future contestant on *Survivor*.[73] As So's literary fiction makes clear, the ability to balance sorrow and humor in relating to the traumatic past is part of what So *gained*, not what he had to overcome, as an inheritance from his Cambodian refugee parents. Vietnamese American writer Thi Bui, in her graphic memoir *The Best We Could Do*, describes this inherited survivalist mentality as a "refugee reflex"— an acute sensitivity to the signs of impending threat, a resourcefulness, and an innate adaptability in the face of hardship.[74] As a subject made and remade by this new world of increasing global precarity, the refugee can embody vital knowledges and resources that will usher in paradigms of planetary humanity. Put differently, the refugee opens up ways of knowing futurity—beneficial knowledge for how we might coexist and care for each other through the protracted temporality of the *long collapse*. In this view, refugees are no longer charity cases and objects of pity. With accelerating waves of climate refugees arriving at the borders, it is the receiving nations who might be characterized as the "lucky" recipients of the knowledge, skills, and flexibility the refugee carries.

That the refugee has the potential to be both a presage of future insecurity and an index of the costs of wars past was an idea articulated by Michel Foucault in 1979, when he wrote that Cambodia's tragedy would also serve as "a foreshadowing of the 21st century's great migration" if the world continued to remain apathetic.[75] As new coordinates of empire have emerged around the world as laboratories of the "New Cold War,"[76] generating newer and newer waves of refugee displacements, the twenty-first century has seen Foucault's predictions come to pass. Driven by interlocking systems of colonialism, war, militarism, climate change, and racial capitalism, the "crisis" of refugee displacement is indicative of a state of permanent wartime that has marked the post–Cold War era. As Ai Weiwei aptly puts it, the "refugee crisis isn't about refugees. It's about us."[77] Instead of erecting more walls and borders to keep refugees out, Ai asserts, "we should look at what is causing people to become refugees and work to solve those conditions."[78] To do so will require that global state powers confront "how they are using political and economic ideology—enforced by overwhelming military power—to disrupt entire societies."[79] At the present moment, there are approximately 70.8 million officially recognized "displaced subjects" worldwide.[80] A 2020 report by the "Costs of War" project at Brown University "conservatively estimates that at least 37 million people have fled their homes in the eight most violent wars the U.S. military has launched or participated in since 2001."[81] According to David Vine, a primary researcher of this study, this human displacement will only continue to accelerate so long as we have "the continuation of endless, infinite war."[82] As the costs of war are borne most heavily by refugees, how might the refugee's knowledge help steer us toward the horizon of war's abolition? Refugee lifeworlds is a lens of critique, a making palpable of politics through embodied ways of knowing and sensing that arise from refugee and disability experience.

To argue, however, that the refugee represents a clue to modern futurity still poses its own conceptual problems as it demands that the refugee be made useful for a broader political agenda. I am not saying that refugees are valuable only because of the resourcefulness they embody. Such a claim instrumentalizes the refugee, like the story of Cambodia, "as epiphenomena" for the primary purpose of mounting a critique of power.[83] Notwithstanding the urgency of such critiques, it is important to underscore that the concept of refugee lifeworlds does not hinge on notions of what the refugee can do for others, or how the refugee can be an example of freedom for others. It asserts the dignity and humanity of the refugee on her own terms.

An Abolitionist Refugee Lens

The term "refugee lifeworlds" signals my desire to bring the fields of critical refugee studies and critical disability studies into closer dialogue, while being mindful of the dangers of an overinvestment in what Hortense Spillers has called "the studies protocol" that dictates the contemporary academic landscape.[84] The zones of intersection between refugee life and disability will always exceed the ossified protocols of institutionalized academic practice, yet I remain committed to what might emerge by routing this analysis through the Cambodian refugee archive. Informed by feminist, crip, queer, transpacific, Indigenous, Black, and critical refugee methods, *Refugee Lifeworlds* asserts the need to envision an intersectional, abolitionist politics of disability and refugee justice that, in Liat Ben-Moshe's words, "is related to one's positionality in relation to power and not identification."[85] Here, we can learn from crip of color critique, Ben-Moshe writes, that urges us "to understand vast social problems through an intersectional lens that has a broader analysis of what we come to call freedom and what liberation might be, not just for the inclusion of some but for the connected liberation of us all."[86] Abolition, Ben-Moshe writes, "is not merely about closures of prisons or institutions; it is a revolutionary framework that transforms the way we analyze and understand the forces that shape our histories and everyday lives."[87] Abolition is a political framework for eliminating slavery, war, carceral systems, and white supremacy, as well as an epistemology that challenges dominant ways of thinking and the status quo. Abolitionist knowledge reconceptualizes notions like crime and innocence; disability, madness, and rehabilitation; ideas of punishment; notions of freedom and equality; and concepts of danger and protection. Ben-Moshe's discussion of abolition specifically relates to what she calls "*race-ability*," a theory that sutures the study of race and disability, racism and ableism, in ways that go beyond neoliberal and multicultural paradigms of minoritized inclusion. According to Ben-Moshe, *race-ability* is defined as "the ways race and disability, and racism, sanism, and ableism as intersecting oppressions, are mutually constitutive and cannot be separated, in their genealogy (eugenics, for example), current iterations of resistance (in the form of disability justice, for example), or oppression (incarceration and police killing, for example)."[88]

An abolitionist refugee lens of critique must seek to account for the depoliticized incorporation and recruitment of the refugee figure into the systems of liberal empire and racial capitalism. To be sure, there is nothing inherently revolutionary about the refugee, or any marginalized identity, as Gayatri Spivak's work on the subaltern subject has long reminded us.[89] The refugee can easily be enlisted to perform the role of the grateful citizen to help perpetuate the empire's projects of war making at home and abroad. As Mimi Thi Nguyen writes, the "refugee patriot" plays an important role in converting the U.S. imperial past into a military rationale for perpetual war.[90] Weaponized as a tool of liberal empire, this refugee patriot helps sustain the U.S. state's myths of a "just war" alongside the demands for the refugee's interminable debt for the gift of freedom.[91]

The refugee's participation in the reproduction of empire can be seen, for instance, in the example of Vietnamese American refugee Nguyet Anh Duong, colloquially known as "the Bomb Lady." Duong has been described as "one of the most important weapons-developers of the modern era."[92] An engineer commissioned by the Pentagon in the aftermath of 9/11, Duong created the first U.S. thermobaric bomb credited with helping "win" the war in Afghanistan. As Achille Mbembe explains, thermobaric bombs are among the cruelest forms of technological warfare in the twenty-first century, "release[ing] walls of fire, absorbing all the oxygen from surrounding spaces, . . . [and] asphyxiating nearly everything that breathes."[93] Duong traces her inspiration for this weapon back to her feelings of indebtedness to "the soldiers and to Americans" who helped her escape from Vietnam.[94] As a refugee-turned-bomb-lady, Duong exemplifies the far reaches of the war machine's ability to incorporate citizens—refugees and nonrefugees alike—into the apparatus of the U.S. forever war.

In the case of Cambodia, the country's conflation with the brutality of Communism helps facilitate a specific narrative of U.S. exceptionalism that invokes Cambodia as a horrifying specter of what can happen when America "abandons" its non-Communist allies abroad. A 2019 television ad from New Faces GOP resurrected this trope again recently.[95] Featuring a Cambodian American woman named Elizabeth Heng, the ad begins with an image of Congresswoman Alexandria Ocasio Cortez's face superimposed with graphic images of the skeletal remains of victims of the Cambodian Genocide. As the camera lingers on these iconic images of the "Killing Fields," Heng questions whether Cortez "knows the horror of socialism," implicitly comparing her policies to those of Pol Pot's regime.[96] The video's graphic sensationalism and mobilization of Heng as an authentic Cambodian voice prompted an outcry from many Cambodian Americans who protested the blatant weaponization of the community's history of suffering. Making no mention of the U.S. war crimes that precipitated the Cambodian Genocide, the political advertisement instantiates a narrative of rescue in which Cambodian refugees are deemed "lucky" recipients of a U.S. liberal humanitarianism that defines itself against a monstrous Khmer Rouge Communism. The example makes visible how easily the refugee figure can be incorporated into U.S. imperial statecraft and mobilized not simply to misremember past war but also to power more cycles of collateral damage.

An abolitionist refugee lens must also contend with the uneasy slippage between the "unsettled" refugee subject and the "refugee as settler," holding the formations of imperial displacement and settler colonialism in productive tension as coconstitutive tactics of white supremacy. There is a need, Dean Itsuji Saranillio has argued, to reckon with "multicultural forms of settler colonialism" in which migrants and refugees reinforce the hierarchies of the white settler-colonial state.[97] Laura Madokoro frames this issue as a matter of "refugee settlerhood," asking "when and how might one start thinking of migrants as settlers? At what cost? And at what gains?"[98] Any consideration of the refugee's agency as a political figure, Madokoro writes, "must equally attend to the manner in which the movement of migrants, including refugees, has facilitated the production of norms and narratives that contribute to the ongoing dispossession of Indigenous peoples."[99] We need to be careful, however, not to flatten out the nuances of this racial reckoning. As Iyko Day argues, our interracial coalitional politics might be better served by a model of racial triangulation wherein we see the "alien" (Black people in the system of chattel slavery and Asian people in that of indentured labor) as triangulated with and against Indigenous peoples to perpetuate the interests of the white settler-colonial state. If we cast our analytics on colonialism's methods of "divide and conquer" rather than on fixed hierarchies of oppression, then we productively resist subsuming all migrants and refugees into "a generalized settler position."[100] To do otherwise, Day argues, risks constraining "our ability to understand how their racialized vulnerability and disposability supports a settler colonial project."[101] Evyn Lê Espiritu Gandhi's work attends specifically to the place of the refugee within settler-colonial contexts, theorizing what she calls "the refugee settler condition," "the vexed positionality of refugee subjects whose citizenship in a settler colonial state is predicated upon the unjust dispossession of an Indigenous population."[102] The work of these theorists emphasizes the importance of refugee lifeworlds as a theory that does not simply condemn all refugees as settlers nor does it absolve them of their participation in settler colonialism and other structures of oppression.

By definition, to be "settled" is to find a condition of stability or security of some sort. Refugees displaced across national borders, such as Cambodian refugees, are settlers in the abstract sense, but they are also often profoundly "unsettled" in other ways. As Eric Tang writes, in the aftermath of the Cold War, Cambodian American refugees were better described as "recaptured" than "resettled" upon arrival in the United States. Warehoused in urban "hyperghetto" infrastructures and consigned to low-wage, precarious labor, Cambodian American refugees found themselves confronting perpetual economic insecurity, criminalization, and fear of deportation.[103] Their unsettled refugee passage—from the Cambodian war zone, to refugee camp, to U.S. hyperghetto, to U.S. prison, to Immigration and Customs Enforcement (ICE) detention, and then "back" to Cambodia as deported "illegal aliens"—complicates the view that the refugee has escaped the circuits of imperial captivity upon arrival in the state of asylum. Like Tang, who rejects the assimilationist teleologies of refugee "resettlement that require one to first acknowledge that a threshold has been crossed, that the displaced have entered entirely new conditions and matrices of power,"[104] I question any universalizing discourses predicated on the refugee's assumed crossing into an uncomplicated settler identity.[105]

Moreover, *Refugee Lifeworlds* strives to illuminate how many refugees might identify as Indigenous peoples themselves. In Cambodia, Indigenous

peoples are variously called ethnic minorities, hill tribes, highlanders, high-
land people, Indigenous people, Khmer Leu, or *Chonheat*. There are an estimated twenty-four different Indigenous groups spread across Cambodia's fifteen
provinces, with the Kuy, Mnong, Stieng, Brao, Tampuan, Pear, Jorai, Rade, and
Bunong being among the largest communities.[106] Known as the caretakers of
Cambodia's sacred forests, waters, mountains, and land, the cosmologies of
these communities affirm a collective obligation of all humankind to care for
the natural world. In particular, the Kuy and Tampuan people are considered
by the Khmer to be the aboriginal inhabitants of the land. Collectively, these
peoples assert the long presence of indigeneity on the territorial land of Cambodia, a nation on the Pacific Rim, as well as on its numerous coastal islands,
all situated in the Gulf of Thailand, itself part of the larger Pacific Ocean.

As in other colonial endeavors throughout history, during the Cold War
in Cambodia, Cambodian Indigenous groups were recruited to fight on different sides of the war. The archives of historian Michael Vickery contain
extensive photographic collections of these groups from the northeastern
Cambodian province of Ratanakiri. Vickery's 1961 collection of the army
in Lomphat community, Ratanakiri, for example, shows images of Indigenous men donning the military uniforms of the Royal Khmer Armed
Forces.[107] Cambodian social anthropologist Krisna Uk has also studied the
history of Indigenous soldiering in her book *Salvage*, an in-depth ethnogra-
phy of the Jorai (ចារាយ) in Cambodia's northeastern Ratanakiri Province.
In the 1970s, some Jorai were enlisted to work with the U.S. Special Forces
during the Cold War. After years of living under the U.S. bombardments,
other Jorai were recruited by the Khmer Rouge, used as bodyguards for Pol
Pot, who felt that the Jorai's "knowledge of the jungle, combined with their
interest in revolutionary ideas and their fighting skills, made them the most
dependable fighters."[108] Uk writes that the Jorai Indigenous peoples' practice
of salvaging the explosive remnants of the U.S. bombing were an "integral
part of their livelihood strategy"—a "harvesting of metal in return for financial gain."[109] For the Jorai, Uk argues, salvaging is not merely a transactional
activity but "lies at the heart of the cultural resilience of the people," enabling
the Jorai "to transform fragments of weapons and painful shards of memory
into refashioned and resymbolized objects used in their rituals and day-to-
day life."[110] After the war, some Jorai were resettled in the United States and
Canada as simply "Cambodian refugees," their Indigenous heritages generally unacknowledged or erased. These Indigenous people turned "Indigenous
soldiers" turned "Indigenous refugees" turned "Indigenous refugee settlers"
embody multiple lines of contradictory affiliations. On the one hand, they
have been entangled within the same militarized currents of U.S. transpa-

cific empire that have disproportionately enlisted Indigenous peoples across the Pacific into the work of U.S. soldiering and war making. On the other hand, their plight is linked to the vast global archipelago of settler-colonial genocide, segregation, land expropriation, racism, criminalization, and cultural and linguistic erosion—as well as Indigenous peoples' ongoing struggles against these systems worldwide.

My own family history has made me attuned to the complicated layering of refugee, Indigenous, and settler identity in many Cambodian families. As a young man, my father (who was a part of the Teochew Chinese ethnic minority in Cambodia) lived for two years with the Kuy Indigenous people in a small village fifty kilometers outside of the city of Kampong Thom known as Phumi O Pou (ភូមិ អូរពោធិ៍). At the time, in the late 1960s, the Chinese Cambodian community and the Kuy worked together in the business of trading and selling rice wine. My father describes his relationship with the Kuy with great fondness. From the Kuy, my father learned how to survive in the wild: how to hunt, fish, work, and live off everything the jungle and forest could provide. He learned how to make medicinal remedies from resin and to forage for food. Without this knowledge, my father often says, he may not have survived the harsh conditions of Pol Pot time, when Cambodian people were thrust into the wild and forced to fend for themselves. In one of his memories of Pol Pot time, my father remembers how a Kuy person helped save his life: Recognizing my father from the "old days," the Kuy helped conceal my father's identity from the Khmer Rouge cadres in the village. The Kuy gave my father two traditional Kuy torches, made of dry preal leaves and rubber, to help him navigate through the dark forest. The Kuy bowed his hands in the gesture of the *sampeah* and said the torches were a gift to repay a debt from the past, when my father had been in good relations with the Kuy people. These anecdotes from my father's memories illuminate the messiness of the multiple contradictions that come to the fore when the lens of refuge seeking, disability, and indigeneity are all brought to bear on the same scene.

The Cambodian Refugee Archive

Responsive to the calls for cultivating methods that are wayward, undisciplined, transpacific, and crip,[111] *Refugee Lifeworlds* assembles an archive of Cambodian writing that enacts the politics of refusal. This is a refusal of imperial, carceral, and white supremacist state violence that has rendered refugee lives disposable and ungrievable—as the collateral damage of imperial wars and global racial capitalism. This refusal is also what critical disability studies scholars have termed a "crip willfulness"—a "refusal to act in accordance with the system of compulsory able-bodiedness."[112] In naming a "crip Cambodian refugee archive," I bring together a lens of critical disability studies and critical refugee studies as I follow the work of scholars such as Ma Vang, in her book *History on the Run*, who imagines a Hmong refugee archive that "reckons with the question of how to engage with memory, the politics of our lack of knowledge about history, and the production of such knowledge."[113] Like Vang's study, which "is neither an empirical study of who Hmong are" nor a positivist recovery of "refugee secrets,"[114] *Refugee Lifeworlds* posits a Cambodian refugee archive that hinges on the unknowable and the uncertain, which is by nature incomplete, partial, and fragmentary.

Transpacific Currents

The Cambodian refugee archive registers the debilitating currents of Cold War transpacific militarism that are the currents of U.S. aerial war, proxy war, occupation, injury, maiming, and killing in Cambodia. As Jasbir Puar writes, "Capitalism, war, forced migration, settler colonial occupation, and . . . U.S. capitalist imperialism are the generators of much of the world's disability."[115] Far from being the routes through which the United States brought "freedom" and "liberation" to Southeast Asia during the Cold War, the "transpacific" represents in many ways the North-South currents of militarized intervention through which the endemic debilitation of Cambodia and the Cambodian diaspora has been produced and reproduced from the Cold War onward.

Invoked as a noun, a critical method, or an adjective, the term "transpacific" references movement back and forth, across and within the Pacific Ocean. The field of transpacific studies leans frequently on the image of ceaseless, intersecting ocean currents as its central structuring metaphor. Whereas the diasporic paradigm in Asian American studies during the 1990s and 2000s tended to focus on the ongoing connections Asian Americans maintained with the ancestral homeland, the transpacific paradigm emphasizes, according to Janet Hoskins and Viet Thanh Nguyen, the "traffic in peoples, cultures, capital, and ideas between 'America' and 'Asia,' as well as across the troubled ocean that lends its name to this model."[116] A response to triumphalist discourse surrounding the economic success of Asia Pacific and Pacific Rim nations in the 1980s, transpacific studies seeks to challenge the largely economic interpretation of the fantasy of the "Pacific Century" favored by the U.S.-led global capitalism. The transpacific thus names a contact zone of "critical engagement with and evaluation of such development and fantasy."[117] As a heuristic of multidirectional traffic, flows, and currents, Yến Lê Espiritu, Lisa Lowe, and Lisa Yoneyama argue that the concept of "transpacific entanglements" makes visible how "U.S. empire and militarism in Asia and the Pacific Islands have been critical, yet underrecognized, parts of the genealogy of the contemporary condition of U.S. neoliberalism."[118] Imperial discourses, they argue, have worked "to naturalize U.S. presence and possession in Asia and the Pacific Islands through the imperatives of national security and wartime necessity, to racialize the peoples it captures, occupies, kills, and governs."[119] The frequent representations of Cambodia, Vietnam, Laos, and North Korea as inert fixtures of communist otherness often have the effect of forgetting America's role in waging war and destabilizing these nations in the first place.

As the field of transpacific studies has developed, scholars have pointed out the need to attend to several currently existing epistemological limitations of the field—to recognize that there are multiple Pacifics at play across the vast space of the ocean. The first critique is that transpacific studies has tended to exclude the Indigenous societies and ecological environments present in the actual space of the Pacific Ocean. Scholars of Oceania studies Tiara R. Na'puti and Michael Lujan Bevacqua argue that this privileging of the periphery treats the Pacific Ocean as "a place meant to be traversed by imperial and world powers, rather than a site from which we can understand the structure of colonial power."[120] As Aimee Bahng and Erin Suzuki write, "We need to resist this 'flyover' model and reevaluate the term 'transpacific' in relation to Pacific studies, Indigenous studies, and Oceanic studies."[121] Another critique involves the call to attend to what Tina Chen calls the "'epistemic asymmetry' of the transpacific [that] presents both a challenge and a promise."[122] For Chen, the multiple transpacific "turns" the field has undergone in the past decade—toward the study of militarized currents, ecological lifeworlds, and Indigenous world making—productively resists the field's reification of a "single preponderant logic."[123] Finally, scholars have argued that there is a need to focus our critical energies on the more "minor nodes" of the Pacific Ocean and the Pacific Rim. As Christine Kim and Helen Leung write, the concept of the "minor transpacific" considers how "imperial desires and practices have shaped minor players such as Canada, Australia, or Singapore."[124] These "minor empires" can be thought of as "privileged, but not entirely dominant, members of the global public."[125] The minor transpacific directs us away from national and imperial sites that have historically dominated the circuits of knowledge production and helps us foreground new perspectives and contexts.[126] As these scholars make clear, it is possible and even desirable to attend to the spaces of the actual Pacific and transpacific at the same time. The two do not need to be mutually exclusive, just as attention to the minor nodes and currents need not subtract from a focus on the major ones.

More so than with earlier waves of Cambodian writing, the Cambodian refugee archive that I examine in this book does not merely celebrate movement across the Pacific Ocean: It engages in the work of theorizing what Lisa Yoneyama terms a "decolonial genealogy of the transpacific."[127] For Cambodian refugees forcibly displaced by the Cold War military interventions of the global superpowers, the transpacific has not been the abstract place of fluid transit, flexibility, or liminality celebrated by global capitalism. Rather, the "Cambodian transpacific" is a current formed in and through the imperial formation of the Cold War. As such, it represents a space of U.S. aerial bombardment, proxy war, debt imperialism, enforced refugee crossing, and ongoing Cambodian American refugee deportation. The "Cambodian minor transpacific" traces lesser-known or unexpected circuits between Cambodia and the transpacific Cold War formation, such as the militarized currents of Black soldiering in Cambodia, linkages between Canada and Cambodia, U.S. carceral circuits of Cambodian American deportation across the Pacific, and intra-Asian circulations between Cambodia and Asian nations such as Vietnam, Thailand, Japan, and China. Attention to these minor flows helps us interrupt U.S.-centric configurations of transpacific studies and spotlights Cambodia's embeddedness within a global web of relations and entanglements.

The transpacific Cambodian refugee archive also disembarks from the familiar shores of the testimonial autobiographical form. As Teri Shaffer Yamada has discussed, the first "phase"[128] of Cambodian writing in the diaspora (exemplified by the works of authors such as Haing S. Ngor, Pin Yathay, Someth May, Loung Ung, and Chanrithy Him) consistently employed the autobiographical testimonial form and remained "narrowly framed around the tragic 1975–79 experience of the Pol Pot era in Cambodia."[129] This body of writing, discussed in depth by scholars such as Shaffer Yamada and Cathy J. Schlund-Vials, reflected the necessity of combating a contested history in Cambodia through the use of nonfiction.

Like many refugees today, the first Cambodian refugees who managed to escape to the border of Thailand to tell their stories were not believed. They were accused of fabricating or exaggerating their accounts.[130] Given the failure of justice in Cambodia characterized by the belated arrival of the Extraordinary Chambers in the Courts of Cambodia, Cambodian American autobiographies throughout the 1990s were propelled by "the need for evidence, to substantiate Khmer Rouge atrocities."[131] The ongoing absence of justice and reconciliation for Cambodians, Yamada argues, "provides one explanation for why there has been more life writing by or about Cambodians than by or about any other Asian ethnic cohort in the United States during the past several decades."[132] The proliferation of Cambodian life narratives in the Cold War and post–Cold War era cannot be disentangled from the context of failed accountability, widespread historical silence about the Khmer Rouge era, and a deep sense of unreconciled wounds among survivors.

The prevalence of the testimonial writing, "an authentic narrative, told by a witness who is moved to narrate by the urgency of a situation,"[133] reflected the Cold War context conditioning the emergence of this writing. In the *testimonio* form, "the witness portrays his or her own experience as an agent (rather than a representative) of collective memory and identity. Truth is summoned in the cause of denouncing a present situation of exploitation and oppression or in exorcising and setting aright official history."[134] Testimony, as Naomi Paik writes, functions as "a first-person narrative told from the perspective of the witness who offers it. But just as crucial, testimony is authentic. It conveys its narrative as true, as emerging from the actual lived experiences of the witness."[135] Beyond a simple recounting of the past, testimony constitutes a "part of a strategy of survival and self-constitution, and it attempts to seize the listener, to insist that we engage."[136] For Cambodian refugees, testimony is about recounting one's firsthand experience of war, genocide, displacement, resettlement, and survival; it is also about reclaiming compromised selfhood and about making appeals to asylum nations to open their borders.

Though useful for its time, the first phase of Cambodian cultural production tended to be limited by the testimonial form, straining as it did to reconstruct *the way things really happened* during the Cambodian Genocide. These texts rendered the meaning of the Cold War in Cambodia exclusively as a story of holocaust survival, often drawing on the form and style of popular Jewish Holocaust testimonials such as Anne Frank's *The Diary of a Young Girl* and Elie Wiesel's *Night* trilogy.[137] Cambodian memoirs of the first phase tended to eclipse any kind of sustained thematic or aesthetic exploration of other wartime experiences that preceded or followed the Cambodian Genocide. As such, they tended to reinforce, whether advertently or inadvertently, the bipolar Cold War frame of containment that required hot war sites in Asia to be viewed as threatening sites of potential Communist expansion that needed to be contained at all costs.[138] Since Cambodia was already viewed by many in America as the ultimate realization of the failure of U.S. Cold War containment, Cambodian testimonial memoirs tended to be easily folded into the "red scare" discourse of the era in which the Khmer Rouge became the embodiment of what the United States was trying to liberate Asia from rather than what the United States had helped create. As Cambodian artist Vandy Rattana, creator of the "Bomb Ponds" photography series, has asserted, it is not enough to just collect testimonies: "This type of artistic practice lacks depth, and most Cambodians don't seek the cause of the genocide."[139] It is this seeking of the deeper causes of the Cambodian Cold War formation that distinguishes the transpacific archive.

Kapok Trees and Aphasia

Saturated by tropes of pain, suffering, loss, illness, speechlessness, silence, muteness, deafness, blindness, prosthesis, and many other modalities of impairment, the Cambodian refugee archive is also an archive of disability. In French Cambodian artist Tian Veasna's graphic novel *Year of the Rabbit*, for instance, a Cambodian elder warns his son that if he wants "to survive under the new regime," he would do well to remember the "old saying": "you need to plant kapok and palm trees around your house" (see Fig. I.4).[140] This piece of survival advice given from a Cambodian elder to his son comes after the sharing of anecdotal information about the Khmer Rouge regime's targeted persecution of "former bureaucrats or intellectuals." One panel depicts this rumored slaughter in the illustration of a refugee boat on the Tonle Sap River under attack by the Khmer Rouge: From a distance, we see the boat surrounded by a bright red patch and the abstract bodies of people being thrown overboard. The next panel zooms in on the image of Khmer Rouge soldiers cleaning the "pools of blood on the deck" of the boat. This four-panel sequence of genocidal violence, debilitating witnessing, and refugee rumor sharing is then interrupted—temporally, visually, and aesthetically—by a panel depicting the Cambodian elder's warning to the younger generation that "you have to be careful." This warning not only interrupts the narration of violence but serves as the frame (indicated by the right-facing positioning of the Cambodian elder) for the very next panel and following two pages in which the kapok tree proverb is introduced and explained. After a panoramic panel depicting a field of kapok and palm trees, we see the text of the proverb, and, below it, a traditional Cambodian home (inhabited by a single person) nestled between a towering kapok tree on one side and an even taller palm tree on the other side. The two trees, in their strength and silence, protect the Khmer person and home. It is also significant that the kapok tree casts a shadow that envelopes the house, a pool of shade that mirrors but also contrasts the pool of blood from the massacre scene on the opposite page. The *act of planting the kapok tree* is emphasized as the undertaking and the state of being that will help Khmer people navigate persecution by the Khmer Rouge.

The scene in Veasna's graphic novel unfolds as a foreshadowing of the dark times to come, as a moment of intergenerational knowledge transmission, and as a visual inscription of Cambodian people's will to survive, what

Figure I.4a Frames from the graphic novel *Year of the Rabbit*, 2019, by Tian Veasna, pp. 86–87, illustrate the Khmer kapok tree proverb, "plant a kapok tree," which means "see nothing, hear nothing, say nothing." (Courtesy of Tian Veasna.)

Figure I.4b

Figure I.4c

some Cambodians have termed "emotional resistance."[141] It is what my mother, in our home while I was growing up, called *kamleang chet* (strength of the heart). Throughout the remainder of *Year of the Rabbit*'s sprawling 368 pages, the kapok tree recurs in frame after frame, a discreet element of the setting infused with rich symbolism: It is a witness and a holder of memory, it is an index of Cambodian people's transformed relationship to language under duress, and it expresses a Khmer epistemology of survival, resilience, and regeneration. As the final landscape panel in the "kapok sequence" of Veasna's graphic novel suggests, planting the kapok tree also means making oneself as small, as silent, and as invisible as possible. In the image, we see two small boats that have left the coast, barely visible as objects against the vast expanse of the Tonle Sap River. Enlarged and almost blending in with the clouds, the proverb resonates and resounds across the skies, loud enough for all Cambodians to hear: "See nothing, hear nothing, say nothing."

In Khmer, the word *kor* means both "kapok" and "mute." It is said that when the wind blows in Cambodia, the leaves of *doeum-kor* make no sound; therefore, the kapok tree is like a person who is mute, or, rather, a person who is mute is like the ancient kapok tree. During the Khmer Rouge years, Cambodian people recited the proverb to each other as a word of wisdom from one Cambodian person to another about how to survive the genocide. To plant a kapok tree (*dam-doeum-kor*), then, exists as a form of refugee knowledge, as an idiom of disability, and as a way of knowing, being, and surviving in a system of genocidal violence and its afterlife.

The kapok tree is a source of livelihood and meaning for Cambodian people: Its silky fibers are used for textile production and cushion stuffing; its plants and seedpods are eaten as snacks, and its bark can be used medicinally to treat illnesses (see Fig. I.5). When I was growing up, my father often told me about the kapok tree. As a child, he loved the dry season in Cambodia when the kapok tree pods would ripen, turning from bright green to brown and growing to the size of corn husks. He remembers the large piles of harvested brown pods at his father's trading business in Kampong Thom, where workers removed the cotton fibers from these pods (see Fig. I.6). To him, the tree was like magic, its fluffy white cotton the material of all the pillows and cushions that lined his household. The kapok tree grew everywhere, belonged to no one, and provided for everyone.

Many years later, after the Khmer Rouge came to power, the kapok tree represented something very different. When my father was away on assignment with a men's work brigade, he came across a field of these trees one day. He knew that it was now forbidden by Angkar for Cambodians to forage for food or plant vegetables of their own. All the resources of the land that

Figure I.5 A kapok tree swaying in a field in the countryside of Cambodia. (Photo by Sothy An, via Shutterstock.)

Figure I.6 Harvested kapok tree fibers, Kampong Cham Province, August 28, 2016. (Screen capture from *Kapok in Cambodia* by Leanghort Sok.)

had provided for Cambodian people for centuries—the trees, the water, the plants—were now the sole property of the state. People were given only two bowls of rice gruel each day. "Stealing" food was punishable by death. And so, many people starved, watched their loved ones starve, even as the natural abundance of the land flourished all around them. On this day, in front of the kapok tree, my father weighed the risks and benefits of defying the regime to feed himself and his family, as he would do hundreds of times over the course of the next four years. Taking the risk, he picked some pods from the tree, cracked them open and savored their delicious black seeds under the cool shade of the quiet branches. For this brief moment, the kapok tree quelled his hunger and reminded him of the old days, the happy times, before the war.

During the Cambodian Genocide, knowing that their words could be overheard by the Khmer Rouge and used as evidence of treason, my father, like most Cambodians, refrained from speaking. In some cases, they witnessed scenes of cruelty and violence that they could not encapsulate in words. Cambodian people, like my parents, possessed an acute awareness of when to speak or not to speak, of whom to trust and not to trust, and to teach their young children how to be quiet *like the kapok tree* in order not to attract attention to themselves.

This silence is described in different ways across the Cambodian refugee archive. Sometimes it is framed as a fearful muteness, sometimes as a protective retreat into the mind, sometimes as a numbed speechlessness in response to witnessing death and violence. At night, the Khmer Rouge cadres, their ears to the walls, would circulate outside or beneath Cambodian people's homes, listening for any evidence of disloyalty to the regime. Faced with the Khmer Rouge's panoptic system of surveillance, Cambodian people went quiet.[142] They advised each other, in hushed tones, to say as little as possible. Becoming mute, in addition to becoming blind and deaf, was linked to the protection of one's kin, for Cambodian people knew that the Khmer Rouge targeted entire families and lineages, even babies, to foreclose the future possibility of revenge. As one Khmer Rouge regime slogan went, "To dig up the grass, one must remove even the roots."[143] With nowhere to hide or escape to, people had to hide deeper and deeper within themselves. Planting the kapok tree, metaphorically speaking, thus became a tactic of survival wielded when most other forms of resistance were unavailable. Other Cambodians witnessed such an extremity of violence that they began to turn inward, toward silence, as a means of psychological survival. In her book *From the Land of Shadows*, Khatharya Um explains that the "surrealism" of the Cambodian experience "rendered many first-generation survivors mute, with tongues parched and heavy with pain and rage."[144] At once a protective mechanism against a threat and a response to it, *dam-doeum-kor* is resistant to a straightforward cause-and-effect teleology.

Curiously, the emphasis on *planting* and *rooting* in the Khmer proverb suggests that, even when language seemed to fall away, Cambodian people still nurtured the possibility of rebirth and regeneration. Silence during Pol Pot time carried an intentionality, a planting of something for an imagined future that was not yet visible. In her book *Unspoken: A Rhetoric of Silence*, the literary scholar Cheryl Glenn writes of silence as a mode of ambiguity against an imposing force, where "unexpected silences unsettle us, often making us anxious about the specific meaning."[145] This ambiguity of silence can open us up to alternative futures by compelling us to question our own predictions and by refusing the authority of language to explain a complex person or event. In this way, planting the kapok tree reflects a modulation of disability and capacity within necropolitical conditions of genocide, wherein there is a blurring of distinctions between the ontologies of "cannot speak"/"will not speak," language loss/language presence, silence/speech, or disabled/nondisabled.

In *Refugee Lifeworlds*, I turn to the Cambodian refugee archive to name the planting of the kapok tree as a Khmer epistemology of disability arising specifically from the history of the Cold War in Cambodia and its afterlife. While "epistemology" generally refers to "thought" or "knowledge,"[146] the concept of "ontoepistemology" signals the inherent blurring between epistemology and ontology. As Karen Barad writes: "Practices of knowing and being are not isolable; they are mutually implicated. We don't obtain knowledge by standing outside the world; we know because we are of the world. We are part of the world in its differential becoming."[147] In her work, Jasbir Puar likewise blurs epistemology and ontology, calling for a critical shift in our methods from "epistemological corrective to ontological irreducibility."[148] As a Khmer epistemology of disability, planting the kapok tree grapples with what crip theorists Merri Johnson and Robert McRuer describe as "the instability of ways of knowing from and through forms of pain that may not register as legible impairments, let alone disabilities."[149] In this way, we might even call planting the kapok tree a "Khmer cripistemology" that eludes Eurocentric definitions of disability. The epistemology of the kapok tree also works to interrupt Cambodia's Cold War episteme, understood in this book as an ableist, racist, and imperialist knowledge project that reproduces the militaristic violence and rationalities of Cambodia's Cold War formation.

The kapok tree proverb is both commensurable and incommensurable with the Western medical condition known as "aphasia," and thus the Cambodian refugee archive might be thought of, in some ways, as an *aphasic refugee archive*. From the Greek etymology *aphatos*, which means to be "speechless" or to be "without language," aphasia, from a medical perspective, is a condition of language impairment resulting from injury to specific regions of the brain. As a disability, aphasia exists along a spectrum, wherein language may become nonnormative with varying degrees of intensity: speech may come and go; the ability to comprehend the meaning of a question may suddenly vanish; the words on the page may suddenly go blurry; speech may become perforated, nervous, and stuttering; or language may fall away gradually and then completely. Many Cambodian people live with medical aphasia. At the same time, their conditions of speechlessness, silence, or difficulty speaking that stem from the survival of war and genocide cannot solely be reduced to the medical classification of aphasia. Their "aphasias"—racialized, gendered, and generational—are shaped by social and political contingencies that necessarily exceed medical, diagnostic truth.

As Palestinian writer Adania Shibli asserts, colonial systems do more than simply silence the sufferer: They produce a kind of "perforated language, a language that doesn't hold itself together."[150] For Shibli, we can learn a great deal about the experience of violence and its ongoing survival by becoming attuned to the sufferer's aphasia—to these intervals when "language abandons us," "when we become speechless, when we miss words, when we scream, when we shout."[151] Shibli's articulation about the difficulty of speaking in the afterlife of violence suggests a way in which aphasia might offer a particularly productive entry point for grappling with the lifeworlds of those who do not fit easily into the disabled or nondisabled binary. Other scholars such as Rey Chow have argued that "aphasia . . . can be conceptualized anew as forms of unveiling, as what expose the untenability of 'proper' (and proprietary) speech as such."[152] The aphasic person's perforated language—full of silences, pauses, hesitations, and inventive substitutions—enacts an embodied, sensorial, relational way of speaking through shared vulnerability that interrupts white, ableist, masculinist hierarchies of valued speech.[153] In Chapter 4 of this book, I consider this aphasic inflection of the Cambodian refugee archive. Where these two cripistemologies of the kapok tree and aphasia differ and/or overlap is not easily parsed. In *Refugee Lifeworlds*, I ask, What happens if we route aphasia through Cambodia and Cambodia through aphasia?

Khmer Renaissance

The Cambodian refugee archive accesses what in recent decades has been heralded as the "renaissance of the Cambodian arts" or "Khmer renaissance." In recent years, terms such as "regeneration," "resurgence," "brilliance," "revival," and others have emerged within global Black, Asian, and Indigenous social justice and artistic movements to characterize community-based responses to the ongoing structures of colonial and settler-colonial violence. The term "renaissance" has perhaps uniquely been attached to the "rebirth" of the arts within Cambodia and the Cambodian diaspora in the post–Cold War era.

This transnational artistic movement hearkens back to a Khmer cosmopolitism and syncretism that characterized the "golden era" in Cambodian history. This was the period immediately after independence from French colonization when Khmer arts and culture flourished—when Phnom Penh was variously known as the "Paris of the East," the "Pearl of Asia," and the "Island of Peace" in Southeast Asia. Upon his state visit to Phnom Penh in 1967, Singaporean prime minister Lee Kuan Yew commented that Cambodia's political neutrality in the Cold War represented "something valuable" that the rest of the world could emulate.[154] Addressing Prince Norodom Sihanouk directly, Yew extolled: "Throughout all the changes of circumstance in the world, your non-aligned policy has never altered its fundamental principles, that the destiny of Cambodia and the Khmers is your paramount consideration."[155] Additionally, Yew marveled at what Cambodia embodied culturally and aesthetically, describing the country's mix of cosmopolitan modernity (Phnom Penh "in steel and concrete") and sublime antiquity (Angkor "in sandstone and laterite") as "monuments to Khmer creativity."[156] Given Singapore's post–Cold War path into the glittering metropolis we know today, it is perhaps most ironic that, in 1967, Yew proclaimed, "I hope, one day, my city will look like this."[157] *Refugee Lifeworlds* seeks to dwell in that spirit of "Khmer creativity" referenced by Yew and to track its rebirth in the social and artistic movement of the Khmer renaissance.

If the current arts movement can be said to exemplify a Khmer renaissance, this prompts the question of what exactly is being revived and refashioned by the new generation of artists? Between 1960 and 1970, an estimated four hundred Cambodian films were produced, many featuring the big film stars of the time, such as Dy Saveth, Kong Sam Oeun, and Vichara Dany. As Southeast Asian film studies scholar Tilman Baumgärtel explains, "Only around 30 of these films survive, remnants of a national cinema that was full of miracles and beauty: Kings with magic powers, giants, witches, flying horses, gods that walk the earth and a girl with snakes instead of hair are only some of the sensations that the film makers of that time put on the screen despite the very limited technical means that they had at their disposal."[158] These mythical-themed films proliferated in the 1960s alongside other kinds of Cambodian films—films with modern stories and plots as well as the nation-building films of King Norodom Sihanouk. As the subject of contemporary Cambodian films, such as Davy Chou's 2011 documentary film *Golden Slumbers* and Sotho Kulikar's 2014 melodrama *The Last Reel*, the bourgeoning film industry of Cambodia's golden era was "part of a much larger renaissance of Khmer culture in the post-colonial period that included architecture, literature, pop music and visual art."[159]

Indeed, we have also seen in the Khmer renaissance a revival of the pop music of Cambodia's golden era. Recent films such as John Pirozzi's 2014 *Don't Think I've Forgotten* and Marc Eberle's *Not Easy Rock and Roll*, for example, have sought to recapture a time when Cambodia, particularly the city of Phnom Penh, was frequently regarded as "cool." Pirozzi, who spent over a decade researching and compiling the archival fragments in his film, expressed his motivation to represent in cinema "the one thing that has allowed the Cambodian people to access a time when their life wasn't about war and genocide."[160] Youk Chhang, the director of DC-Cam and an executive producer of *Don't Think I've Forgotten*, has characterized the film as a "completely different way to tell the history than about prison, about killing, about tribunals. . . . It restores the missing part of us, the identity of who we are."[161] As the film demonstrates, Phnom Penh in the 1960s embodied a style of culture influenced by a zeitgeist of free love, progressive thinking, and creative autonomy represented in the nation's hybrid rock and roll music. Cambodia's "coolness" as a musical and cultural haven during the 1960s was produced through its unique geopolitical positioning at the crossroads of European, American, Latin, and Southeast Asian musical influences and circuits of cultural exchange.

To be speaking of the renaissance of Cambodian arts in the present moment almost fifty years after the Cambodian Genocide is a telling signal of the extremity of the repression that took place in the past. The Cold War in Cambodia left not only a devastated national infrastructure but also a void of artistic representation resulting from the Khmer Rouge regime's targeting of writers, musicians, filmmakers, dancers, and other artists. A generation later, Cambodian artists have acquired a degree of psychological space and distance from the traumatic past. Combined with a general acceptance by the international community that Cambodian refugee testimonies were not fabricated tales, time and distance have allowed a new generation of Cambodian artists to approach the past with more experimentation and flexibility. These artists have insisted that Cambodia not be simply conflated with war and genocide.

The renaissance of the Cambodian arts signals, at last, an interval of reprieve for the Cambodian community from the insecurity of perpetual war—a condition necessary for artistic experimentation to take place. And yet, the presence of the genocide is still palpable in contemporary Cambodian writing, reflective of Cambodian author Soth Polin's apt remark that, "even if you are reaching in your imagination for a new destination, you cannot get past their cruelty. When you try to write something without mentioning the Khmer Rouge, you can't."[162] Khmer renaissance does not mean forgetting the past but rather channeling that difficult history into a wholly unique hybrid

Figure I.7 "The Rising Phoenix," created in Phnom Penh, Cambodia, 2014. Graffiti blends traditional Kbach Khmer style with contemporary 1960s Cambodian golden era iconography and imagery. (Courtesy of FONKi Yav. Photo by FONKi.)

creative form, mixing the legacy of collective pain and the new generation's impulse for revival, that could only emerge from Cambodia and the Cambodian diaspora. As FONKi Yav explains in a recent *CBC* television profile, "the wave of that Khmer renaissance" is what propelled him to Cambodia in 2012 to continue his artistic graffiti practice from the land of his parents' birth. In FONKi's words, "We had the golden era back in the 60s and then April '75 we had our genocide . . . now we've been able to heal and we're witnessing a renaissance not only in the art but in the music, in the film industry. The city's really developing in its own way. So there's room now for contemporary art and for us [in the] new generation to get back our history."[163] FONKi's graffiti art is distinctive, in particular for its melding of *kbach*—a traditional style of Khmer decorative arts that dates back to the Angkorian era—and 1960s Cambodian golden era iconography and imagery (see Fig. I.7). This syncretism of styles is seen in the example of FONKi's mural "The Rising Phoenix," painted in Phnom Penh in 2014, during his first trip back to Cambodia since the completion of his 2012 documentary biopic *The Roots Remain*. "The Rising Phoenix" tethers the present (kbach graffiti) to the past (the Khmer mythical figures of the *apsara* and phoenix), generating a fluid and dynamic image of the renaissance and rebirth of Khmer culture. As FONKi has explained, the mural is in "the exact same spot where they erased [his] first version of Kbach Khmer graffiti you see in [his] movie."[164] Khmer renaissance is marked by both the rebirth of collective identity and the struggle over the reclamation of public space that has been eroded through over three decades of neoliberal authoritarian rule in Cambodia under Prime Minister Hun Sen.

As the form of graffiti suggests, Khmer renaissance challenges received ideas about art and aesthetic hierarchies. The teleology of presumed "progress" in literary style and form, from testimonial content to avant-garde experimentation, does not hold within the Cambodian context. On this point, I appreciate literary ecocriticism scholar Rob Nixon's reflection on the false binary often maintained by scholars between the political and the aesthetic. When literary studies become demarcated from critical engagement with worldly issues, Nixon notes, "we frequently witness, alongside an excessive regard for ahistoric philosophy, an accompanying historically indifferent formalism that treats the study of aesthetics as the literary scholar's definitive calling."[165] In this branch of literary aesthetics, the study of *literature* is lamented as a disappearing art and "formal categories such as rupture, irony, and bricolage assume an inflated agency."[166] When this happens, form rather than politics is seen as the literary scholar's proper purview, and any transgression of the disciplinary boundaries between politics and aesthetics is easily dismissed as sociological or political interpretation. The study of "aesthetics" becomes the specialized domain, "severed from the broader sociopolitical environmental contexts that animate the forms in question."[167] If there has been in the recent decade an impetus to return to questions of form in literary studies,[168] how can we keep such a turn from lapsing into an abstract, apolitical celebration of the aesthetic, the rhetorical, or the formal? One way of approaching this issue, as Timothy August argues in his book *The Refugee Aesthetic*, is to analyze the refugee narrative on its own terms, "whether it challenges, avoids, or even reinforces [the most] common geopolitical narratives."[169] Another way of undoing the false binary between politics and aesthetics is to assert, in Saidiya Hartman's words, that we have a responsibility as scholars and as people of color to finds ways "to tell a story capable of engaging and countering the violence of abstraction."[170] In addressing a topic such as the afterlife of the Cold War in Cambodia, for which there has yet to be a proper reckoning, countering the violence of abstraction by returning to the site of the embodied, the personal, and the political is a way of doing justice to the rich aesthetic dimensions of the Cambodian refugee archive.

The renaissance of the Cambodian arts is a movement propelled not only by the work of Cambodian refugee artists proper but also by those adjacent to the community. Many of the authors, artists, and filmmakers whose works I discuss in this book—Viet Thanh Nguyen, Madeleine Thien, and Masahiro Sugano—are not of Cambodian ancestry. As authors, their engagement with the Cambodian community and the legacies of the Cold War in Cambodia

resides in their struggles with what Trinh T. Minh-ha calls "speaking nearby"—
a form of "speaking that does not objectify, does not point to an object
as if it is distant from the speaking subject or absent from the speaking place."[171]
Speaking nearby "reflects on itself and can come very close to a subject without, however, seizing or claiming it."[172] This position of ethical proximity,
as opposed to appropriation, is sustained through not only what the writer
chooses to tell but also how the form or style employed can resist a voyeuristic
or appropriative gaze. To speak nearby "is not just a technique or a statement
to be made verbally. It is an attitude in life, a way of positioning oneself in
relation to the world."[173] Speaking nearby the Cambodian community entails
the cultivation of a lifelong ethics and commitment to dialogue, a respect of
privacy and mental health, and a prioritization of relationality over monetization or cultural currency.

This persistent accountability to the ethics and politics of speaking nearby is perhaps best articulated by acclaimed author Madeleine Thien, a Canadian author of Malaysian-Chinese ancestry, in an interview about why she
chose to write a book about Cambodia: "I hoped that *Dogs at the Perimeter*
would be able to stand behind the historical and witnessing books, to say that
all of us have a stake in understanding what happened there, that we are all
connected."[174] Time and again, Thien has underscored the point that Cambodia's twentieth-century tragedy must be understood as a global event connected to the world. "The history of the Cambodian Genocide," Thien asserts, "is also American history, and is inextricable from the repercussions of
American policies and decisions. We need to look at it, think about it, mourn
it, be angry about it, and at least live in it for a little while."[175] In the Global
North, where Cambodia's collective tragedy was witnessed from a distance,
the public still has a stake in revisiting Cambodia's history for a multitude of
reasons: among them, the fact that the United States was complicit in bombing Cambodia; that many Western intellectuals and journalists were apolo-
gists for a genocidal regime; that the world remained largely apathetic to the
plight of an entire nation that suffered on an unprecedented level. As Thien
has stated, *Dogs at the Perimeter* was propelled by her belief that "there is no
us and them, we are all entwined and responsible to one another. Geopolitics
and the movement of people across borders has made this so."[176] For Thien,
then, the difficulty of reckoning with Cambodian history is a responsibility
that must be carried by Cambodians and non-Cambodians alike.

This view of the need to distribute the labor of reckoning is also articulated in Rithy Panh's *The Missing Picture*, which ends with the narrator saying, "And so, I make this picture . . . this missing picture I now hand over to
you, so that it never ceases to seek us out."[177] The responsibility to remember

cannot be the duty of the survivor to bear alone. For decades now, Cambodian survivors and their descendants have labored to assert that our histories cannot be reduced to the material of mere footnote, anecdote, or silence. As Panh writes in *The Elimination*, for Cambodian survivors, the return to the past "isn't some sad passion; it's a struggle against elimination . . . it gives us back our humanity, our intelligence, our history."[178] We search for a language and form that can give meaning to the dark void of the past because we do not want to be stranded there, alone at the edge of that mass grave.

Outline

Refugee Lifeworlds unfolds across four chapters and a coda. The book has a temporal structure as it moves (in a nonlinear way at times) through the chronological periods of the Cold War in Cambodia from the U.S. bombing of Cambodia (1965–1975), to the Cambodian Genocide (1975–1979), to the history of Cambodian refugee resettlement (1979–present). There is also a spatial movement throughout the book that traces the Cambodian refugee's transpacific passage from Cambodia to the United States/Canada and back to Cambodia again. Finally, each chapter develops my theory of refugee lifeworlds a little differently by bringing a specific aspect of critical disability studies (namely, the concepts of debility, cripistemology, and aphasia) to the analysis of the Cambodian refugee archive.

A framing chapter for the book, Chapter 1, "Cambodia's Cold War Episteme," examines the construction and circulation of racial fantasies of Cambodia from the colonial French protectorate era to the present. Cambodia's Cold War episteme operates through the repetition of a familiar set of orientalist and racist repertoires as well as what I call the logic of minor anecdoting. This is the invocation of Cambodia as a "minor detail" in the narration of something else—the "main story"—that is expressly *not* about Cambodia or Cambodian people. The logic of minor anecdoting renders Cambodia simultaneously hypervisible as a frame of reference and mystifyingly opaque and unknowable as a site of meaning and knowledge unto itself. Cambodia's Cold War episteme also disavows the disability and pain of Cambodia through the inscription of colonial tropes about the Cambodian body-mind as outside of the teleologies of Western modernity and liberal progress—as exotic, savage, and damaged matter. I track this episteme across different texts and archives such as Cold War photojournalism, the 1970s Henry Kissinger telecons, Joel Brinkley's 2011 *Cambodia's Curse*, the French 1906 Colonial Exposition in Marseille, and the form of the "Cambodia travel anecdote." These works illustrate how Cambodia's Cold War episteme operates not only to sustain the ongoing debilitation of Cambodian populations but also to shore up the capacitated humanity of white liberal personhood seen as the antithesis to this population marked as always already defective.

Chapter 2, "Debility and the U.S. Bombing of Cambodia" examines the intersection between disability and refugee life in relation to the U.S. secret war in Cambodia, an "off the map," disavowed coordinate in the U.S. imperial cartography of the Cold War. I examine the *longue durée* of endemic debilitation produced through the U.S. bombing of Cambodia as an imperial formation coextensive with the global Cold War confrontation. Debility in the context of the U.S. bombing of Cambodia and its afterlife is multivalent: It relates to the incapacitation of Cambodian populations subjected to the brunt of the U.S. war machine's imperial violence and "right to maim," to the predation of the Khmer Rouge war machine as this regime sought to recruit disposed of and disenfranchised populations to the cause of Communist revolution, to the extraction and deployment of the Black American body's soldiering labor as war fodder for the front lines of the war in Southeast Asia, to the reproduction of ableist fantasies of military masculinity and disability economies of humanitarian labor, and, finally, to the ongoing crip incarcerations and displacements of the Cambodian American refugee-deportee. Through their narrativization of the U.S. bombing of Cambodia and its long afterlife, texts such as Rithy Panh's film *Shiiku, the Catch*, Viet Thanh Nguyen's short story "The Americans," and Kosal Khiev / Masahiro Sugano's film *Cambodian Son* illuminate how debility operates by suturing the operations of war to the racial capitalist accumulation of bodies made available for injury and maiming.

In Chapter 3, "Cripping the Kapok Tree and the Cambodian Genocide," I address the disabling legacies of the Cambodian Genocide through attention to the Khmer proverb "to plant a kapok tree," a Khmer idiom of disability that means "see nothing, hear nothing, say nothing." Reading this proverb as a composite of being blind, deaf, and mute, I argue the kapok tree makes visible the multilayered valences of Cambodian people's forms of "emotional resistance" (*kamleang chet*) during Pol Pot time. Inclusive of an array of corporeal, affective, and psychological tactics—such as intentional blindness, deafness, and muteness—the situated practices of emotional resistance and performative disability adopted by Cambodian people during the genocide continue to remain illegible within Western paradigms of resistance and subversion. In this chapter, I bring crip theory to bear on a reading of the Cambodian refugee archive, as exemplified by works such as Vaddey Ratner's novel *In the Shadow of the Banyan* and Rithy Panh's film *The Missing Picture*. I argue that the kapok tree can be seen as opening us up to a Khmer cripistemological way of knowing refugee disability in the afterlife of the Cold War in Cambodia.

Chapter 4, "Aphasia and the Nervous Condition of Refugee Asylum," explores the psychic and affective refugee afterlives of the Cold War in Cambodia. Aphasia has been theorized as both a speech impairment resulting from brain injury and a socially and racially inflected condition of being made speechless in moments of racial violence and destabilization. Through analyzing Madeleine Thien's novel *Dogs at the Perimeter* and short story "Alice Munro Country," this chapter brings disability studies to bear on refugee lifeworlds by theorizing *refugee aphasia* as a critical tool that accounts for the ruptures of silence and speechlessness in the Cambodian refugee archive, and considers what this aphasic form might mean. Unsettling the disabled/nondisabled binary, refugee aphasia, I argue, can be read as an ontoepistemology of refugee being and knowing that arises in the afterlife of war and genocide.

Finally, in the book's Coda, I conclude with a discussion on the afterlife of the Cold War in Cambodia in the longer genealogy of U.S. permanent war, from Cambodia to Iraq, Afghanistan, and Syria. The Coda ends with a personal essay of refugee autotheory titled "Boneyards of the Cold War." This essay is a reflection on my experience of walking through the War Museum Cambodia in Siem Reap—a boneyard of decommissioned war material leftover from the Cold War in Cambodia. As I move through this unsettling space, I find myself captivated by the image of a lotus flower taking root in a bomb crater. What grows in the ruins of war? This remains an open and indefinite question by the book's end.

My mother often tells me the story of how she saved her husband, my father.

In 1976, my family lived in a *pom*, a village in the jungle created by clearing the bush and building huts made of bamboo. One day, my father was sent to work in a work cooperative with a group of around fifteen other men. My mother, a twenty-eight-year-old woman, stayed at home with their two young children, my brothers. It took the group two days to walk through the dense jungle to the work site. Many could not endure the unremitting labor, the harsh tropical elements, and the lack of food. One by one, people died of exhaustion and illness. After days or weeks, only about five men returned to the *pom*. My father was not among them.

Hearing rumors that my father was ill, my mother begged the village leader to let her go see him. The cadre felt pity for my mother and gave her a transit letter to walk to the work site to see about my father. She walked for days, by herself, through the jungle, foraging for food along the way, stopping to rest and to sleep on the earth. When she arrived at the work site, she found my father, gravely ill, left outside under a tree, where they left people to die. He was unconscious, on the brink of death, but his heart was still beating. She pleaded with the work cooperative leader to transport my father to a hospital in Kampong Thom. "Please, look, he's still alive," she said. Eventually, they agreed to transport him. The vehicle arrived, full of Khmer Rouge soldiers. They stopped my mother from entering the vehicle, pointing a rifle at her and ordering her to stop. She got down on her knees and begged them to let her go with them. Somehow, miraculously, they agreed. She traveled in the vehicle with the Khmer Rouge soldiers, protecting my father's unconscious body.

The city of Kampong Thom, her hometown, was barely recognizable— a ghost town, almost empty. The hospital was scarcely a hospital. The sick and dying laid on flat wooden beds. Some patients were given basic IVs, but modern medicine was not available. My mother sat on the floor at my father's bedside waiting for him to regain consciousness. She thought of her children back at the *pom*, sent out daily to work in the children's work cooperative. She thought of her youngest son who was frail and showing signs of dysentery. How much longer would he survive?

Two or three days passed before my father finally stirred. He had regained consciousness, but it would be three months before he left the hospital. My mother could not stay. She had to return to her children. She made the journey on foot, alone, through the jungle. It took her an entire day to walk back to the *pom*.

"No one would believe how people survived in Pol Pot time," my mother says as she ends this story.

1

Cambodia's Cold War Episteme

One day, in my twenties, while conducting research on Cambodian refugee history, I came across a newspaper article in the *Montreal Gazette* dated December 4, 1980, with the headline, "Snow Looks Nice to Asian Refugees." The article showed an image of my mother and me, a baby of eleven months at the time.[1] I remember having a mixed reaction—a feeling of both warmth and misrecognition. I recognized something in my mother's expression, yet there was also something out of alignment in the framing. What caught my attention was my mother's unrestrained, radiant smile. I had seen my mother smiling in photos before, smiling for white people in ways that made me feel ill, but never quite this way. The expression looked real to me, as if she was not aware of the camera. I also wondered: After so much loss, could this photo be true? Was she not supposed to look sad and downtrodden, the picture-perfect charity case? (See Fig. 1.1.)

I looked closer at the photo: In it, my mother's gaze is cast downward at me. I am bundled in baby's winter clothing and look directly into the camera with wide brown eyes. The woolly winter hat I am wearing forms a perfect circle around my face. My mother wears the same kind of hat. These are the winter clothes that have been collected for us in advance by our refugee sponsors and the government. We are standing outside against the night sky. A light dusting of snow appears to cover us. The article explains that "in high spirits after a grueling 17-hour flight from Bangkok to Mirabel Airport, the Troeungs peered out at the white stuff on the ground and said: 'It looks nice—because it's different.'"[2] These details create an impression of serenity,

Figure 1.1 Front page of the *Montreal Gazette*, December 4, 1980. A human interest story about the Troeung family's arrival in Canada and my (baby Y-Dang's) first look at snow. (Material republished with the express permission of *Montreal Gazette*, a division of Postmedia Network.)

purity, and innocence. A small Canadian flag peeks out from my coat, and the caption under the photo reads: "Hello, Canada: Cheaung Yok Troeung with her 11-month-old baby Y Dang Troeung."[3] The dash is left out of my name. My mother's maiden name Cheaung (莊) is spelled in English with an unusual transliteration, like the surname Troeung. The article explains that "the Cambodian baby waved a Canadian flag as the Troeung family set foot on Canadian soil—or rather snow—for the first time last night. It was a fitting start for the family of refugees about to start a new life in Goderich, Ontario."[4] "Wearing a woolly balaclava," the article recounts, "Bouy Sou Troeung said through an interpreter that the refugees had been warned about the rigors of the Canadian climate."[5]

This image is all about drawing the reader's attention to the experiential "firsts" of refugee landing: the Cambodian refugee child's first look at Canada, her first breath of its pure and untainted air, her first toy (the Canadian flag), and her bewildered first dusting of snow. In this story of arrival, it is the great Canadian climate that takes center stage. It is an account of goodness—of good refugees entering the good refuge being welcomed by the good man (the prime minister). It is a tale of refugees encountering an awe-inspiring foreign land, a feel-good arc that forever fixes the refugee in the gaze of whiteness. In this story, the refugees are "the lucky ones" who have made it to Canada with nothing except the clothes on their backs, ready to embrace all that the good nation has to offer: "Clothes are all they packed in their suitcases; after a year in three different refugee camps it's all they have left. Baby Y Dang Troeung was born in a refugee camp in Thailand last January."[6] The story aims to charm, delight, and inspire. What could be more delightful than the account of snow looking nice to Asian refugees? What could be more inspiring than a refugee child who comes from nothing being given the opportunity to now have everything? The story of arrival is an account of white charity and white mobility: "Parishioners in Goderich, a small town on the shore of Lake Huron, set up a fund to buy the families food for their first few months. They held 'work bees' to fix up an old convent for them to live in."[7] These things will make the refugees more "Canadian" with each passing year—preparing them for taking on a new language, a new religion, a new diet, and a new way of life. These piles of charity will also teach the refugees that there is little room for remembering the past, for stepping "out of line," or for disobedience of any kind in the harsh winter climate. Survival in rural Canada will require a blanketing of all that came before.

Staring at this account on the screen of my laptop, I began to replay different scenes in my mind. I thought about the daily battle against the sun, rain, and earth that my parents had faced just a year before this photo was taken. I pictured them sleeping on the bare earth, exposed to the torrential monsoon rains and floods. I saw them foraging for food in the raging rivers, amid the wild forest animals. I envisioned them walking for days, for four years, through the jungle, land mines, and mountains, parched dry by the burning hot sun, terrified by the earth itself. I thought of the clothes and styles that my mother had cast off many times in her past: her bell-bottoms and flower print shirts; her sarongs and chi paos, discarded immediately in the rush of April 17, 1975; the revolutionary attire of Democratic Kampuchea, thrown off and burned after January 7, 1979; and the salvaged apparel of the old days traded in at the border camps for the donated garb arriving off foreign aid trucks. I thought of my mother's family in Cambodia, the Cheaung family, who were all killed in Cambodia, with the exception of one younger sister and brother who remained in the country. In this photo, she leaves them and so many others behind. Only thirty-three years old, after living so many lives already, here she crosses into a new life, a new start. There is something true captured in her smile, something the story of arrival leaves to the wind.

I begin with this family anecdote to suggest the ways in which the Cambodian refugee archive pushes back against what I call "Cambodia's Cold War episteme" (Fig. 1.1). In his memoir *The Elimination*, published almost concurrently with the release of *The Missing Picture*, Rithy Panh relates an anecdote that illuminates the racial fantasies that underlie Cambodia's Cold War episteme: On the radio one day, Panh hears "a historian, speaking on a French radio station, explain that the Cambodians have been fighting among themselves since the building of Angkor."[8] Panh finds this interpretation "unacceptable . . . given the fact of 1.7 million dead" and writes to the program's director to "let him know that Khmers were not some man-eating tribe."[9] The incident is more troubling to Panh because the radio broadcasters chose to support their interpretation of Cambodia by playing two clips from Panh's film *S-21: The Khmer Rouge Killing Machine*. The film focuses on two survivors of S-21 who return to the prison many years later to confront a number of former Khmer Rouge guards and torturers who Panh has managed to gather at the compound. *S-21* has been seen by critics as a film intended to catalyze the arrival of the Khmer Rouge Tribunal, a film that would serve as "evidence against those who would deny the genocide's severity or the fact that it even happened."[10] Yet, as Panh reveals, the documentary impulse to chronicle violence can have unintended consequences. The clips from his film have been used, without Panh's consent, to reproduce the spectacle of trauma, and, even worse, to deploy this spectacle in the service of genocide denial. As Panh concludes, "That's where we are: confusion. Or silence. Silence about Cambodia."[11] Confusion and silence are linked here as corollary conditions: The silence about what happened in Cambodia has led to widespread confusion, and vice versa. This is the case both within and outside the Cambodian community, for the most common response to the question about the Cambodian Genocide is that it is a confusing and opaque history.

A knowledge project that extends from French colonial imaginaries to U.S. Cold War logics to liberal multicultural repertoires, Cambodia's Cold War episteme constructs Cambodia, variously, as a "red menace" to be contained by the West, as a savage and tragic land cursed by its primitive culture, as a zone of inhumanity to be solved through humanitarian development, as a place for a cheap holiday sojourn amid exotic temples and dark tourism, and as a "black hole" of third world underdevelopment. Within this episteme, the Cambodian refugee can appear as a human interest story to shore up myths of Canadian or American exceptionalism or as a minor anecdote in the major story of white suffering, benevolence, or metamorphosis. In this chapter, I track the making of Cambodia's Cold War episteme across a range of archives—Cold War photojournalism, the 1970s Henry Kissinger telecons, Joel Brinkley's 2011 *Cambodia's Curse*, the French 1906 Colonial Exposition in Marseille, and the form of the "Cambodia travel anecdote."

The Minor Anecdote

Cambodia's Cold War episteme operates through what I call the logic of "Cambodia's minor anecdoting." To offer an example, I turn to an image of the aftermath, Christine Spengler's 1974 photograph, "The Bombardment of Phnom Penh" (see Fig. 1.2). This image captures one fragment of the transpacific proxy war that transformed Cambodia into a hot battleground of the Cold War. In the frame, a man turns to face the camera in bewilderment after gazing at a scorched landscape in the city's southwestern suburban district of Boeung Tumpon. Friends of mine, Davi Hyder and Colin Grafton, remember this deadly battle at the end of the dry season in 1974 like it was just yesterday. Davi Hyder recalls spending days digging a hole under her home in the hopes that a bunker would protect her family from the ceaseless bombardments.[12] Colin Grafton, a teacher of English at a local school at the time, remembers the student who came limping back to the school one day, numbed by the reality that his entire family had been killed.[13]

Zooming in on this photo, we can see that the two people in the foreground are military personnel, dressed in the berets and boots characteristic of the U.S.-backed Lon Nol army. In 1974, this army was at war with the Khmer Rouge, but, during this particular battle, both armies were fighting

Figure 1.2 Christine Spengler's 1974 photograph, "The Bombardment of Phnom Penh." (Photo by Christine Spengler/Sygma/Sygma via Getty Images.)

with U.S. made weapons: the Khmer Rouge powered by U.S.-made 105 mm Howitzer guns and the Lon Nol army by U.S.-made T28 aircraft trainers (adapted as fighter-bombers). For over two months the fighting continued, killing hundreds of people and destroying over ten thousand homes.[14] From the charred terrain left in the wake of the battle, Cambodian civilians salvaged what remained of their collapsed and incinerated dwellings. In the background of the photo, a group of people, some who appear to be children, search through the wreckage and debris. If we listen to the image, we might hear the sounds of hot war: billowing plumes of smoke, choking coughs, crackling embers, crumbling buildings, and the screams of people.[15] The ground is anything but cold: It is burning hot, as is the fury and grief of the Cambodian people lost in the hellfire.

This image serves as the cover image of several books I have come across over the years. These include Spengler's two books, *Années de guerre* (2003) and *L'Opéra du monde* (2016), and American historian Paul Thomas Chamberlin's *The Cold War's Killing Fields: Rethinking the Long Peace* (2018). While Spengler's books read as a celebration of the French war correspondent's heroic escapades in various armed conflicts around the world over the past four decades, Chamberlin's *The Cold War's Killing Fields* is a sweeping 640-page military history of the "deadliest military theatre of the Cold War" as it played out in Asia.[16] These books undertake a centering of Cambodia visually and linguistically, while still managing to evade any kind of sustained attention to the actual lives of Cambodian people. Even as the image of Cambodia occupies center stage, its meaning remains formless and obscure.

From the Greek etymology "*anekdota*," which means "not to publish," an anecdote is a "short narrative of an interesting, amusing, or biographical incident."[17] Anecdotes circulate primarily in the realm of the spoken and the conversational but find their ways into all forms of communication. Anecdotes often make people laugh. They are stories meant to entertain, that are regarded as inconsequential or trivial. In the logic of Cambodia's minor anecdoting, we see a familiar pattern—Cambodia is made to perform a specific kind of discursive work, supplying a malleable staging ground for Western liberalism to define its own humanity. There is a persistent *minoring* of Cambodia, a passing over of Cambodian lives to get to something else deemed *more important*. What does this pattern tell us about the inability or unwillingness to look at the thing itself? The logic of Cambodia's minor anecdoting is akin to what erin Khuê Ninh describes in her work on narratives of sexual violence as the treatment of "rape as epiphenomenal."[18] This is the narration of rape "only as illuminating a structural base, so to speak, of other violences. Its *victims* interesting mainly as forensic evidence, in the pursuit of a larger pattern of destruction."[19] When rape becomes epiphenomenal, it becomes "little more than a stepping-stone" for the illustration of a phenomenon deemed more significant, urgent, or pressing.[20] When Cambodia becomes epiphenomenal, it is generally enlisted to tell a story about whiteness and about the benevolence of whiteness.

Minor anecdoting is not exactly the same as erasure or secrecy. In her book *History on the Run*, Ma Vang argues that the U.S. "secret war" in Laos functions as a Cold War knowledge project that is structured through secrecy—not only in terms of the redactions about the war in the U.S. state archive but also because the war being referenced was itself a secret in the first place.[21] In the absence of an existing official "secret war" archive, Vang argues that "this war exists as an archive which produces knowledge through epistemic erasure and violence in its attempts to reproduce the traditional record about the war and refugees."[22] The Hmong refugee's embodied history of the war and its violence is thus "multiply concealed and secreted because of the nature of this archive."[23] As I discussed in earlier parts of this book, secrecy was central to the U.S. intervention in Cambodia. As in Laos, the U.S. war in Cambodia, entailing the secret U.S.-backed coup to install the pro-American Cambodian leader General Lon Nol in 1970 and the dropping of over 2.7 tons of ordnances on Cambodia from 1965 to 1970, was never officially declared, even as it galvanized the U.S. antiwar movement, particularly at Kent State University in 1970. As an "open secret," the U.S. bombing of Cambodia reinforces Vang's argument that secrecy itself generates the refugee archive as a "repertoire of deferred histories."[24] Yet, Cambodia's Cold War episteme goes beyond secrecy: There is a logic of minor anecdoting at work as Cambodia is there, yet not there, in the archive—prominent and central, yet vacated of meaning. The U.S. state's archives are replete with references to the war in Cambodia, invoked not so much as a secret to be obscured and quieted but rather as the most minor and inconsequential of the U.S. military's Cold War foreign policy priorities, even as these policies unleashed a catastrophic amount of violence.

The Kissinger Telecons

Suturing white supremacist and masculinist fantasies of U.S. imperial rescue of Cambodia to the ableist logics of targeting the Cambodian population as deficient and inhumane, Cambodia's Cold War episteme rationalizes the need for a wholesale "correction" of a foreign population through military intervention and imperial statecraft. "The Kissinger Telecons," declassified in 2004, serve as an example of this logic. When the news of the secret U.S. bombing of Cambodia began to break in the 1970s, the U.S. media often reported on these bombings as one-off incidents of "wayward bombs"—stray or misdirected bombs that supposedly deviated from their intended target.[25] This language of "collateral damage" was used to evade accountability for one of the deadliest U.S. airstrikes waged on Cambodia during the Cold War— a bombing massacre in the Cambodian town of Neak Luong in August 1973. After the massacre at Neak Luong, Richard Nixon conveniently shifted from a rhetorical position of disavowal to one of justified preemptive attack. Now admitting to the approval of "secret bombing raids in Cambodia," Nixon "vigorously justified them as necessary to protect American lives."[26] In the face of mounting pressure by the Senate and the House to stop the illegal bombing of Cambodia, Nixon avowed: "We could cop out, but if we do, *our children* will live in a very dangerous world" [emphasis mine].[27] The designation of Cambodian children's lives as utterly expendable in the service of purportedly safeguarding American children's lives lays bare what Judith Butler describes as the "frames of war" that "produce iconic versions of populations who are eminently grievable, and others whose loss is no loss, and who remain ungrievable."[28]

The "accidental" death, maiming, and suffering of Cambodian lives becomes rationalized by the U.S. military and participating American public in a way that is analogous to the justifications of a child's suffering made by the citizens of the fictional city of Omelas in Ursula Le Guin's classic 1973 dystopian tale, "The Ones Who Walk Away from Omelas." In Le Guin's story, when the citizens of Omelas are confronted with the reality that the city's blissful state of utopia is predicated on the suffering of a single child locked away in a basement cellar, their reactions gradually turn from shock and outrage to acceptance and ableist rationalizations, as the narrator explains: "Perhaps it [the child] was born defective, or perhaps it has become imbecile through fear, malnutrition, and neglect." To maintain the "health of *their children*, the wisdom of their scholars, the skill of their makers, even the abundance of their harvest and the kindly weathers of their skies," the citizens of Omelas must accept and justify the child in the cellar's "abominable misery" [italics mine]. The suffering child who makes possible the happiness, health, and safety of the people of Omelas is, ultimately, ungrievable because they do not see it as human in the first place. Likewise, in the eyes of the U.S. military and the complicit public, Cambodian lives were seen as no loss at all, inhuman from the outset, and, thus, ungrievable in the final accounting. Whether the U.S. bombing of Cambodia offers a blueprint for reading dystopic narratives such as Le Guin's story, or vice versa, Le Guin, writing in 1974, was no doubt influenced by the pathological and commonplace rationalizations made by the United States for waging war in Vietnam, Cambodia, and Laos for over twenty years.

Until today, Henry Kissinger continues to maintain that the areas bombed by the United States "contained next to no Cambodian population"[29]—this despite "The Kissinger Telecons" that exposed the planned and coordinated nature of the operation (see Fig. 1.3). In the telecons dated December 9, 1970, Kissinger instructs General Haig to carry out Nixon's orders for "a massive bombing campaign in Cambodia. . . . Anything that flys [*sic*] on anything that moves."[30] This order is stated by Kissinger as the second agenda item in a banal list of four, which also included: a request for insider information about an upcoming military hearing, an order that General Haig carry out a military equipment inventory, and instructions about a specific army airlift operation. The directive to "use anything that flys" to indiscriminately bomb "anything that moves" in Cambodia is expressed as a routine and mundane instruction, prompting General Haig's laughter presumably because he recognizes the absurdity of the order: At the time, not all aircraft were equipped to be bombers, so grenades would have had to be thrown out the window of smaller prop planes, F-15 planes (which would have been an impossibility), or whatever the inventory turned up.[31] Next, Kissinger says, "Thirdly, now hold on to your hat. He wants an inventory of every prop plane that is suitable for operations out there. He wants a report on it by Saturday morning, for possible movement out there."[32] The killing of hundreds of thousands of Cambodian people and the political destabilization of a neutral, decolonizing

Mr. Kissinger/General Haig (tape)   (General Haig extremely difficult to hear)
December 9, 1970 8:50 p.m.
jlj

H: Yes sir.

K: I just had a call from our friend. First, he wants to know by noon tomorrow whether the Coast Guard is going to be court marshalled because if they are going to be court marshalled he can avoid all questions.

H: No they're not.

K: Why not?

H: I understand that they have decided that there was no criminal culpability involved.

K: Well, what are they going to do - reprimand them?

H: Yes. XXXXXXXXXXXXXXXX They'll use administrative _____
                                        you
K: Well XX better get a written report from Volpe by 10 o'clock tomorrow morning. Can you get that?

H: (Can't hear)

K: Two, he wants a massive bombing campaign in Cambodia. He doesn't want to hear anything. It's an order, it's to be done. Anything that flys on anything that moves. You got that?

H: (Couldn't hear but sounded like Haig laughing.)
                                        to find out, he wants
K: Thirdly, now hold on to your hat. He wants/an inventory of every prop plane that's suitable for operations out there. He wants a report on it by Saturday morning, for possible movement out there.

H: (XXXXXXXXX) For close air support.

K: Yes. That's actually not a bad idea. Fourthly, he's now gung ho on the operation. Have you got Moorer yet?

H: Yes, I talked with him.

K: Is he happier?

H: Much. I didn't go too far.

K: No, but did you tell him I talked to the President?

H: Yes, I did. I told him _____ *(completely unintelligible.)*

Figure 1.3 Transcript of "The Kissinger Telecons," December 9, 1970, in which Kissinger instructs General Haig to carry out four instructions—including the B-52 bombing of Cambodia on the order of Richard Nixon. (Source: NSA Archive.)

territory in the Cold War would be so inconsequential, so minor, in Kissinger's framework that it would not even merit a prefacing that Haig brace himself by "holding on to [his] hat."

The U.S. bombing of Cambodia, far from being a one-off, wayward, or misdirected bombing accident, as was claimed in the media at the time, was a planned and coordinated attack intended to have *massive* consequences in Southeast Asia. Because "killing from above and from a distance" had become the primary means of military assault since World War II, the order to bomb Cambodia reflected the standard operating procedure (with the novelty, in this case, being that the order was directed at a country not officially at war with the United States). Hence, Haig's laughter derives from the absurdity and banality of being asked to quickly get *every* prop plane on hand to engage in an illegal war, from the standpoint of the Senate and the House. Haig laughs ironically at the difficulty of the new predicament he suddenly finds himself in, while the death, debilitation, and destruction of Cambodian lives and infrastructure is normalized as part and parcel of the war, exemplary of what I call Cambodia's Cold War episteme, itself part of a longer genealogy of U.S. permanent war. As Nikhil Pal Singh writes, "The criminal burglary and scandal that brought down the Nixon administration are better remembered than the international crimes that initiated them, especially the illegal bombing of Cambodia."[33] Such a rationality of disposable Cambodian life would exemplify the U.S. Cold War policies in Cambodia for years to come as the country would go to become one of "the most heavily bombed countr[ies] in history," as well as the most heavily mined with antipersonnel devices and other unexploded ordnances.[34] The telecons, here and elsewhere in the declassified archive of over twenty thousand pages, illustrate the suturing of white imperial masculinist fantasies of military power to the ableist logics of the need for a wholesale "correction" of a targeted population. Perhaps, more importantly, this conversation demonstrates the fact of U.S. military power as a system of endemic debilitation with the destruction of Cambodia as the result, regardless of any fantasies these figures might have been entertaining.

Cambodia's Curse

If the Kissinger telecons and other Cold War–era U.S. state archives reflect the casual and mundane way through which the decisions to collateralize Cambodian lives were made, then the most popular books about Cambodia today participate in the reproduction of Cambodia's Cold War episteme through a different kind of trope: that of the "curse."[35] Foremost among these accounts is Joel Brinkley's *Cambodia's Curse: The Modern History of a Troubled Land,* one of the best-selling and widely translated social histories about Cambodia. A former *New York Times* columnist, Brinkley won a Pulitzer Prize in 1980 for his reporting on Cambodian refugees in the Thai border camps. Brinkley's book opens with two anecdotes about the author's trips to Cambodia: the first trip as a twenty-seven-year-old American reporter for the *Louisville Courier-Journal* in 1979 and the second trip as a reporter for the

New York Times in 2008. In 1979, Brinkley went on assignment to interview survivors of the Cambodia Genocide stuck in Thai refugee camps; in 2008, thirty years later, Brinkley returned to Cambodia to find out what had happened to the country after the "world had come together out of guilt and concern (and self-interest) to help pull this little nation out of the mire and give it an opportunity to start over, to enter the modern age."[36] By the end of the preface, it is clear that these anecdotes serve to set up a familiar narrative frame: that of one American man's heroic quest to diagnose the problem of Cambodia's stubborn inability to "enter the modern age"—to shake off its inexorable "curse" of catastrophe, poverty, and suffering.

Frequently referenced by NGO workers and general readers alike, *Cambodia's Curse* attributes Cambodia's modern history of suffering to an affliction of cultural traits—namely, passivity and violence—inherent to the nation's people.[37] Integral to this argument is the conjuring of an image of the country as a place of incomprehensible violence, failed transition, and arrested progress. The book's cover displays a decrepit urban residential neighborhood, where electrical wires hang haphazardly and precariously close to the dusty, unpaved, and chaotic streets. The location is Sothearos Boulevard in Phnom Penh, at the site of the infamous White Building.[38] Up to its demolition in 2017, the historic White Building was a place of stigma associated with poverty, drugs, and sex work. Connoting danger and antimodernity, anarchy and unruliness, the cover image projects an unmistakable "slum tourism" gaze.[39] We are invited to gaze on Cambodia in a way that recalls Achille Mbembe's argument about the portrayal of the African subcontinent in the colonial imaginary as an image of "the half-created and the incomplete, strange signs, convulsive movements—in short, a bottomless abyss where everything is noise, yawning gap, and primordial chaos."[40] Describing Cambodia as a country "still living in the Middle Ages," rife with poverty and government corruption, and "stagnant while most of its neighbors prosper,"[41] Brinkley downplays the U.S. bombings and the Khmer Rouge years as factors affecting the nation's contemporary socioeconomic problems.[42] Commenting on the high rates of post-traumatic stress disorder that continue to afflict the Cambodian population, he asks, "Won't the nation grow out of it? After all, nearly two-thirds of the population is now under thirty; they were born after the Khmer Rouge fell from power."[43] For Brinkley, the inherited trauma of survivors is something that exists largely in the minds of the sufferers. Brinkley concludes that this intergenerational trauma is a "learned behavior" that reinforces an already existing cultural essence.[44]

Cambodia's Curse exemplifies how the white American man's travel anecdote about Cambodia is enlisted in the service of propagating the "culture

of passivity/violence thesis" about Cambodia, a colonial trope at the heart
of Cambodia's Cold War episteme. Referenced commonly by journalists,
scholars, and NGOs,[45] this thesis suggests that Khmer belief systems instill
in the population cultural traits of emotional repression and absolutism that,
ultimately, lead to the irruption of violence. *Cambodia's Curse* posits "Cambodian passivity" as both the *cause* and *effect* of the mass suffering that took
place during the Khmer Rouge era. Cambodian refugees in the aftermath of
the genocide are presented as a permanently damaged, traumatized, and helpless community incapable of embracing the tenets of neoliberal rationality.
Writing about the destruction wrought by the Khmer Rouge regime, Brinkley
quickly qualifies his statement: "In truth, though, the nation was quite primitive
on April 17, 1975, when Pol Pot's army marched into Phnom Penh. There
were few schools, factories, hospitals, or other features of twentieth- or even
nineteenth-century life to raze."[46] Prerevolutionary Cambodia is represented
here as a backwater landscape devoid of all signs of modernity and progress.
In this recounting, the magnitude of loss suffered by Cambodia at the hands
of Pol Pot's Khmer Rouge regime, a regime erected from the ashes of the U.S.
bombings of Cambodia, is rendered null and void. Cambodia is seen as a place
having nothing to lose and, therefore, having lost nothing during the years of
Democratic Kampuchea. The curse finds its most insidious iteration as an
explanatory framework for why Cambodians supposedly did not resist the
Khmer Rouge during the years of Democratic Kampuchea. Describing Cambodians as "a conflicted people, generally passive, quiet, non-threatening—
but also capable of extraordinary violence and brutality,"[47] *Cambodia's Curse*
traces the trait of Cambodian passivity back to "the time of the great kings
of Angkor 1,000 years ago."[48]

   Brinkley's book suspends temporality, freezing Cambodia and Cambodians in a fetishistic image of ancient time. The trope of the curse as a diagnosis for Cambodia's contemporary situation again recalls the way in which
many African societies have been constructed as cursed landscapes incapable
of progress. In the same vein as popular books such as Dambisa Moyo's
Dead Aid or Robert Calderisi's *The Trouble with Africa*, *Cambodia's Curse* is
disguised as an impassioned plea for restructuring international aid to Cambodia by first understanding the "problem" of a Cambodian culture that dis-
courages "a drive to succeed."[49] Such books illustrate Achille Mbembe's view
of how colonial discourse constructs places in the Global South as "being
moved by the blind force of custom" and "living under the burden of charms,
spells, and prodigies."[50] The trope of the curse also recalls Frantz Fanon's
discussion of the "colonial vocabulary" that constructed and maintained the
physical and ideological borders of a "world divided."[51] As Fanon argues,

colonial discourse designated the "colonized's sector" as a space character-ized by the absolute negation of values, ethics, and aesthetics in opposition to the colonizer's world of security, order, and humaneness.[52] Constitutive of a colonial orthography and a Cold War episteme, *Cambodia's Curse* relegates Cambodia to a space of absolute otherness, forever outside of the time and progress of Western modernity.

The 1906 Colonial Exposition

While the articulation of Cambodia's third world degeneracy and devel-opmental failure makes for an easily digestible narrative for contemporary Western audiences looking to affirm a sense of their moral and cultural superiority, the roots of this discourse go back much further to the era of French colonial rule in Indochina and its conjuring of *Cambodge* as an exotic and mystical landscape in need of European patronage. As Penny Edwards explains in her book *Cambodge: The Cultivation of a Nation, 1860–1945*, French colonial propaganda held that "Cambodians were changeless, sus-pended in cultural time and political space."[53] French colonial magazines such as *l'Illustration*, published in Paris from 1843 to 1944, described Cam-bodia as "a fallen country, which has preserved only two parts of its glorious past: its improbably grandiose ruins and its dancers, strange relics of a dead past."[54] This characterization reflected France's broader program of *la mis-sion civilisatrice* (the civilizing mission) that dictated the philosophy of the French empire's responsibility to uplift and develop the colonies. Arising out of this colonial context, the 1906 Colonial Exposition in Marseille promised its French audience "panoramas" of the faraway colonies, including pavil-ions and performances from Tunisia, Algeria, Madagascar, and Indochina. Attracting more than thirty thousand spectators per night, the exposition was aimed at promoting France's cultural policies in the colonies. It was also a tourist attraction of the highest order, drawing large audiences from all parts of France eager to experience the mystique of the faraway colonies. As Edward Said argues, the Orient has since antiquity been seen as "a place of romance, exotic beings, haunting memories and landscapes, remarkable experiences."[55] According to Panivong Norindr, Indochina, in particular, rep-resented "an elaborate fiction, a modern phantasmatic assemblage invented during the heyday of French colonial hegemony in Southeast Asia. It is a myth that has never existed and yet endures in our collective imaginary."[56]

As illustrated by the exposition's advertisement, this phantasmatic projec-tion of Indochina was best embodied in the mythical figure of the Khmer apsara dancer (see Fig. 1.4). The event's main attraction was a Khmer court dance troupe consisting of eighty dancers accompanied by the Cambodian king Sisowath himself. According to the French colonialists, Cambodia was seen as a vanishing and declining "traditional" culture, vulnerable to threats of encroachment from its neighboring Siamese and Vietnamese enemies as well as other foreign occupiers.[57] With Cambodia as its "protectorate," France had a duty, it was argued, to preserve and protect the precious Cambodian paintings, sculptures, monuments, and other art forms (especially dance) that were seen as being in "crisis" and in "decline." As Edwards puts it, the French colonial ethnographers and travel writers were not so much concerned that actual Khmer people "would die or disappear, but that their customs and culture might vanish."[58] The exposition was meant to showcase, above all, that the preservation of the traditional Cambodian arts was dependent on enlightened French colonial management. This view that Cambodia was indebted to France was perhaps best observed when the Cambodian royal family was burdened with the entire bill for its excursion to France in 1906, even going so far as to charge Cambodia retroactively for the presents given to King Sisowath during his visit.[59] The colonial "gift" bestowed on Cambodia by the French turned out to be no gift at all but rather a colonial debt that Cambodia could never fully escape.

Over time, the story of the exposition in Marseilles acquired what art historian Anna Blair describes as "an epic dimension" in French circles, an anecdote about the reanimation of French culture through colonial encounters with Cambodia.[60] This legendary aura was partly owing to Auguste Rodin's famous sketches of the Cambodian dancers, which immortalized the 1906 exposition. Mesmerized by the image of these dancers who, for him, embodied the "timelessness of Cambodian culture," Rodin drew the dancers in an abstract, expressionistic style that stripped them of all background, context, and individual identity.[61] For Rodin, it was as if the dancers had sprung to life directly from the bas-reliefs of Angkor Wat, personifications of the great apsaras "engraved in the stone ten centuries ago."[62] Rodin desired to capture the beauty of the Cambodian dancers as a means to electrify and animate his own treatises on mankind, art, and civilization. Setting himself up with the task of translating, for the French public, a new form, style, and aesthetics embodied in the Cambodian dancers, Rodin produced over 150 sketches of the Khmer apsara dancers. Long after the royal court returned to Cambodia, Rodin's drawings would be extolled as masterful works of French modern art. The sketches would go on to help cement Rodin's "lofty position in the Western artistic canon."[63] Like so many works of this canon formed through colonial conquest and encounters, Rodin's drawings showcase a striking di-

Figure 1.4 Advertisement of 1906 Colonial Exposition in Marseille, France, depicting Khmer apsara dancers alongside icons of other colonial pavilions staged at the exposition. (Via Wikimedia Commons.)

mension of colonial conquest: the theft of cultural resources alongside the extraction of natural ones.

As works such as Amitav Ghosh's 1998 travelogue *Dancing in Cambodia* demonstrates, the orientalist imaginaries embedded in the 1906 Colonial Exposition in Marseille and Rodin's sketches can be seen as a mirror for the logics that underwrite the contemporary human rights economy in Cambodia. *Dancing in Cambodia* begins with a historical anecdote about Cambodian king Sisowath's journey to France in 1906 aboard a French liner called the *Amiral-Kersaint*. Ghosh explains that he was fascinated by the detail about how the liner was also "carrying a troupe of nearly a hundred classical dancers and musicians from the royal palace of Phnom Penh."[64] From these scenes set in 1906 France, the text moves to 1990s Cambodia under the occupation of the United Nations Transitional Authority in Cambodia (UNTAC), where Ghosh meets three UN workers described as "the smallest of cogs in the vast machinery of the UN," and "whose vision of the country was organized around [their] part in saving it from itself."[65] These UN workers from Russia and Bangladesh had lived through their own countries' civil wars yet saw Cambodia as a nation cursed with infancy and barbarism apart from all others. The Bangladeshi humanitarian worker tells Ghosh that Cambodian people's motivation to participate in the country's demining efforts is purely economic since "for them it's all dollars, dollars, dollars."[66] Reminiscent of the paternalistic attitudes of the French colonial tourists at the 1906 exposition, the UNTAC humanitarian worker sees his own role in the UN occupation solely through the lens of the white man's burden, incapable of imagining any kind of interiority or ethical dimension to Cambodian lives. The UN workers in Ghosh's story narrate the righteousness of their work in Cambodia with an attitude of unqualified moral superiority that echoes the tones of the French protectorate regime. Carrying these insidious imperial attitudes, the humanitarian workers imagine their mission in Cambodia as an ushering of the country into a future of Western imitation. Through Ghosh's story, we can discern how Cambodia's Cold War episteme cuts across time and space, from the "civilizing" fantasies held by the French colonial regime in Indochina to the human rights economies purporting to deliver Cambodia from its endemic illiberalism.

The Travel Anecdote

Whereas the colonial expositions of the French protectorate era turned Cambodian people into grotesque displays of the exotic Orient, tourists who visit Cambodia today are often drawn to the brutality on display at the mass graves of Choeung Ek and at the torture cells of Tuol Sleng. In the former, Cambodia is seen as untamed and organic (ancient temples, the heat of the tropics, natural abundance); in the latter, Cambodia is machinelike and inorganic (Communism, the Khmer Rouge, the "wheel of history"). Both imaginaries, however, are braided strands of Cambodia's Cold War episteme.

Cambodian people today are frequently praised by outsiders for overcoming their history of tragedy, for their hospitality, and for the famous "Cambodian smile." At the same time, the experience of visiting Cambodia may inspire outsiders to shake their heads in bewilderment at how such a gentle people could have *let such a horror happen*. Tourists gaze at the skulls, bones, and bloodstained walls at Cambodia's various atrocity tourist sites and wonder *why these people would choose to memorialize their tragedy in such a way*. As in the long tradition of Western imperial discovery in the "exotic Orient," the desire for Cambodia is the desire to consume the sensuous, but simultaneously horrifying, pleasures of the East. What is seen through the eyes of the tourist viewing Cambodia through a reductive binary of (exotic) temples and (horrific) trauma, then, is a selective act of negation, an unconscious or, perhaps, willful act of nonseeing.

Take for example, Elizabeth Gilbert's 2006 memoir, *Eat, Pray, Love*, and its 2010 film adaptation starring Julia Roberts, both of which begin with the protagonist Elizabeth's voice-over recounting an anecdote told to her by her psychologist friend Deborah. As Elizabeth is seen on camera riding a bicycle into a Buddhist temple complex while on holiday in Indonesia, her voice-over explains that Deborah was asked "if she could offer psychological counselling to Cambodian refugees, boat people who had recently arrived in the city."[67] Deborah is at first "daunted by the task," of trying to help these Cambodians who "had suffered genocide, starvation, relatives murdered before their eyes, years in refugee camps, harrowing boat trips to the West."[68] Soon enough, however, Deborah is delighted to discover that the task will not actually be daunting at all, as the refugees do not seem to have any complex psychological needs beyond that of the average American. According to Deborah, for the Cambodian refugees, "it was all, 'I met this guy in the refugee camp. I thought he really loved me, but when we got separated on the boat, he took up with my cousin, but now he says he loves me and he keeps calling me. They're married now. What should I do? I still love him.' This is how we are."[69] This anecdote serves to set the stage for a film about a white American woman's pursuit of romantic love and spiritual awakening. No matter the traumatic experiences at hand, the scene suggests, we can turn to the interpersonal and the romantic to glimpse the universal humanity of all beings. Aside from the historical inaccuracy of Cambodian refugees' "harrowing boat trips to the

West," what makes this opening scene particularly vexing for viewers like myself is the way in which the Cambodian refugee experience is presented as emblematic of the *worst* kind of suffering imaginable for white Western women seeking to find meaning in their own lives.

With their midlife crises marked by breakups, travel to exotic Asian countries, and the seeking of spiritual enlightenment, these women are reassured of the Cambodian refugees' humanity only insofar as it reminds them of their own preoccupations with the romantic banalities of white American middle-class life. Indeed, the film does not interrogate Cambodia as anything more than a site of violence. While Elizabeth's other travel destinations (Italy, India, and Bali) are eroticized and orientalized as foreign playgrounds for her self-discovery, Cambodia is enlisted merely as an anecdotal vehicle that delimits the inhumanity of the world and thus the humanity of the white protagonist. Even more explicitly than the film, Gilbert's memoir uses the Cambodian anecdote to suggest a nascent humanitarian ethos within Elizabeth. After thinking about Deborah's story, Elizabeth says, "When I tried this morning, after an hour or so of unhappy thinking, to dip back into my meditation, I took a new idea with me: compassion."[70] In the true spirit of neoliberal self-care regimes, the Cambodian anecdote here reminds the narrator to be compassionate *to herself*, catalyzing Elizabeth's transformation from an unhappy and psychologically detached person to a fulfilled life of sexual awakening, spiritual awakening, and compassion for herself as a white American woman.

While representing a best-selling memoir and a box office sensation, Elizabeth Gilbert's *Eat, Pray, Love*, has hardly been taken seriously as a work of feminist writing. Yet, we find similarities in Gilbert's memoir with theoretical feminist works such as Maggie Nelson's memoir *The Argonauts*, a book that has been heralded as an exemplary work of feminist autotheory for the twenty-first century. In the genealogy of queer and feminist autobiographical writings, along with Roland Barthes, Susan Sontag, Eve Sedgwick, and others, *The Argonauts* is at once a memoir of Nelson's experience raising a child with her transgender husband, Harry Dodge, and a theoretical rendition of the language and ideas of queer theory and psychoanalysis. In one scene, Nelson recounts an anecdote about her mother's visit to Cambodia:

> Recently my mother visited the Killing Fields in Cambodia. After she returned, she sat in our living room showing me her trip photos while Iggy motored around the shaggy white rug, doing "tummy time." *I barely want to tell you about this, because of the baby*, she said, nodding

in his direction, *but there was a tree there, an oak tree, called the Killing Tree, against which the Khmer Rouge would kill babies by bashing their skulls. Thousands and thousands of babies, their brains smashed out against this tree.* I get the point, I say. *I'm sorry*, she says, *I really shouldn't be telling you this.*

A few weeks later, talking about her trip again on the phone, she says, *Now, there's something I shouldn't really mention, because of the baby, but they had this tree there, at the Killing Fields, called the Killing Tree . . .*

I know my mother well enough by now to recognize, in her baby-killing-tree Tourette's, her desire to install in me an outer parameter of horror of what could happen to a baby human on this planet. I don't know why she needs to feel sure I have this parameter in mind, but I have come to accept that she feels it necessary. She needs me to know that she's stood before the Killing Tree.[71]

In this anecdote, Nelson's mother is referring to the place known to Cambodian people as *Choeung Ek*, a former mass execution center used by the Khmer Rouge. Inside the compound today, tourists often crowd around a majestic tree with an umbrella-shaped crown known colloquially as the "Killing Tree." Native to South and Central America and known for its sensitivity to light, the Killing Tree today is adorned with hundreds of colorful bracelets. Reminiscent of the Khmer Buddhist symbol of compassion, protection, and connection, these bracelets have been left by visitors to commemorate the lives that were ended, cruelly and brutally, at the base of this tree.[72] For Cambodian people, the Killing Tree embodies a collective pain and suffering extending from Pol Pot time that remains so difficult to articulate that it often manifests as silence, shame, and self-abjection. It stands as a visceral reminder of what Cambodian people did to each other, of the planned waste of life that most Cambodian people still find incomprehensible, and of the indignity of death in mass graves suffered by millions of Cambodian people, including children, which continues to haunt the consciousness of all survivors.

In Nelson's mother's anecdote, however, the Killing Tree circulates as something quite different. Conflated with Cambodia writ large, the Killing Tree is invoked as a synecdoche of horror, as the distinctly violent "other" that gives greater value to the white child's safety in the West. Returning from her holiday, Nelson's mother comes away with only one image of Cambodia imprinted on her mind: that of Cambodian babies thrashed against trees by the Khmer Rouge. What she "learns" from her trip to the Killing Fields is not an account of Cold War geopolitics, Western complicity, or Cambodian survival but a reaffirmation of what whiteness has to continually fear and safeguard itself against.

Cambodia, in the eyes of Nelson's mother, is invoked as a lesson from a white mother to her pregnant daughter about the need to protect one's child against the horrors that exist in the world. Cambodia becomes a warning about what happens to babies "over there," where there is a supposed void of humanity. The implicit suggestion is that Nelson's mother now has firsthand experience of a place where "life really has no value,"[73] a racist tourist dictum that goes back to the infamous statement by U.S. general William Westmoreland during the Vietnam War era: "The Oriental doesn't put the same high price on life as does a Westerner. Life is plentiful, life is cheap in the Orient. And as the philosophy of the Orient expresses it: Life is not important."[74] In the anecdote, Nelson's mother cannot stop herself from bringing up what she saw during her tour at the Killing Fields memorial. Her incessant repetition of Cambodia as the "outer parameter of horror" becomes a "baby-killing-tree Tourette's." Likened to an involuntary tic, the utterance of Cambodia's history of tragedy becomes an irrepressible, uncontrollable urge.

In repeatedly apologizing for bringing up the horror of the Killing Tree, Nelson's mother becomes, like Marlow in Joseph Conrad's *Heart of Darkness* or Willard in Francis Ford Coppola's *Apocalypse Now*, the courageous Westerner who has dared to venture into Cambodia at her own physical and psychological peril.[75] Cambodia has been figured as Asia's "heart of darkness," the site where Kurtz has "gone native" among the Indigenous people in *Apocalypse Now*. Cambodia is the threatening and untamed landscape into which Willard must travel in order to witness the horror of Indochina directly. Just as these anti-imperialist white men are transformed through their voyages into the heart of colonialism, Nelson's mother emerges from Cambodia physically intact, but deeply affected, having witnessed the remains of unimaginable brutality. Now plagued by a stuttering tic, Nelson's mother also becomes like Kurtz in *Heart of Darkness*, beset by a condition of madness, which in Nelson's mother's case manifests as a figurative form of Tourette's syndrome. In this story, Nelson's mother is now the one with the disability. As Nelson writes, "She needs me to know that she's stood before the Killing Tree." In this portrait of white witnessing, *standing* before the tree is more important than the tree itself as Nelson's mother is positioned at the center of the story. Cambodia's tragedy and debilitation becomes nothing more than a transformative vehicle of self-discovery, enabling Nelson's mother to prove her worldliness, her humanity, and her self-sacrifice. A scene so brief that it is easily glossed over, this travel anecdote about Cambodia functions as a tourist spectacle that merely results in a shoring up of white womanhood.

It could be argued, of course, that the attitude toward Cambodia is *not* Maggie Nelson's but expressly that of Nelson's mother; far from sanctioning her mother's ignorance, one might say, Nelson is satirizing it and holding it up to ridicule. In this narrative separation of mother and daughter, it is only Nelson's mother who is culpable while Maggie Nelson, the author, emerges in the foreground as the enlightened, antiracist feminist. Regardless of Nelson's intent, Cambodia becomes incidental and collateral, the raw material through which white liberal personhood is made and defined.

Conclusion: Crip Refugee Crossings

If the examples discussed above highlight the production of Cambodia's Cold War episteme through the logic of minor anecdoting, then the rest of this book endeavors to show how the Cambodian refugee archive wrestles with and unsettles this logic through various forms of aesthetic and artistic experimentation. The remainder of this book queries what it means to bring the fields of critical refugee studies and critical disability studies to the afterlife of the Cold War in Cambodia—three decades of hot fighting on Cambodian territory that resulted in the widespread physical and psychological impairment of over four million Cambodian people. We might begin to explore this question by looking at how Cambodian refugee and Cambodian refugee–allied artists have redeployed the minor anecdote itself, investing it with new meaning by locating the crip Cambodian refugee body-mind at the center of the narrative to highlight how refugee "bodies and minds are unevenly caught up in, or differentially materialize around, global processes of uneven development,"[76] including the disabling structures of war, imprisonment, resettlement, deportation, and neoliberal divestment. These systems form the matrices of domination that Liat Ben-Moshe describes as "race-ability"—the way in which criminalization "entails the construction of both race (especially blackness) and disability (especially mental difference) as dangerous."[77] This framework is not simply about inclusion but about interrogating the systems that make populations vulnerable to and available for capture in carceral locales. The rest of this book thus seeks to elaborate my ideas about refugee lifeworlds—an intersectional, abolitionist lens through which we can interrogate the multivalent ways in which refugee life and disability come together in the afterlife of war. Circling back to where this chapter began, with the story in the *Montreal Gazette*, this chapter concludes with a short essay of refugee autotheory that carries the momentum of the book with the force of the refugee's ongoing journey.

In 1979, after years of Khmer Rouge territorial incursion into Vietnam, the Vietnamese army invaded Cambodia and overthrew Pol Pot's regime. My mother and father found themselves back in their hometown of Kampong Thom. They had survived, but shame washed over them when they thought of those who did not. Most survivors believed that just one more year under Pol Pot's rule and all Cambodians would have been dead—the extinction of an entire people. My parents and brothers, now just barely skin and bones, staggered out of the labor camps and made their way to an abandoned building in Kampong Thom—an apocalyptic-looking city full of destroyed and ransacked homes that had been deserted in haste four years earlier.

The Khmer Rouge was no longer in control, but the war continued to rage on and on. Cambodian people feared the return of the Khmer Rouge, enlistment into the Vietnamese military, and outright starvation due to the U.S. sanctions on foreign aid getting into Cambodia. My mother always said about this time, "We didn't have enough of anything. Not enough water. No money. Nothing." One day, my mother could no longer bear my brother's cries of hunger. Watching her children live on the brink of starvation for four years had led my mother to a place beyond sanity, beyond madness, to something more excruciating, more feral. No mother should have to live with the memory of her children in such pain.

With a bag of jewelry stashed near her waist, my mother set out for the market to buy a hen. She had managed to hide this bag of jewelry throughout Pol Pol time by burying it in the ground, for the day when things could be bought and sold again. The only hen still available at the market looked demonic, as if it were possessed by the devil. When my mother went to pay for it, she suddenly noticed that her bag of jewelry was gone. With this loss, she felt as if something inside her had finally come undone. Inside the bag were two diamond bracelets given to her by her mother whose body was never found, whose spirit wandered restlessly. These items were all that my mother had left of her mother. And without the jewelry, she could not barter and trade for food. She wondered how her children would survive. I went so crazy during this time, she recounted. She remembered how she cried and cried uncontrollably, and how a friend tried to comfort her by saying to her in her native Fujian language, 你哭有什么样? (My child, what is the use of crying now?)

As the days passed, my mother started to feel ill. She began to vomit frequently and then one day she realized that she was pregnant. It had been eight years since her last pregnancy. She could not believe that she was bringing a child into this world. It was a crime, she thought. Surely, the gods would punish her for such an act. She could barely take care of the two children that she had.

Around this time, my mother and father began hearing the stories about refugees going to the Thai border. They heard about how people were getting food and water in the camps, how some refugees were being sponsored to France or America. Thousands and thousands of refugees were leaving every day, making the journey on foot, by bicycle, on top of trucks. My parents heard about the three-hundred-kilometer route that went from Kampong Thom to Svay Sisophon, and then on to Chumrum Thmei at the border of Cambodia and Thailand. They knew the route was dangerous, filled with Vietnamese checkpoints, land mines, malaria, and wild animals in the jungle. They heard the stories about refugees being driven back at the border by Thai soldiers firing at them.

In one story about this border, recounted to me many years later in Canada, Thai soldiers shot at a Cambodian refugee woman as she held her newborn child in her arms. Later, a Red Cross vehicle came, and—after dispersing the soldiers scavenging her body for gold—they found the refugee woman unconscious but still alive, a bullet in her leg and her dead child in her arms. The woman survived and eventually made it across the border to Thailand, and then to Canada, where she settled in the small town of Goderich, Ontario, the rural hometown where I grew up, and where I knew her as the mother of the only other Cambodian family in town. My memories of her are of a woman with a prosthetic leg who could speak some English but conversed with me mainly in Khmer. With a husband who had also left behind a family in Cambodia, she had two children, one of whom was my best friend growing up. The refugee mother communicated her story to the refugee communities and to my parents, who repeated it to me. The story encapsulates two absences: the child, and the mother's past as a dancer for the Royal Ballet. The last time I saw the woman's living daughter, I promised her that I would one day communicate her mother's story to others through the written page.

My parents knew of the stories like my friend's mother's, of the absolute brutalities, of all the unforeseeable risks, yet they still believed it was the right decision to go. From their squatter home in Kampong Thom, my parents and my two brothers rode on top of a large oil truck with other refugee families for the daylong journey to Svay Sisophon. The bouncing motion of the vehicle made my mother, now eight-months pregnant, completely nauseous, and she threw up many times along the way. After arriving at Svay Sisophon, the family prepared for the most dangerous leg of the journey to the next destination: Chumrum Thmei. They ran out of transportation options and so my mother and father resorted to paying local people to take the family by bicycle and then on foot through the jungle. My mother was riding on the back of a bicycle, when suddenly the cyclist stopped. He told my mother that she was too heavy, and he demanded she pay more. My mother begged him to take pity on her, and eventually he continued.

The family arrived at a checkpoint controlled by the Vietnamese army. Many Cambodian refugees were being stopped at this checkpoint, where they searched my father's body and found a letter in his pocket written in Chinese. It was sent to him by his father in Laos with instructions on how to go to the refugee camp in Thailand. It was the only correspondence my father had had with his father in almost five years. The guard could not read the letter, but anything in the Chinese language at this time was deemed suspicious, as Vietnam was at war with China.

At the checkpoint, my father was detained while my mother and two brothers were allowed to pass through. At the sight of my father being left behind, my second oldest brother screamed and cried uncontrollably. Seeing this, the guard turned to ask my father if the boy was his son. My father said no, that he did not know the woman and two boys, that it was just another refugee boy crying. The guard let my mother and brothers go on, while my father had to stay and wait to be questioned further. But, when the guard was not looking, my father ran away, back into the jungle. It took him another two days to reach Chumrum Thmei where he was reunited with my mother and brothers. From there, they prepared for their next crossing, to Khao-I-Dang.

2

Debility and the U.S.
Bombing of Cambodia

In 1971, the Cambodian Civil War began to permeate every aspect of my mother and father's life in their hometown of Kampong Thom. They remember how the skies above the city were regularly filled with U.S. military drones and fighter jets. Every day, the drone planes circled above, scanning the terrain and quietly snapping aerial photographs. Meanwhile, the jets swooped down from the skies and made deafening sounds, leaving the city's residents in constant fear of impending bombs. Everyone knew these were U.S.-made planes, as it was common knowledge that the two armies at war—the Khmer Rouge guerillas and the Lon Nol army—did not have access to this kind of technology. One night, when the bombings got too close to the city, my mother and father packed up their two young children (my brothers) and took shelter overnight in a Buddhist pagoda, a site rumored to be safe from the U.S. bombs. When they returned to the city the next day, they found that their home had been taken over by the Lon Nol soldiers, who wanted to use the rooftop to launch rockets at the Khmer Rouge. The incoming shelling happened every morning, and, out on the streets, people would go from buying coffee and noodles in one instant to throwing their bodies down on the streets in the next. One morning, outside a café, a rocket hit a man standing just meters away from my father, who was also wounded by a piece of shrapnel from the blast. With the sound of the explosion ringing in his ears, my father stared in horror at the lifeless body of this man, his neighbor, on the street.

For years, the war continued to rage on, bringing daily scenes such as this one to the lives of Cambodian people, particularly those in the rural countryside. In 1973, my mother and brothers were evacuated by helicopter from Kampong Thom to Phnom Penh, a capital city beginning to expand with waves of refugees arriving from the countryside. At the last minute, my father was prevented from boarding the helicopter and had to watch in disbelief as his family lifted off without him. It took seven months until he, too, was able to evacuate on a cargo boat filled with hundreds of Cambodian people. The journey by boat along the Tonle Sap River was dangerous. To try to stop the refugees from fleeing to Phnom Penh, the Khmer Rouge hid in coconut trees along the river. When refugee cargo boats slowed down at a bend in the river, the guerrilla fighters took this opportunity to fire at the boats from the tree-tops. To this day, my father finds it difficult to talk about this period of time, often lapsing into a repetitive monologue about how many close encounters he had with death in those years of Lon Nol time, and then afterward, when the Khmer Rouge took over. It was only when I was in my twenties, when I began asking many questions about the past, that I learned that my family had lived through a brutal civil war and a U.S. bombing campaign that made them into refugees before the horror of the Cambodian Genocide had even begun.

I begin with this fragment to frame this chapter's discussion of debility in the afterlife of the U.S. bombing of Cambodia. Despite its vivid central-ity within the collective psyche of Cambodian people, the U.S. bombing of Cambodia remains only faintly legible in the episteme of the Cold War knowledge formation that, as Lisa Yoneyama argues, continues to obscure the regional manifestations of the Cold War as they played out in places such as Cambodia.[1] Here, starting in 1970, the Cold War unfolded as a violent hot war, as the scenes from my mother and father's memories make viscerally clear. In the words of Australian journalist John Pilger, in 1979, "The official aim of the bombing was to wipe out a Viet Cong base in Cambodia—a base that existed only in the imagination of American generals. President Nixon's aim was to show the Vietnamese Communists just how tough he could be—a policy he once described as a madman's theory of war. The Cambodians who died were called 'collateral damage' and their burning villages, 'friendly fire.'"[2] Linked to the military calculation of "acceptable" levels of killing during wartime, the term "collateral damage" was first popularized during the Vietnam War era to describe the U.S. military's "unintentional" killing of Southeast Asian civilians.[3] Today, Jasbir Puar explains, the language of collateral damage continues to disarticulate "the effects of warfare from the perpetration of violence" through terms such as "unintended" or "accidental" killings while never calling into question the *justness* of the war in the first place.[4] Also obscured is the collateral damage that continues to unfold for long after the initial violence—damage that manifests as what Puar describes as "deeply entrenched forms of belated disability caused by U.S. imperial occupations."[5] To read the U.S. bombing of Cambodia as a structure of endemic debilitation is to move away from a trauma-based framework that individualizes the nature of wartime injury.

This shift from trauma to debility seeks to acknowledge, in Puar's words, that "the production of most of the world's disability happens through colonial violence, developmentalism, war, occupation, and the disparity of resources."[6] For Cambodian people who have lived through war, genocide, and refugee displacement, many of whom continue to live in perpetual fear of being maimed and killed by unexploded ordnances, the "elsewhere" zone of endemic debilitation is already *here*: There is no clear before or after becoming disabled. Debility complicates the notion of the violent "accident" by emphasizing "the statistical likelihood by which certain populations are expected to yield themselves to bodily debilitation, deterioration, and outright harm."[7] Puar focuses on the tactical debilitation of Palestinian inhabitants of Gaza and the West Bank, insisting on the carceral-ableist and settler-colonial structures of power that make and remake the disability of Palestinian people. Unsettling the disabled/nondisabled binary, debility is about "the slow wearing down of populations instead of the event of becoming disabled" and is witnessed, for example, in the Israeli state's "shoot to maim but not to kill" policy in Palestine.[8] Debility also destabilizes assumptions about the disabled subject's capacity to "voice" or "speak" their pain within a framework legible to a listening public.[9]

In this chapter, I examine Rithy Panh's 2011 film *Shiiku, the Catch*, Viet Thanh Nguyen's 2010 short story "The Americans," and Masahiro Sugano and Kosal Khiev's film *Cambodian Son* as works that explore the U.S. collateralization of Cambodian refugee life during the Cold War. In Panh's film and Nguyen's story, debility implicates not only the lifeworlds of refugees injured and maimed by war but also that of the Black U.S. soldier enlisted in the transpacific currents of militarized labor.[10] As Nikhil Pal Singh argues, undeclared wars such as the U.S. bombing of Cambodia have always been inextricably linked to the domestic "inner wars" on American soil.[11] In his 1970 foreword to the 1951 petition *We Charge Genocide*, American civil rights activist William Patterson wrote, "The wantonly murderous and predatory racist attacks on Korea, Vietnam and Cambodia . . . are inseparably related to the equally criminal murders of rebellious black youth in Chicago, Illinois, New Haven, Connecticut, Augusta, Georgia, and Jackson, Mississippi."[12] For many of these young Black men caught in the impossible binary of "the choice to kill or be killed," military enlistment in the outer wars in Asia proved to be their only option to escape the racial violence of the inner war at home.[13] While Panh's *Shiiku, the Catch* and Nguyen's "The Americans" explore the channeling of surplus Black bodies into the military and to the "off the map" zones of undeclared wars in places such as Cambodia, the film *Cambodian Son* demonstrates how surplus refugee bodies are channeled into prison or deportation exile. Focusing on the story of Cambodian American spoken word poet Kosal Khiev, *Cambodian Son* explores the carceral disciplining of the refugee body, resettled and recaptured in the U.S. hyperghetto, prison system, and deportation land of exile. These works that constitute the Cambodian refugee archive limn a landscape of refugee physical and mental impairment that arises as a product of the carceral-ableist military-industrial complex. What emerges through a reading of these works are a reckoning with the enduring remains of war and an understanding of how those remains have been salvaged and remade among refugees and racialized subjects in war's afterlife.

Rithy Panh's *Shiiku, the Catch*: Debility "Off the Map"

Rithy Panh's film *Shiiku, the Catch* centers on a community of villagers living in the rural, Cambodian countryside as it is being ravaged by U.S. bombings in 1972.[14] The film's story is adapted from Japanese author Kenzaburo Oe's classic novella, *Shiiku* (*Prize Stock*).[15] Oe's novella is a fictional account of an unnamed Black American pilot whose fighter plane crashes into a small secluded Japanese village near the end of World War II. Oe's story narrates the pilot's capture by the village people, focusing on his interactions with a group of Japanese boys left in charge of guarding him. In intense, often uncomfortably graphic detail, Oe recounts the exoticization and violence the Black pilot is subjected to as well as the semblance of a growing kinship between the pilot and the Japanese boys. In the novella's climax, the Black soldier captures one of the Japanese boys as a hostage, prompting the Japanese villagers to exact a brutal revenge. In her book *A Violent Peace*, Christine Hong argues that Oe's *Shiiku*, published five years after the formal end of the U.S. occupation of Japan, serves as an "ironic meditation on the U.S. occupation and postwar democratization of Japan."[16] Reading the novella in relation to discussions of "the black Pacific," Hong asserts that the text illustrates "dramas in comparative subhumanity in which the operators of machineries of death and the inhabitants of the target have been unevenly placed into inexorable kill-or-be-killed motion against each other."[17] Panh explains his reasoning for choosing to adapt Oe's story as the following: "I thought there were some good parallels with the original 1957 Kenzaburo Oe story and I thought we could set the story in Cambodia under the Khmer Rouge rather than WWII Japan."[18] Stressing the parallels between the history of U.S. imperialism in Japan and Cambodia, Panh aligns himself with an artistic genealogy of Asian authors and auteurs known for their antiwar, anti-imperial writing and filmmaking.

In Panh's *Shiiku, the Catch*, the B-52 plane of a Black American bomber pilot, named Lieutenant Simon Jefferson Louis, crashes behind Khmer Rouge enemy lines in 1972. Captured by Cambodian villagers, Louis's imprisonment becomes a part of the military training of a group of young Cambodian boys as they live amid the relentless U.S. aerial bombardments and the intensifying civil war between the Khmer Rouge regime and the Lon Nol army. A coming-of-age narrative about Cambodian childhoods silenced and curtailed by war and military recruitment, Panh's *Shiiku, the Catch* rests specifically on the perspective of a tough orphan Cambodian boy named Pang, who must navigate the U.S. bombings and the military hierarchies of the Khmer Rouge. As the narrative unfolds, we see how Pang's debilitation is linked to the regime's gradual reformation of Pang's personhood into a hardened militarized cadre. Disciplined into the language and codes of Communist military manhood, Pang is no longer allowed to be a carefree, wayward child.[19] Seated at the edge of a crater made by a U.S. bomb, Pang and his friends are instructed on how to sit and stand in formation, how to obey military hierarchy, and how to speak or not speak. As Achille Mbembe writes, necropower works by disaggregating local populations into "rebels, child soldiers, victims, or refugees, or civilians who are incapacitated through mutilation or simply massacred on the model of ancient sacrifices."[20] In Cambodia, what we saw was a deep blurring of these categories, with children such as Pang inhabiting multiple categories all at once. Pang is a refugee and a victim of the U.S. bombs as well as a child soldier and a rebel. Incapacitated by multiple overlapping systems of necropower (both the U.S. empire and the Khmer Rouge), Pang's deepening silence is conveyed through his increasing externalization of violence. The symbol of debility in the film is thus the rifle that comes into Pang's possession. His new toy, the rifle, figures as Pang's predicament in the film: He is given repeated opportunities to exercise violence while still being a child himself. He represents the generation of abandoned young children, uneducated and often orphaned, who were taken in and trained to see Angkar as their only family.[21] As Khatharya Um points out, "Whether on the side of the government or of the [Khmer Rouge], it was more often that individuals *found* themselves there rather than they *chose* to be there . . . the Khmer Rouge did build their organizational force from a small community of 'true believers.' Most Cambodians, however, simply 'asked to stay alive.'"[22] In an environment saturated with ideological indoctrination and an economic context of rural disenfranchisement, young Khmer Rouge recruits were often caught in a situation of survival by necessity.[23]

In the "vertical sovereignty" of necropolitical war, Achille Mbembe writes, "underground and airspace are transformed into conflict zones" and "occupation of the skies" is of critical importance.[24] We see this U.S. occupation of the skies in Panh's film as the camera cuts back and forth between the imperial "view from above" and the sight lines of Cambodian refugee lives on the ground.[25] The film's opening sequence strategically combines historical archival footage with dramatic voice reenactments to situate the viewer directly in the aerial perspective of the bomber pilot, who drops cluster bombs while commenting boastfully in English about the success of the mission.[26] From this vantage point, the U.S. pilot, in radio communication with his fleet, exclaims as the bombs explode, "That was an outstanding target! Alright, we bomb first of all and we can see the people running everywhere. Fantastic! We know we got them."[27] The pilot's casual commentary, as if he were leading a mission in a video game, combined with the scene's upbeat musical score, conveys the indiscriminateness of the bombings and the imperial state's presumed right to extraterritorial killing. Sighted as objects of the U.S. military's "kill-chain" that names "the grim relation between pilots and the masses below,"[28] the Cambodian lives on the ground become meaningless and formless targets to be eliminated for sport. In the film, we see that the U.S. bombings have not targeted specific Vietnamese military sanctuaries as purported by the U.S. government but have turned Cambodian landscapes, dwellings, and communities into unspecific sites of collateral damage.

If *Shiiku, the Catch*'s opening bombing sequence introduces the imperial cartographies and rationalities that transformed Cambodia's ground into expendable terrain, the rest of the film moves the viewer into the perspective of the lifeworlds on the receiving end of the U.S. bombs.[29] The routinization of necropolitical war is expressed in the film's exploration of the deafening sonic impact of air war. As the bombings intensify, the idyllic sounds of the Cambodian countryside (cicadas and children's laughter) are interrupted by the fragmenting sounds of war and chaos. In one scene, a village elder named Uncle Vorn sits polishing a rifle when he suddenly hears a shift in the distant airwaves. He cries out "it seems bombing us day by day is not enough now!"[30] Where previously the bombs arrived predictably by day, villagers now have to adjust to the anticipation of death or maiming at any moment. The scene gives sensory density to what James A. Tyner, writing about the U.S. bombing of Cambodia, has termed "everyday death," where "the palpable fear of being maimed or killed becomes 'routine'; and where the simple, seemingly trivial task of washing a shirt or cooking dinner becomes infused with the prospect of being shot."[31] In this environment, the villagers' eyes and ears have become attuned to the threat of bombs, their senses telling them when to take shelter underground and when to brace themselves for impact. For instance, a young Cambodian boy named A'Siet warns the villagers that the sounds of the planes are getting "louder and louder" and that they need to run.[32] Soon all communication between the villagers is drowned out by the sound of war. As the sounds of distant explosions and rattling objects reverberate, we observe how the villagers have become habituated to what Ian Hill terms "sonic torture."[33] As Hill writes, "All noise can produce headaches, nausea, impotence, hypertension, slowed digestion, reduced bodily functions, altered diction and intellectual capacities, as well as disorientation, anxiety, fear, and terror."[34] Prolonged exposure to loud noise can produce hearing loss, interrupt rest and sleep patterns, and break down social communication. Sonic torture thus produces debilitation at the corporeal, psychological, and sensory levels. Sonic torture also produces a debilitating form of aphasia, termed as the "altered diction" of sensory disordering and psychological distress.

Near the end of this bombing sequence, the camera lingers on Pang as he wields a long bamboo stick (his only weapon) and glances up at the sky. Unlike the other villagers who have taken shelter underground, Pang stands alone on the ground and gazes up at an invisible enemy in the lit-up sky. Confronted by the utter intensity of the war, Pang is rendered speechless. Pang's world—the Cambodia of the 1970s—is referred to in a later scene by the captured U.S. pilot as a location "off the map" of the world's media radar and global consciousness.[35] Cambodia is also "off the map" of the U.S.'s officially declared territory of war, what Jasbir Puar calls an "elsewhere" zone of disavowed debilitation in the U.S. circuits of empire. As Puar writes, "Via this circuitry, disability—or, rather, debility and debilitation—is an exported product of imperial aggression. This exportation not only is disavowed but is done so through the belated arrival of such disability."[36] In Cambodia, this belated debility continues to arrive in the form of unexploded ordnances leftover from the U.S. bombs. In *Shiiku, the Catch*, the escalating war and increasingly militarized landscape of the countryside inspire in the children a sense of both terror and wonder. Without any school to attend and few adults around to care for them, the boys are easily seduced by the lure of militarism. In one scene, a group of boys are shown cleaning up the wreckage of a B-52 bomber plane. They have been assigned this dangerous work by the adult Khmer Rouge cadres, heedless of a villager's earlier observation that the plane is "full of bombs. It'll go off!"[37] In an overhead shot, the camera pans across the ruins of the U.S. military aircraft that has begun to blend in with the foliage. We look down at a row of nine Cambodian boys pretending to fly the bomber plane, simulating the sound of the aircraft while extending their arms as wings. The ruined aircraft has become their new favorite toy, and the cratered landscape, filled with the toxic detritus of U.S. militarism, has become their new playground.

This image of Cambodian children surviving among the toxic ruins of war, during the 1970s, highlights how in many "elsewhere" zones of the Global South, such as Cambodia then and now, the aftereffects of war such as unexploded ordnances and chemical exposure guarantee ongoing forms of belated and disavowed debility and toxicity. As Mel Y. Chen argues, narratives of toxicity in the Global South, including the toxic legacies of U.S. wars and interventions abroad, minimally register for Western publics located in the "seat of U.S. empire."[38] It is important, Chen writes, to retain within our analyses "a fine sensitivity to the vastly different sites in which toxicity involves itself in very different lived experiences (or deaths)."[39] As Panh's film demonstrates, the work of salvaging empire's waste material becomes the primary form of labor available in a local economy that has had its agrarian base destroyed by B-52 bombings and civil war. For instance, we watch a scene where three of the Cambodian boys sit in a circle surrounded by an assortment of military waste material they have salvaged from the wreckage (see Fig. 2.1). As the boys scrutinize the various pieces of equipment from the plane, they wonder about each item's specific function in waging war against them. Looking at a digital piece of equipment, one boy attempts to explain it to his friends, "It shows the number of bombs. When they drop a bomb, it burns down all our houses, and now there's no more bombs. The circle is for zero."[40] Orphaned from their parents who have been killed or conscripted into war, the Cambodian boys entertain themselves with the literal debris of empire in their hands. With their homes and schools transformed into ground zeros of bombing raids, these children have only each other to try to make sense of the violence of war and its never-ending nature. They are inhabitants of the "elsewhere" target points, always somewhat hazy and undefinable, in the U.S. imperial cartography.

In this emerging militia economy, the salvaged war material—what Angela Naimou calls "the physical debris of collapsed economies"[41]—performs multiple functions: to preoccupy and amuse the boys who have nothing else to play with, and to serve as tools of recruitment used by the senior Khmer Rouge cadres to "educate" the children about the terror being wrought on their land by foreign Western powers. One of the most important interventions Panh's film makes in the narration of the Cold War in Cambodia is the depiction of how the Khmer Rouge regime (before becoming the genocidal

Figure 2.1 Village boys play with salvaged war material while discussing the U.S. bombs that drop at night. (From *Shiiku, the Catch*, directed by Rithy Panh, 2011.)

regime that they would become during Democratic Kampuchea) preyed on the ruination caused by the U.S. war machine to fuel the expansion of its militia insurgency. As Taylor Owen and Ben Kiernan explain in their essay "Bombs over Cambodia," "Civilian casualties in Cambodia drove an enraged populace into the arms of an insurgency that had enjoyed relatively little support until the bombing began, setting in motion the expansion of the Vietnam War deeper into Cambodia, a coup d'état in 1970, the rapid rise of the Khmer Rouge, and ultimately the Cambodian Genocide."[42] The rise of such insurgencies is not unique to the history of Cambodia. As Achille Mbembe writes, in necropolitical zones, "war is no longer waged between the armies of two sovereign states but between armed groups that act behind the mask of the state against armed groups that have no state but control very distinct territories, with both sides having as their main targets civilian populations that are unarmed or organized into militias."[43] We see this played out in *Shiiku, the Catch* as Cambodian children become pawns of recruitment. Immersed in an atmosphere of militarism and traumatized by years of U.S. airstrikes, the Cambodian boys in the film become particularly vulnerable to recruitment by the Khmer Rouge regime that promises them both safety from and retribution against the Western imperialists.

Panh's film explores the relationship between debility and salvage work—the labor of repurposing waste material—perhaps most poignantly in a scene where Cambodian children and the Black soldier are depicted literally speaking through an object of military salvage—the tin can radio. Developed in 1962 by U.S. designer Victor Papanek, the tin can radio emerged out of the U.S. Army's need for help with "designing a device that could deliver a radio signal to people living in remote parts of the world: villages which were primarily illiterate, unaware of the fact that they lived in a nation-state, and had no electricity, money for batteries, or access to broadcast news."[44] The solution came when Papanek discovered that "the tin can was able to act as a one-transistor radio, and it was non-directional, which meant it could only pick up one radio signal."[45] Like in the Vietcong-controlled villages along what was known as the "Ho Chi Minh Trail," villagers on the Cambodian side of the trail made homemade weapons out of salvaged material: "Materials ranged from scavenged tin can[s] to discarded wire, but the most important ingredients were provided by the enemy. In a year, dud American bombs could leave more than 20,000 tons of explosives scattered around the Vietnamese countryside. After air-raids, volunteers retrieved the duds and the dangerous business of creating new weapons began."[46] In *Shiiku, the Catch*, the salvaged tin radio represents not only the Cambodian redeployment of U.S. imperial design and debris as a tactic of local survival and resistance but also a means of cutting across the Cold War and racial divides between the Cambodian refugees and the Black American soldier.

In this scene, Lieutenant Louis, the Black American soldier, plays a child's game of radio with his Cambodian captors (see Fig. 2.2). Sitting casually side by side, Louis and the Cambodian boys smile and joke with each other, with Louis speaking in English and the boys responding in Khmer. The scene's composition and playful performances symbolize the gradual breaking down of silence and hierarchy between Louis and the boys. Speaking into a tin can, Louis pretends to radio the outside world for help. Knowing the children cannot understand him, he uses the game as an opportunity to voice his frustrations: "This is Lieutenant Simon Jefferson Louis, sent here by the American war machine. . . . But I'm happy because I've finally made contact with the so-called enemies of democracy: kids. [This machine] sends a bunch of dead meat over here to bomb more dead meat. Fuck this goddamn war."[47] In turn, the Cambodian children use the radio game to speak back to the pilot: "You've destroyed my rice field. We can't grow rice anymore. You haven't spared even a small dyke. You destroyed the canals."[48] The boys and Louis, both recruited and channeled into the military as disposable fodder of their respective armies, are having the same conversation, but in different languages. In Khmer and in English, they are arriving at similar realizations about the costs of war but are prevented from connecting due to the barrier of language. Through the tin can radio, a form of paralingual speaking emerges—one that cuts through the difficulty of communication as racial-

Figure 2.2 Louis, "the catch," using a salvaged tin can radio. (From *Shiiku, the Catch*, directed by Rithy Panh, 2011.)

ized peoples taught to hate each other. With the salvaged and repurposed fragments of U.S. empire in their hands, the Cambodian boys and the Black soldier edge closer to a mutual recognition of their shared plight as fodder for the war on both sides of the Cold War divide.

Confronted up close with the devastation that his military has wrought on the ground in Cambodia, Louis starts to become a wayward, disobedient soldier, no longer able to buy into the moral fiction of the United States' role in Southeast Asia as one of freeing the world from the "enemies of democracy." He sees, instead, a group of alienated, orphaned children affected by years of U.S. airstrikes. Louis also begins to question the domestic conditions of structural racism, poverty, and compulsory militarism that have propelled him to the front lines of this war. Held captive by his Asian enemies—a bunch of "kids"—Louis begins having nightmares and flashbacks of the aerial war that he has been complicit in, coming to the realization that he is now part of the abandoned landscape that has been targeted for eradication by his government. The film highlights the tragedy of the imperial war machine that pits racialized subjects at the bottom of the social hierarchy against each other.

In many ways paralleling the scene of speaking through salvaged tin can radios, *Shiiku, the Catch* also depicts a developing comradery between Louis and the Cambodian boys that centers on the music that plays through a salvaged radio. As Louis fixes the radio and 1960s Cambodian rock and roll music suddenly comes on the air, we witness another moment of brief levity

Figure 2.3 Louis and the boys dancing to Cambodian rock and roll that plays on a salvaged radio. (From *Shiiku, the Catch*, directed by Rithy Panh, 2011.)

and communication that takes place through the act of salvage and the language of music (see Fig. 2.3). As the music plays, the soldiers dance the twist in a circle to this Western-influenced Cambodian music that would soon be completely banned by the Khmer Rouge and replaced by the revolutionary songs of the regime. An overhead shot is used to show the spontaneous moment of intimacy and friendship that has broken through the militarized order of everyday life. In contrast to the aerial view of the war machine with which the film begins, we can see from this angle the people on the ground as wayward, playful subjects, connecting across linguistic and political divides through the language of Khmer rock and roll music—itself already a hybrid form resulting from Cambodia-American cultural cross currents. The scene reflects Alexander Weheliye's discussion of an "assemblage of humanity" that "insists on the importance of miniscule movements, glimmers of hope, scraps of food, the interrupted dreams of freedom found in those spaces deemed devoid of full human life."[49] In this case, it is the act of salvaging the remains of war that makes the assemblage of humanity possible.

In yet another scene, communication is mediated by a salvaged object—this time an old photograph. Pang has retrieved a photograph of Louis's wife and son back in America from the wreckage of the B-52 crash. Bringing it to Louis, Pang says in Khmer, "Uncle Enemy, why are you a soldier? My father's a soldier, too. And I'm on my own. You're also on your own, Uncle Enemy. Your child is on his own too. What will I do when I grow up?"[50] Here again, due to the language barrier, Louis is unable to understand what Pang is asking, yet Louis's expression suggests that he has caught the essence of Pang's question. Pang's words here express his awareness of the absurdity of adulthood and the cyclical dispossession engendered by war. Like that of the Cambodian children, Louis's youth has been lost to war. Louis recognizes that he has been used as "a dog of war" by the war machine that will soon render his son fatherless.[51] Louis and the Cambodian boys do not speak the same language, but their lives are brought together as militarized subjects caught within a global system of racial disposability at the intersection of the Cold War and the afterlife of slavery. At this intersection, both the children and the Black soldier share a common condition of captivity in a war created and sustained by the West but fought far from its borders.

If Panh's film posits a horizon of justice, then it resides not in any kind of universal humanitarianism in which the West will suddenly manifest itself as a heroic white savior but, rather, in the emergent possibilities of interracial solidarity that, however fragile, offer some momentary disruptions in the logics of the war machine. Such disruption occurs in the film's climax when Louis manages to escape from his makeshift prison. When the boys track him down at the site of his downed aircraft, he takes one of the boys, A'Siet, hostage. Pang, inexperienced with the rifle, accidentally shoots A'Siet in the arm, wounding and debilitating the boy. *Shiiku, the Catch* constructs an ending that sees Louis lifting up the wounded A'Siet and carrying him back to the village, where the boy is ultimately able to make a partial recovery. This gesture of salvage—of saving a wounded and debilitated boy—temporarily interrupts the war's circulation of hatred and violence.

That Louis commits this act of rescue, despite his knowledge that his own freedom will never be given in return, signals the film's unsettling of any kind of idealized discourse of interracial solidarity. The Cambodian villagers may be like the Black soldier—disenfranchised by poverty and war and caught in a cycle of compulsory militarism—but they do not recognize him as such, conditioned, like American soldiers are, to think of the enemy as inhuman. To the Cambodian people, he is simply another "catch," an imperial *and* racial enemy. At the end of the film, Louis is shown being led away from the village to be transferred to higher-level Khmer Rouge authorities in the city. In the line of soldiers leading the pilot away is Pang. Now donning the official uniform of the Khmer Rouge, he declares to a village elder that he is "going to the frontline . . . to fight the imperialists and landowners."[52] The Black American soldier has crossed enemy lines to salvage what remains of his own humanity as a perpetrator in an illegal secret war, yet we know no rescue awaits him. His ideological military training in the expendability of

Figure 2.4 The boy, A'Siet, searches for his village on a salvaged war map as the movie ends. (From *Shiiku, the Catch*, directed by Rithy Panh, 2011.)

Cambodian lives is predicated on the same logic that makes his own life as a Black soldier just as disposable.

The film *Shiiku, the Catch* ends with the image of A'Siet, a debilitated boy with one arm in a sling, fiddling with a salvaged compass and map (see Fig. 2.4). Running his fingers down the map, he searches in futility for the location of the coordinates of his village. The Cambodian location is nowhere to be found since the U.S. bombing of Cambodia, carried out secretly and illegally, was never officially declared as a site of war in the first place. The cartographic metaphor implies the world's indifference to the fate of a small foreign country like Cambodia, littered with the detritus of war that becomes the only objects through which Cambodian people on the ground can begin to make sense of their predicament. When the camera zooms out to an extreme long shot, we see that the wounded Cambodian boy A'Siet is sitting at the edge of a bomb crater—the image with which the film began. Injured by Pang's rifle (the symbol of necropolitical debilitation), A'Siet is now its keeper. Before Pang departed for the front lines, he passed the rifle on to A'Siet, who is now positioned to become the new leader of the children's unit. Necropower has descended down the chain of command to the youngest members in the hierarchy. As the end credits roll, the film returns to the archival footage of the U.S. bombings—fragments of the U.S. imperial archive retrieved and redeployed by Rithy Panh to signal his own art of speaking through the salvaged material of war at the film's metalevel. The narrative's formal circularity reinforces the film's sympathy for all those differentially, yet not equivalently, caught in a dialectical spiral of militarized violence and vulnerability.

Viet Thanh Nguyen's "The Americans": Economies of Disability

Like Rithy Panh's *Shiiku, the Catch*, Viet Thanh Nguyen's short story "The Americans" explores themes of debility in relation to the U.S. bombing of Cambodia. In the literary tradition of the U.S. veteran's "return" narrative to the site of war, "The Americans" is a short story told from the perspective of James Carver, a Black American veteran of the Vietnam War. Originally published in the *Chicago Tribune* in 2010 as a story set in Cambodia, Nguyen republished "The Americans" in 2017 as a part of his short story collection *The Refugees*. In a Twitter post from his now-deleted account, Nguyen explains that the change in context from the U.S. bombing of Cambodia to the U.S. bombing of Vietnam was purely pragmatic in nature—a response to his editor's suggestion to make *The Refugees* more cohesive as a book of short stories focused on refugees from or within Vietnam.[53] While Nguyen should not be individually faulted, the industry's demands for him to replace the Cambodian story with a more coherent Vietnamese one speaks to a larger discursive and representational pattern of "Cambodia's minor anecdoting" that I discussed in Chapter 1. This includes the persistent sidelining of Cambodia in order to tell a different story—in this case, a story about the American inheritances of the Vietnam War. Cambodia's presence as a landscape and population in ruin during the Cold War haunts the ground of literary projects such as "The Americans," yet the interrogation of its meaning as a place unto itself remains perpetually deferred in place of telling a story that is perhaps seen as more legible to a Western, liberal, antiwar audience. The dearth of available stories about the U.S. bombing of Cambodia remains a remarkable lacuna in the post–Cold War global imaginary, especially given the centrality that events such as Watergate, the Vietnam War, and the Kent State shootings continue to occupy as flashpoints in twentieth-century American history.

If Panh's film explores the relationship between the U.S. bombing and Cambodian refugee debilitation, Nguyen's story delves more deeply into the debilitating legacies of war on the Black soldier. Like Panh's film, Nguyen's text spotlights the incorporation of the Black soldier into the war machine without drawing a false equivalence between the suffering of soldiers and targeted civilians. At the age of sixty-nine and walking with a limp due to an injury a few years earlier, Carver has returned to Cambodia with his Japanese American wife, Michiko. Carver originally met Michiko in Japan while on military "R&R from Okinawa," the U.S.-occupied Indigenous territory where he was stationed during the Vietnam War and from which he launched his B-52 bombing missions. The story's linking of Japan/Okinawa and Cambodia here recalls Rithy Panh's inspiration in the works of Japanese author Kenzaburo Oe. The insertion of Japan into the U.S./Cambodia/Black soldier triad (in both Panh's film and Nguyen's story) sketches the contours of a complex Cold War formation that Christine Hong describes as "a vast militarized archipelago stretching westward from California and Alaska to Hawai'i, Okinawa, and South Korea, and southward from East Asia to Singapore, Guam, the Marshall Islands, and Australia."[54] This formation also produced the transpacific currents of Black soldiering that emerged in part in response to what Hong calls "the color-line propaganda" of both the Japanese imperial army and the Vietcong military. The interracial family at the center of Nguyen's story, then, embodies the traces of this U.S. Cold War formation. Over three decades after the U.S. war in Southeast Asia, the family is back in Asia. Carver and Michiko are in Cambodia visiting their adult mixed-race daughter, Claire, who is now working in Cambodia as a foreign teacher of English. Far from a conventional U.S. veteran's return narrative, the story explores the complex entanglements between race, disability, militarism, soldiering, humanitarianism, and empire, illuminating war's persistence as a debility in the life of the former U.S. soldier.

Reluctant to travel to Southeast Asia in the first place, Carver continues to disidentify with all that Cambodia represents. To him, Cambodia remains "a country about which he knew next to nothing except what it looked like at forty thousand feet."[55] His uninformed, disengaged, and indifferent attitude is presented in the story as somewhat unexceptional: It is the view of the everyday man or Western tourist who conceives of Cambodia as having nothing of value, a country requiring a stopover at the beaches in Thailand in order for the trip as a whole to be worthwhile. On the ground of this land that he once bombed but now walks on as a tourist, Carver approaches the local culture with little sense of humility or renewed perception. Fixating only on the signs of what he sees as poverty, underdevelopment, and incivility all around him, Carver experiences Cambodia as a "land of bad omens and misfortunes so severe he had been content just to fly over it."[56] Accustomed to "ascending ever higher" in his life's pursuits by pushing all doubts and discomforts into his "peripheral vision," Carver finds himself psychologically and viscerally incapable of connecting to the local people on any level.[57] While in Cambodia, he does his best to keep himself walled off and sanitized from the local environment. On one adventurous day, Carver rolls down his window and then immediately regrets it, seeing it as "an invitation to inhale the reek of the land and the people."[58] Carver thus feels validated in his condescension toward Cambodian culture and in his disapproval of Claire's decision to make the country her new home. The relationship between father and daughter here is thoroughly punctured with silence and difficult communication, with Carver regarding his daughter as weak and naive and Claire viewing her father through a lens of unqualified villainy.

Carver is reminiscent of literary archetypes such as the Black American pilot in Kenzaburo Oe's *Shiiku*, the Igbo warrior Okonkwo in Chinua Achebe's *Things Fall Apart*, the Black American pilot Todd in Ralph Ellison's *Flying Home*, and the Black American Korean War veteran Frank Money in Toni Morrison's *Home*.[59] Deploying extended tropes of masculinist virility and aggression, Nguyen's story highlights the rape mentality that often configures the logics and rationalities of U.S. war. In a flashback, the narrator recounts: "He had never explained to Claire the difficulty of precision bombing, aiming from forty thousand feet at targets the size of football fields, like dropping golf balls into a coffee cup from the roof of a house. The tonnage fell far behind his B-52 after its release, and so he had never seen his own payload explode or even drop, although he watched other planes of his squadron scattering their black seed into the wind, leaving him to imagine what he would later see on film, the bombs exploding, footfalls of an invisible giant stomping the earth."[60] Propelled by a fetishistic sense of excitement and danger, Carver approaches the act of "killing from a distance" like a game of golf or football, a sport for him to prove his militarized masculinity, irrespective of the game's consequences to human and nonhuman lives and ecologies.

In its aestheticized description of Carver's inability to sense or even see Cambodian lives on the ground, the passage also troubles the military logic of precision that rationalized the aerial bombings of the Vietnam War era and that underwrites contemporary drone warfare. As Rob Nixon explains, "The emotional sanitation of war involves, in entangled ways, technological, geographical, temporal, and linguistic strategies for distancing."[61] As in the drone wars of today that mask their war casualties through linguistic euphemisms such as "precision," Carver's relationship to bombing is highly mediated and disembodied, for he never once even witnessed the direct consequences of his actions, except in retrospect through watching war film reenactments. The aerial bombing perspective, rape imagery, and Hollywood war film tropes all coalesce in this passage to illuminate the contours of what Puar describes as the "biopolitical assemblage of control that instrumentalizes a spectrum of capacities and debilities for the use of the occupation" and war.[62] Carver has never atoned, or even spoken about, his participation in this system of militarized debilitation. The violent past remains lodged within him not so much as a repressed memory or a noticeable silence but as an unfeeling and unremorseful blankness—one that only later manifests in his nightmares of a gaze fixed on "the cockpit windows" of a ghostly aircraft, "the empty pilot's seat waiting for him."[63] In Carver's inability to see beyond the horizon of war, Nguyen's story illuminates a soldier's psychological debility as a condition marked by the interior crowding out of anything but militarism's enduring conditioning and discipline.

While Carver continues to see Cambodia as nothing more than a third world abyss, Claire, his mixed-race Black Asian daughter, sees Cambodia as her "mission" in life, seeking to "make up for some of the things" her father has done in the past.[64] Claire has a salvage mission of her own—one rooted both in a desire to atone for her father's participation in the war and in the affinities she feels with Cambodian people as someone who professes to have a "Cambodian soul."[65] Claire's boyfriend is Chanthou Vanneth, a Cambodian American graduate student at MIT who has returned to Cambodia to work at a demining site on the outskirts of Phnom Penh. One day, Carver agrees to go with Vanneth and Claire to the demining site to see the robots in action. When the group arrives, they are greeted by two Cambodian teenage boys with prosthetic limbs, disabled by "playing with cluster bomblets when they were kids."[66] The insidious nature of the slow violence of cluster bombs relates in part to the differential vulnerability these bombs create for rural and poor children in the Global South. As Rob Nixon writes, "The submunitions that cluster bombs dispense are often gleaming and colorful—inquisitive children readily mistake them for toys."[67] In Nguyen's story, these once inquisitive children have turned into debilitated quasi tour guides—teenagers with mismatched prosthetic limbs wearing used clothing donated from Canadian charities who are overseeing the demining site. As Jasbir Puar argues, debilitation is "not just an unfortunate by-product of the exploitative workings of capitalism; it is required for and constitutive of the expansion of profit. Certain bodies are employed in production processes precisely because they are deemed available for injury."[68] Like in Panh's story, these Cambodian teenagers have lived their lives walking and existing on a land littered with the remnants of war. Where they once stumbled across these ordnances in the process of salvaging metal for bare survival, or while simply looking for toys, these debilitated boys now make their livelihood guarding and offering tours of the lethal landscape. The image of these boys in prosthetics confronts the reader with the material reality of belated debility and its intersection with the NGO and tourist industry that turns disability into profit in the Global South.

In "The Americans," the tin can reappears. At the demining site, Carver observes a somewhat retrograde system of robotic demining that leverages a mongoose's light body mass and acute sense of smell alongside robots "cobbled together from what looked like two tin milkshakes."[69] Reminiscent of Panh's film, the salvaged tin cans here acquire a symbolic valence: While Cambodian people have resourcefully worked within the constraints of their predicament, the tin can robots serve as an indictment of the West's failure of accountability to safely resource its demining endeavors abroad. Debilitated subjects like the two Cambodian teenagers that Carver simply refers to as "Ben and Jerry" have few economic options but to make their living through the hazardous labor of demining with the use of technology "cobbled together" with tin cans. In the scene's triangulation of the debilitated Cambodian tour guides, the disabled Black American veteran, and the "returning" racialized Americans—all on the physical landscape of war remains—Nguyen dramatizes the difficulty of salvage work, as war remnants tend to unravel previously unspoken tensions within the group.

At the demining site, Carver becomes indignant at what he perceives to be Claire and Vanneth's attitudes of moral superiority. Here, Nguyen astutely captures the predicament of humanitarianism where the lines between humanitarianism and liberal empire have become increasingly blurred in the global era. What we see in places such as Cambodia and Palestine, where foreign NGOs have a marked presence, is that disability may be instrumentalized as a means of facilitating funding flows and infrastructure projects that largely serve to benefit international actors rather than local populations. In short, Jasbir Puar argues, "Debilitation is extremely profitable economically and ideologically" for settler-colonial and imperial regimes, as many "NGO actors who are embedded in corporate economies of humanitarianism" rush to partake in the "rehabilitation" of places such as Gaza.[70] What we might term the "crip economy" or the "debility dollar," Merri Lisa Johnson and Robert McRuer explain, is "one of the most sought-after currencies in the world; in the United States alone, money spent on actual or seeming impairments represents 17.6 percent of the GDP."[71] Nguyen's story situates Vanneth squarely within this NGO extension of the military-industrial complex as Vanneth is conducting applied research as a part of his MIT supervisor's project on robotic demining, a project funded by the U.S. Department of Defense. While Claire is in awe of the demining technology, Carver is cynical of the research agenda, bristling "as the humanitarian jargon of cost efficiency, improvement of the land, moral obligation, employment of local technicians, and so on spooled forth."[72] For all of his patriotic sensibilities, Carver is frustrated by Claire and Vanneth's naive investment in the humanitarian project, exclaiming in the story that "some brilliant guy at a university working on a defense contract will figure out a way to put a landmine on this robot. Then the Pentagon will send it into a tunnel where a terrorist is hiding."[73] The story here alludes to humanitarian militarism's reproductive capacities through the establishment of a complex network of state and nonstate actors, research projects, academic institutions, and a local and transnational labor force. Readers are invited to grasp the transnational and transtemporal scale of U.S. empire that sees the ruins of yesterday's Cold War laboratories (i.e., Cambodia) as salvage grounds for the expansion of today's laboratories of empire (i.e., Iraq and Afghanistan). Nguyen's story thus exposes the palimpsest temporalities of the U.S. forever war, wherein the collateralized landscapes of the past serve as new testing grounds for future cycles of war and debilitation.

Like in Rithy Panh's *Shiiku, the Catch*, Viet Thanh Nguyen's "The Americans" explores the Black American soldier's existence at the interstice of the U.S. "inner war" and "outer war." During the Vietnam War era, military airmen who were involved in the B-52 bombings of Southeast Asia, including Black American veterans, were particularly reviled by American antiwar activists upon their return home from tours of duty, even as this antiwar movement recognized from early on that impoverished Black Americans were being sent to the front lines of the war as what Toni Morrison and war resisters called "cannon fodder."[74] As discussed above, the attempts by racialized Americans to prove their patriotism and value through dedication in war stretches back to World Wars I and II. As Elizabeth Reich writes in her book *Militant Visions* about cinematic representations of Black soldiering, "The black soldier performed his hopeful inclusion in the nation through his participation in U.S. imperialism and, by implication, his disavowal of alliance or affiliation with the other oppressed races and peoples of the world."[75] In Nguyen's story, this desire for inclusion is apparent in Carver's disidentification with his "childhood passed in a rural Alabama hamlet siphoned clean of hope long before his birth."[76] As an adult, Carver strives to get as far away from this rural past as possible. He slowly works his way up through college, military training, and, ultimately, to "his B-52 and later his Boeing airliner."[77] For Carver, ascending to these ranks marks his sense of transcendence of "where he was supposed to be" in life.[78] As a Black man in an "airman's uniform," Carver has defied the racialized parameters of social mobility set out for him, acquiring a sense of pride after living a life of indignity in a white supremacist society.[79] Indeed, the text suggests that part of Carver's visceral distaste for Cambodia actually stems from its invocation of the "dirt farmers and sharecroppers of his childhood, their skin as brown and cracked as the soil they tilled, the earth desiccated during summer's simmering months."[80] Through these details, Nguyen's story conveys the fugitive flight lines of racialized subjects like Carver, who have little choice but to escape the landscape of the "inner war" of racialized abjection through participation in the "outer war" of empire.[81]

Nguyen's narrative also challenges assimilationist myths of intergenerational progress by showing how Carver's military legacy gets reproduced through his son William's enlistment in the military. We learn that "one of the proudest moments in Carver's life" is "William's graduation from the Air Force Academy" and when he begins his job piloting a military tanker.[82] Tasked with "refueling bombers and fighters patrolling the skies of Iraq and Afghanistan," William describes his work as "boring" and wishes he could engage in more direct aerial war as his father did.[83] Here, in this parallel drawn between the wars in Cambodia, Iraq, and Afghanistan, Nguyen traces an unbroken line between old and new Cold War laboratories. That this narrative line is established via a focus on the figure of the Black American soldier and his mixed-race Afro-Asian son underscores the story's commentary on the war machine's ceaseless incorporative capacity: not only does the military-industrial complex work to recruit disenfranchised citizens into patriotic soldiers but it is also adept at transforming its "failed" wars into lessons for future imperial projects. The U.S. military only "lost" the Vietnam War insofar as America could not claim this war as an official victory. The war machine's perpetual existence and expansion in the post–Cold War era, as the wars in the Greater Middle East have shown, complicates any straightforward notion of winning or losing.

In "The Americans," Nguyen offers very little in the way of narrative resolution or redemption for any of the characters caught up in the entanglements of the war machine. Instead, the story explores the provisional and temporary moments of critical insight born out of Carver's fleeting moments of interracial and intergenerational reparation with his daughter Claire. While in Cambodia, Carver reflects that more than all the discomforting physical sensations he feels as a foreigner in Cambodia, what has been the hardest for him to endure during the trip has been "Claire and Michiko's silent treatment of him."[84] For Claire, her father's blatant dismissal of her humanitarian endeavors in Cambodia simply reinforces a lifetime's worth of anger and resentment she feels as the daughter of an unyielding patriarch and military man. At one point, Claire beats her head in frustration, wondering why she ever thinks "things will be different with [her father]."[85] Carver, on the other hand, resents the fact that Claire sees him not as an American hero and patriot but as a villain in a loathsome story of unjust and illegal war. That Claire "empathized with vast masses of people she had never met, total strangers who regarded her as a stranger," only serves to incense Carver more.[86] The brewing storm in the story functions as a symbol of Carver's intensifying inner turmoil—an accumulation of difficult thoughts and sensations accrued over the course of his days in Cambodia and perhaps over the course of many years or decades of his life. In his advanced age, Carver now walks with a limp after falling down the stairway of his own house and breaking his hip three years earlier. Unprepared to psychologically confront an embodied vulnerability and impaired masculinity brought on by disability, Carver prefers instead to view himself through what Jasbir Puar describes as "ableist fantasies of endless capacity"—the belief in life and the able-body as an "endless resource" of self-sufficiency.[87] To be disabled and dependent on the care of others, it is implied, is a fate worse than death for a man such as Carver.

As tensions rise and simple mobility becomes more difficult, Carver's sense of frustration and purposelessness begins to mount, culminating in a scene of physical collapse that brings Carver face down in the murky ground, just meters away from the Cambodian land site littered with land mines: "The mud was wet and cold against his belly and face, its odor and taste evoking the soil in the distant yard of his childhood, the one where he had so often lain prone on the earth and played soldier."[88] Immersed in the foreign "red earth" of the Cambodian land that he once ravaged with the "black seed(s)" of his B-52 bombers, Carver is now met with an uncomfortable realization of grounded familiarity.[89] What he senses in being brought down to the earth is the palimpsest landscapes of rural Black America and rural Cambodia. Both landscapes are zones of divestment or collateralization, "off the map" of the American public consciousness and, therefore, deemed expendable. The scene brings the story's comment on the irony of war full circle when it is Vanneth, a Cambodian man, who helps Carver "to his feet and into the idling land cruiser."[90] If in Rithy Panh's film it is the Black soldier who lifts up and carries a wounded Cambodian boy, in Nguyen's story we have an image of the opposite—a gesture of momentary care extended from the Asian man to the Black soldier.

Carver's recognition of mutuality and interdependence across racial and generational divides is further reinforced in the story's final scene, as Carver is taken to a rural, Cambodian hospital to recover. Here, Carver notices "his fellow patients in the three other beds, silver-haired, aging Cambodian men, tended by crowds of relatives who chatted loudly and carried bowls and things wrapped in towels."[91] The sense of being cared for by a large network of kin is not something that Carver readily relates to; rather the texture of Carver's life of alienation and familial estrangement better resembles the feverish dream he has of being "in a darkened airliner," filled with Asian passengers, but with no one piloting the plane.[92] The dream is symbolic of the military—his purported family—that has left him with nothing at the end of his life except blood on his hands, broken intimacies, and a debilitated mind and body. To Carver's surprise, however, when he wakes up from his dream, Claire is there at his bedside, having slept on the hard hospital floor for three days. She helps hold up her frail and aging father as he struggles to the bathroom—a reversal of parent/child roles as Carver has become dependent on his daughter for his basic needs. As Carver cries quietly in the darkness of the bathroom, his masculine bravado softened, Nguyen ends the story with a provisional sense of intergenerational salvage. In this interval of mutual dependency, a different sight line begins to come into focus as "Carver saw the tiled floor as if from a very high altitude."[93] What emerges by the story's end is a messy entanglement of relationality between Carver (a Black soldier brought down to reckon with the terrain of refugee life) and Claire (an Afro-Asian daughter with a "Cambodian soul" who cares for her disabled father in his time of need). Such grounded alliances herald the conditions of possibility for a politics of disability justice and refugee justice rooted in intergenerational dialogue, radical care, and the abolition of the war.

Masahiro Sugano and Kosal Khiev's *Cambodian Son*: Carceral Debilities

A documentary set over thirty years after the U.S. bombing of Cambodia, Masahiro Sugano and Kosal Khiev's 2014 film, *Cambodian Son*, interrogates the processes of debility that mark what Eric Tang describes as "the long, unbroken interval" of "refugee temporality."[94] The very moment the refugee crosses into the space of asylum, Tang argues, "is the very moment in which the terms of liberal warfare—violence, captivity, collateral damage—are reinvigorated."[95] The *longue durée* of refugee captivity extends from the war zone, to the labor camp, to the hyperghetto, to the prison, and back to the deportation homeland. While these carceral regimes maintain ableist social structures in myriad ways, they rarely figure in discussions about disability and accessibility. Important work is emerging, however, in the field of southern disability studies that explores the relation of disability to U.S. incarceration, racial capitalism, and settler colonialism.[96] As Jasbir Puar writes, "Warfare, exploitative laboring conditions, occupations, incarceration [should] count as a large component of these structures, part of an inaccessible ableist social, as much as buildings, curbs, ramps, elevators, service animals, cognitive normativity, and chemical sensitivities."[97] The film *Cambodian Son* explores how Cambodian American refugees have specifically been impacted by this system of making disabled bodies through U.S. practices of racialization and incarceration. If Rithy Panh's *Shiiku, the Catch,* zeroes in on debilitation in the "elsewhere" zone of U.S. imperial cartographies, *Cambodian Son* connects the spaces of the "elsewhere" to the "here" of Cambodian American refugee life.

Focusing on the story of Cambodian American refugee and spoken word poet Kosal Khiev, *Cambodian Son* follows Kosal's life in deportation exile after serving a fourteen-year prison sentence in various U.S. prisons. Like me, Kosal Khiev was born in Khao-I-Dang refugee camp in 1980. We are the same age and linked by the same birthplace and geopolitical history. While my family resettled in Canada, Kosal Khiev and his family went to the United States in 1981. Settling in Santa Ana, California, Kosal grew up living in a two-bedroom public housing apartment with seven other family members until he was sent away to a boys' home at the age of fifteen. This home was later shut down by the state for child abuse.[98] At the age of sixteen, Kosal was involved in a gang shootout, in which two people were injured, and he was subsequently convicted and sentenced to sixteen years in prison for attempted murder. On his parole fourteen years later, Khiev was deported as a result of a 2002 repatriation agreement between the United States and Cambodia, an agreement made possible by Bill Clinton's signing of the 1996 Illegal Immigration Reform and Immigrant Responsibility Act. The act dramatically expanded the U.S. government's ability to deport U.S. residents by making common misdemeanors, such as drug possession, grounds for removal and by establishing mandatory deportation for crimes like burglary and fraud.[99] The law also eliminated the discretionary ability of immigration judges to overturn deportation orders on a case-by-case basis. Kosal Khiev's family had been living in the United States as legal permanent residents and had not yet gone through the complicated and financially prohibitive process of obtaining U.S. citizenship.

Conditioned by systemic poverty into the status of "irregular citizenship,"[100] many Cambodian refugees have not been aware that legal permanent residency can offer no protection against deportation in the event of prosecution and time served for an aggravated felony. This legal technicality has proven to be consequential as many Cambodian American youths involved with gang activity, like Kosal, have ultimately found themselves in prison, only to be deported upon release.[101] Upon completing his prison sentence, Kosal was seized by ICE for another year of detention until his deportation to Cambodia in 2011. Permanently barred from the United States and dropped off in Phnom Penh with no passport or identification, Kosal joined the self-described Khmer Exiled American community, a group consisting of approximately eight hundred Cambodian American men and women who have been deported to Cambodia.[102] This Cambodian American "deportation diaspora" or "deportspora" continues to expand, with nineteen hundred Cambodians holding removal orders in the United States and ICE reporting a 279 percent increase in Cambodian American deportations from 2017 to 2018.[103] This evolving situation illustrates the way in which irregular citizenship links up with deportation, upending liberal humanitarian narratives of U.S. refugee rescue.

The film *Cambodian Son* explicitly locates the contemporary crisis of Cambodian American refugee deportation in the imperial genealogy of the Cold War in Cambodia. In the opening scene, we see an animation of U.S. B-52 bomber planes moving across the screen as ordnances fall on a map of Cambodia. As the bombs drop, we hear the audio voice-over reenactment of Henry Kissinger's orders from the Kissinger telecons: "I want a plan where every goddam thing that can fly goes into Cambodia and hits every target that is open. . . . Go in there and crack the hell out of them."[104] With this opening, the film gestures to what is frequently elided from the replay of the Kissinger telecons in contemporary media and cinema: the debilitated Cambodian refugee body on the receiving end of those bombs as well as the long-term repercussions on the Cambodian community. From the animation of the U.S. bombing, the film cuts to an image of an unidentified older Cambodian man, speaking to the camera in French. With strong emotion in his voice, he laments the losses of war: "It's the war that separated all the families. That's it. The whole world has to recognize that this is what war does. War has to stop. All over the world, war has to be stopped. Arms all around the world have to be destroyed."[105] The man's identity remains a mystery until the third act of the film when we find out that he is Kosal Khiev's father, Sophal, who has been living in France, separated from his son for over thirty-two years. The family was separated at Khao-I-Dang refugee camp in 1980 after Kosal's father incorrectly responded to questions on the U.S. immigration forms, leading the immigration screening officials to deny his application to the United States. While Kosal, his siblings, and his mother went to the United States, Kosal's father went to France. Moving backward and forward in time, *Cambodian Son* establishes a filmic pattern that situates Kosal's life, and the fragmentation of kinship ties that have defined it, in the context of U.S. empire in Cambodia, the immigration bureaucracy of the refugee camps, and the U.S. prison and deportation systems in the United States that have targeted and segregated Cambodian refugee populations.

Being kept "in place" by the U.S. prison system for over fourteen years is one reason Kosal's father was never able to get in contact with his son after the war. While Kosal never explicitly pinpoints the U.S. state as a culprit in the long drama of his captivity, displacement, and familial separation, the film uses expository techniques to fill in the causal links that remain unspecified by Kosal. In one scene, we see how the harm of family separation, as well as the response to reunion, is inarticulable to Kosal. After meeting his father, Kosal says, "I feel all sorts of stuff right now. . . . But I can't help but feel anger too. . . . Angry at why. Why the separation happened in the first place. Angry at . . . at even the Khmer Rouge."[106] Kosal's relationship with his father frames the broken intimacies of the present as an ongoing legacy of the Cold War in Cambodia. As Kosal puts it, efforts at reconciliation and healing cannot help but rouse feelings of anger for "why the separation happened in the first place."[107] This scene is telling for the way in which Kosal struggles to name the object of his anger, which is directed at both the specific ("at even the Khmer Rouge") and the nonspecific ("at why"). While he is able to speak about his anger, all the other things he is feeling become unspeakable, almost bowing to anger as the only emotion that can be expressed. Later in the film, Kosal says, "Most men don't show their grief or their sadness, you know. In fact, most rage, most anger, is just the cork that keeps all the grief in the bottle."[108] Kosal articulates here what Cathy Park Hong calls "minor feelings"—"the racialized range of emotions that are negative, dysphoric, and therefore untelegenic, built from the sediments of everyday racial experience."[109] Kosal's minor feelings of anger and rage have accrued over the course of decades of uprooting and precarity as a formerly incarcerated and deported racialized subject. In *Cambodian Son*, the production of the refugee's minor feelings is another outcome of war and the prison's system of debility.

Key to the film's analysis of the long and continuously unfolding collateral aftermath of the U.S. bombing of Cambodia is its exploration of racial criminal pathologization that has consigned Kosal Khiev and others like him to the category of the "bad refugee"—a figure attached to signs of deviance, criminality, and rebelliousness. Typically gendered as male, the bad refugee is seen as bad in and through his acquisition and embodiment of the signifiers of a criminalized Black masculinity. According to some scholars, the putative discourse on Southeast Asian American youths "has been grounded in the notion that they are immigrant youth who are hindered in their socioeconomic mobility because of their proximity to blackness."[110] In her analysis of Cambodian American deportee mug shot photos, Thy Phu argues that "the identification of the refugee as criminal, specifically as alien felon, helps erase the former category and any claims to compassionate, humane treatment that could otherwise be made on its behalf."[111] The refugee-deportee as a "bad subject" exposes the modern nation-state's fictitious claims to hospitality and "the tenuousness of the refugee's welcome."[112] For Mimi Nguyen, the bad subject is built into the debt economy prescribed by the "gift of free-dom" since certain conditions of disciplinary governmentality that envelop the lives of refugees, such as welfare dependency, "operate as signs of latent criminality."[113] This bad subject is seen as endemically and culturally amoral and irrational, and, as such, a threat to public security.[114] Specifically, legalis-tic discourses depict Southeast Asian gang members "as especially incapable of moral action, allowing their infinite detention and, after 2002, eventual deportation as criminal aliens."[115] The deportation of the Cambodian refugee criminalized as a bad subject illustrates the overlapping of refugee criminal-ization and carceral ableism.

Cambodian Son explores the material and psychological effects of this long interval of carceral captivity in the lives of Cambodian American refu-gees. In one of the film's opening scenes, the camera lingers on Kosal's tat-tooed upper body, as if to lay bare for the viewer the signs of deviance and gang affiliation that have repeatedly rendered Kosal a target of state profiling (see Fig. 2.5). Suggesting the depth of psychological vulnerability that exists beneath his tough masculine exterior, Kosal speaks to the camera while in the shower: "I get nightmares. Nightmares where I'm crying. Sometimes I'll have nightmares that I'm still doing time. And sometimes I'll get nightmares of me getting killed. And sometimes, I have like, dreams of me still being in the States waking up like I'm at home."[116] Kosal's expression of his ongo-ing psychological pain here acquires an uncanny quality when set against the testimonies of Cambodian Genocide survivors, such as Kosal's mother and father, who frequently describe their lingering trauma. For Kosal, it is not just the knowledge of what the Khmer Rouge regime did to his family members that continues to haunt him. Kosal has survived his own kind of "killing fields": the U.S. hyperghetto and the U.S. prison system, both part of the same pipeline of the prison industrial complex that have led to the impairment of Kosal's body-mind in ways that remain inarticulable beyond Kosal's allusion to his ongoing nightmares. Disability and impairment are inseparable from the incarceration matrix. The majority of the incarcerated in the U.S. prison system are poor people of color who arrive in prison with numerous disabilities acquired over a lifetime of exposure to impoverishment, insufficiency, and everyday violence.

Moreover, as Liat Ben-Moshe writes, "The prison environment itself is disabling so that even if an individual enters prison without a disability or mental health diagnosis, she is likely to get one—from the sheer trauma of incarceration."[117] It is estimated that 70 percent of the incarcerated popula-tion in the United States has a physical or developmental disability.[118] From the debilitation of hard labor, solitary confinement, prison violence, and lack

Figure 2.5 Kosal Khiev's tattooed upper body. (From *Cambodian Son*, directed by Masahiro Sugano, 2014.)

of medical care, there is no disputing the reality that disability is pervasive in prison settings. In *Cambodian Son*, Kosal's incarceration and subsequent deportation have made it difficult for him to imagine a future without similar experiences of violence. Notable in Kosal's speech is his reluctance to speak about his dreams and plans for the future. When a friend asks him what he wants to do with his life, Kosal simply responds, "I have no idea." Barred from returning home to his family in America and left to his own devices to rebuild his life in Cambodia, futurity becomes unimaginable.[119]

The pattern of Kosal's unpredictability, low self-esteem, and depression is evidenced in other scenes as well, marking his persona in the film as something far from an idealized or heroic victim. In one scene, he is a "no-show" at a school where he is expected to tutor disadvantaged Cambodian children in the art of spoken word. Accustomed to his regular appearance at the school, the kids are filmed expressing their disappointment that "Teacher Kosal never came back."[120] We also see Kosal's nervous agitation in a scene where he works on a spoken word track. Here, Kosal pauses midsentence, holding his stomach, but once his friends and the filmmaker bring him to the intensive care unit he suddenly "feels better."[121] In an argument with the film's producer Anida Yoeu Ali on screen, Kosal says, "There are so many thoughts in my head that are like, you could just leave. You could just disappear."[122] Kosal's friend KK echoes Kosal's sentiments: "We been down so long, we been locked up so long, that we confused in life too."[123] As Ben-Moshe asserts, even if inmates entering prison are already disabled, "conditions of confinement may cause further mental breakdown for those entering the system with diagnoses of 'mental,' psychiatric, or intellectual disabilities."[124] Quantifying the number of prisoners with psychiatric disabilities is difficult as the incarcerated represent one of the most invisibilized disabled populations in the world.

Through spoken word poetry, Kosal grapples with the difficulty of speaking about his experiences. The film includes a video of Kosal's performance of "Moments in between the Nights" onstage at the London Cultural Olympiad in 2012. In it, Kosal describes how he wrote the poem in prison one night, "warehoused in a room with 200 bunks, 400 people."[125] This prison, Kosal recounts, was "crazy, a madhouse. It breeded hatred and so many other things."[126] In discussing the themes of refuge and disability, it is useful to turn to the text of the poem itself. Written in three long stanzas with a repeating refrain, "Moments in between the Nights" oscillates between the temporalities of the poet's days and nights while in prison. His days consist of the monotonous, repetitive routine of prison life. Here, the poet is "cold" and "alone." He becomes a "vacant body," a "hollow tomb," and "branded cattle."[127] He fights for daily survival in "a part of the world where tragedies happen every day."[128] This battleground is not the poet's ancestral homeland in Cambodia but rather the American prison system. The poem underscores the poet's feelings of despair and hopelessness as he counts down the number of years of his life that have been taken away from him: "Too much time has elapsed / 8 years to be exact."[129] Khiev's parents spent four years in a Khmer Rouge labor camp, marking the passage of time through the brutal toil of work; Kosal's prison sentence—fourteen years in total—is a decade longer than what his parents endured during Pol Pot time.

If the poet's days are rendered as repeating cycles of routinized "senseless violence," then his nights are the moments when time slows down, when the war with his memories and ruminations begins.[130] At night, scenes from the poet's childhood replay in his mind: "What's replaced is a face who I can hardly wait to embrace."[131] The poet's flashbacks tell a story of a young boy whose circumstances of poverty and gang violence haunt him. Alone in his prison bunk at night, he is tormented by the memories of his many near-death encounters, "laying in the gutters."[132] These thoughts overwhelm him in the night hours when he is incapable of shutting off his thoughts of grief, shame, and regret: "My thoughts keep going black / I can't help it."[133] For Kosal, the scripts going on in his mind constitute a form of psychological imprisonment that coincides with the violence of his physical captivity. The accumulation of stress and suffering inevitably leads him to thoughts of suicide, "When crying wouldn't suffice but you take it with a sigh."[134] The poem questions whether there is any movement out of the pain of the poet's own tormented thoughts. By its end, the poem locates this movement in the poet's expression of vulnerability and retrospective awareness of his fallibility as a young man who got caught up with the allure of being in a gang: "I've checked in with my chips of sin and this is the life I had bought."[135] The poker metaphor expresses Kosal's refusal to see himself as a pure victim of the system, but rather as a person whose circumstances do not excuse his mistakes. The U.S. government, on the other hand, refuses to concede to its wrongdoing in handling the cases of Cambodian American deportees, a refugee diaspora it was in part responsible for making.

As Eric Tang explains, poor housing conditions, the cycle of working poverty, punitive welfare conditions, and the pipeline to prison—these are all hallmarks of the "hyperghetto," a space of carceral regulation "reserved for the isolation and enclosure of the poorest urban residents."[136] The hyperghetto is a site of domestic war in which poor racialized communities are abandoned by the state and pitted against each other for scarce resources. Extending the connotations of collateral damage to the hyperghetto, Tang argues that just as Cambodian refugees "were once 'incidentally' violated by the destruction wrought by their ostensible saviors, so they continue to function as collateral damage in the war against the hyperghetto's long-standing residents, specifically African Americans and Puerto Ricans."[137] Held captive in urban abjection even as they are celebrated as model minority figures who are destined to transcend this abjection, Cambodian refugees have become collateralized subjects of U.S. racial statecraft and carceral capitalism designed to punish the hyperghetto's existing racialized others.[138] State divestment, interracial/ethnic violence, and forms of everyday crisis coalesce in this space to perpetually foreclose interracial solidarity, turning Cambodians and African Americans into mutual enemies. The hyperghetto is also what Robert McRuer terms the "inhabitable spaces" of inaccessible urban housing that warehouse "unruly bodies, or bodies inconvenient to and for processes of neoliberal development."[139] This space of "crippling" neoliberal development and predatory debt "not only ensnares already disabled bodies or minds, but inescapably produces more disability and illness."[140]

Traversing locales such as the hyperghettos of Riverside, Sacramento, and Los Angeles, *Cambodian Son* explores the inhabitable spaces of Cambodian American refugee life—the "killing fields" on American soil. In fact, the "killing fields" is precisely the term Ta-Nehisi Coates has used to describe not the battlefields of Cambodia but the "caged neighborhoods on the West-side [of Baltimore]."[141] For Coates, these spaces constitute "an elegant act of racism, killing fields authored by federal policies, where we [Black people] are, all again, plundered of our dignity, of our families, of our wealth, and of our lives."[142] Premised on "the reduction of the black body," "the killing fields of Chicago, of Baltimore, of Detroit, were created by the policy of Dreamers, but their weight, their shame, rests solely upon those who are dying in them."[143] Whether conscious or not of his allusion to Cambodia, Coates's use of the killing fields metaphor exhibits the logic of Cambodia's minor anecdoting in its own way as Coates elides a consideration of the racial battlefields that ensnare both Black life and Cambodian refugee life through the coexisting temporalities of America's wars at home and abroad. Both the killing fields "over there" and "over here" are premised on the injuring and elimination of racialized bodies and spaces deemed surplus to the racial capitalist nation-state.

A polyvocal work that incorporates multiple perspectives, *Cambodian Son* sets the story of Kosal Khiev alongside that of other deportees, constructing a "gangster bricolage" that conveys the system of Cambodian American deportation as a state instrument of what McRuer terms "crip displacement," wherein "uprootedness, eviction, and relocation have been quotidian effects of a transnational neoliberal consensus."[144] In this gangster bricolage, we get the story of Sokha, a deportee who verbally reenacts the crime that led to his incarceration at the age of seventeen. As a teenager, Sokha fired his gun one night in a college dormitory in Amherst in a drug deal gone awry, injuring one person. The film uses black-and-white monochrome footage of Sokha, rapidly intercut with an image of a bloodied chicken, to portray Sokha's agitation in recalling this memory. The breathless, disorderly montage, reminiscent of a noir gangster cinematic style, conveys the masculinist conditioning of gang members like Sokha who feel they have no alternative but to prove themselves to their peers through performances of violence. In Sokha's animated voice and body language, we can see and hear that, even decades later, this conditioning remains a deeply embedded mode of survival. Like Sokha, "who would get picked on" as a boy, other deportees featured in *Cambodian Son*, such as Thea, WicCed, and KK, describe how their tough upbringings were defined by the barrage of racial violence directed at the community: in WicCed's words, it was "chink this, chink that" at school; out in the streets, gun violence and death were normalized to the point where "that's all you see in life."[145] Troubling the linear narrative of refugee progress and ascent to model minority "success," *Cambodian Son* portrays the banal forms of both every day racism (racial slurs, gang fights) and systemic racism (poverty, police violence) through which Cambodian refugee lives are wasted and disposed of, either through prison or deportation.

Cambodian Son takes the viewer to the specific park in Riverside, California, "where Kosal got put-in" (street slang for being initiated into a gang).[146] Here, Sugano interviews Kosal's former friend and codefendant, Po, who served fourteen years in prison. As the camera follows him through the park, Po recounts spending most of his youth in this playground-turned-battleground. He remembers that the "cops [would] always swoop on [them]" and that he was recruited to fight in a gang "pretty much [as] a soldier."[147] Recalling the bloodshed of his youth, Po feels lucky to have just made it out alive: "Out of all of us," Po remarks, "I'm the only one left out here. Everyone else is out of the country" or "doing life."[148] In Po's self-characterization as a lucky survivor, we hear an account of childhood marked by perpetual fear, insufficiency, and racialized criminalization. The playgrounds of Cambodian American youths in *Cambodian Son* have become carceral enclosures in which these youths live on the edge of anticipated violence, bracing for the next explosive moment.

While Kosal's new life in Cambodia signifies his movement from the crip refugee temporality of incarceration to that of deportation, his displacement illustrates McRuer's argument that "perhaps paradoxically, crip displacements generate unpredictability and precarity *and* a generative longing."[149] In deportation exile, Kosal now inhabits a crip time marked by poverty, separation, being without status, and psychological debilitation, yet in many scenes we see how his life in Cambodia is not as restricted and precarious as it once was in the U.S. "killing fields," if you will. In the film, Kosal's recitation of the "Moments in between the Nights" in London is split apart by a montage of Kosal performing the same lines in different times and spaces. As he lyricizes, "knowing full well with a full heart that I should be there not here," the "here" of a prison cell is transformed through the film's editing to the "here" of both the London poetry stage and various locations around Cambodia.[150] The poet's days and nights are now filled with other experiences in Cambodia and elsewhere where the poet is trying to rebuild his life in exile. Kosal's desire to move away from hate, resentment, and violence is suggested through the film's splicing together of various contexts where Kosal recites the poem in Cambodia: on a river, near the beach, in the streets of Phnom Penh. The poem ends with a call to responsibility: "This is the life that I bought," a life that takes ownership of one's "sins" but also confirms the commitments of the exiled "bad refugee" artist.[151] "This is the life that I bought" is no longer a life in prison but a life of secondary refuge with the responsibilities of representing Cambodia on the world stage and trying to make amends with his friends and family back in the United States.

For Kosal, spoken word poetry becomes a vehicle for working through the anger and grief he feels at the private and familial level as well as the rage and aspirations for structural change to the carceral system that has caused so much pain within the Cambodian community. Reflecting on his time in prison, Kosal explains in an interview, "When you're in an environment of monsters you almost become a monster in order to survive."[152] Spoken word poetry offered him an emotional lifeline while in prison as a way out of his own anger: "I was angry. I was sad. I was lost. And then I heard somebody read some poetry."[153] The climax of *Cambodian Son* occurs when Kosal manages to reunite with his father after decades of separation. Outside his father's restaurant in France, Kosal recites a poem titled "Love U I," written originally for his mother, bringing his own form of artistic refuge to share with his father's family. As Kosal writes in the poem, "This is my extension. Mind heart body and soul plus a spiritual dimension written thru a pen."[154] The poem underlines the capacity for joy, a "pure joy, sublime noise," as Kosal names it.[155] As Vinh Nguyen argues, in the testimonies of Cambodian American deportees, "Love is not a ruse for the articulation of resentment, nor is resentment somehow disguised as love in order to be heard or felt. Rather, the messiness of affective experience tells us that love and resentment can coexist or overlap, where the expression of love is simultaneously the utterance of resentment."[156] In the film, Kosal freestyles in plain dialogue, breaking with the rhyme form to voice his anger, invoking the multiple intersections of oppression that he has been subjected to: the U.S. bombings, the Khmer Rouge, Western immigration policies that forced his family to separate, the prison industrial complex, and the U.S. deportation regime that exiled him from his home in America. These structures have produced thirty-two years of separation.

By its conclusion, *Cambodian Son* refuses a sentimental ending in which individual redemption is achieved through a facile "coming to voice." As Kosal's sister Victoria says in the film, "He didn't make the right choice, but he served his time. He should be given a second chance to stay with us. It's just unjust."[157] As in the past, deportation represents another temporality of forced dislocation marked by traumatic upheaval, family separation, homesickness, and economic precarity in which Cambodian Americans have had to negotiate complex strategies of survival. The film ends with intertitles that provide an update, as of January 2014, on the status of the various Khmer Exiled Americans featured in the documentary. Some deportees such as WicCed and KK have managed to find fulfilling work, but others are struggling to stay afloat. As Thea comments, their struggle is ongoing: "Coming to Cambodia,

Figure 2.6 Kosal Khiev performing on train tracks, showing the word "abandoned" tattooed on his left arm. (From *Cambodian Son*, directed by Masahiro Sugano, 2014.)

at first I felt like it's so hard to fit in with Cambodia. Because I'm not . . . I'm not a local, and I'm not an expat. We're exiles. We're in between."[158] While they remain stranded in extraterritorial limbo as subjects of irregular citizenship, they form a community in exile that sets them apart from the local Khmer and the expatriates. As the final credits roll, Kosal is filmed walking alone along a railway track in Cambodia as he performs his spoken word poem, "Take Me Home." We see the word "abandoned" tattooed on his left arm, a reminder of his scars, but his spoken word tells us that he is "ready to roll" (see Fig. 2.6). The railway track symbolizes Kosal's uncertain future and his new journey as a Cambodian American poet in exile. In his new home, Kosal moves at his own pace among a newly formed community of deportees like him and with the newfound opportunity for rebuilding kinship ties severed by empire. Unlike flight, the train implies slow, grounded movement.

Conclusion: Debility, Debt, and the Afterlife

In the afterlife of war, debt and debility go hand in hand. As Jasbir Puar asserts, "Tropes of disability are used to describe the past as well as the future of capitalism, such that debt functions as debility. The concept of 'crippling debt,' for example, reveals the ways in which fiscal 'health' is a form of capacitation or capacity."[159] If the U.S. Cold War formation "crippled" Cambodia's economic infrastructure in the 1970s through bombing campaigns, the backing of secret coups, and the loaning of money that caused massive currency inflation, then this system of debilitation persists in the afterlife of war through what Jodi Kim calls "debt imperialism"—"a multiscalar process through which the United States imposes imperial power by rolling over its significant national debt indefinitely and not conforming to the homogenous time of repayment that it imposes on others."[160] In February 2017, at a press conference in Phnom Penh, U.S. ambassador to Cambodia William Heidt told a Cambodian audience that "it's in Cambodia's interest not to look at the past, but to look at how to solve this [debt] because it's important to Cambodia's future."[161] "Until it takes care of its debt with America and its other creditors," Heidt elaborates, Cambodia "cannot have a normal relationship with the IMF."[162] Here Heidt is referring to Cambodia's $500 million dollar (USD) Cold War–era debt to the United States. Tying Cambodia's prosperity and health as a nation solely to its fiscal condition within a system of "normal" neocolonial capitalism, Heidt exposes the ableist assumptions embedded within the U.S. statecraft of debt imperialism. In the early 1970s, the U.S. bombing of Cambodia devastated the country's civilian and agricultural infrastructure and contributed to a massive food shortage that paved the way for the United States to then step in with a loan to the Lon Nol government (installed by the United States through a coup) in the form of agricultural commodities. Presumably out of fear that it would have to repay reparations to Cambodia, the U.S. government continues to use the debt as a means of evading its own culpability.[163] More than just demonstrating U.S. hypocrisy, the demands for Cambodia's debt works to silence the argument voiced by many Cambodians that *it is the United States that owes a debt to Cambodia*, not the inverse.

Cambodia's economic fate continues to be welded to the U.S. empire through the Cold War legacies of U.S. currency substitution and national monetary debt. This irony is illustrated perhaps most poignantly in the scenes of Qingming, the annual festival to honor the dead in Cambodia. During Qingming, Cambodians traditionally burn fake money or gold in remembrance of their ancestors, transferring to the afterlife the commodities that are of most value in Cambodian society at any given time in history. Today, the Cambodian riel as a national currency remains too devalued; piles of fake U.S. dollars are frequently set alight for the dead instead.

On April 19, 1975, my mother and father, along with my two brothers, walked outside of the front door of their home in Kampong Thom, Cambodia, their arms full of food and gifts to welcome the Khmer Rouge soldiers who marched into the city. Their faces showed expressions of relief as they walked out onto the street. The war, the bombings, and rockets had come to an end. My mother, a slight woman, resourceful and beautiful, and my father, a gentle rebel, huddled their young boys close to them.

The Khmer Rouge told people to pack up their belongings and prepare to leave their homes for three days. My mother and father's expressions turned to worry, then fear, then dread. The Khmer Rouge announced warnings that the Americans were planning to bomb again. All those in possession of arms were ordered to lay them down in the town square. My mother went to dig up a jar of *riel*, Cambodian currency she had buried in preparation for this day, when the Khmer Rouge announced that money too was now abolished in the new Democratic Kampuchea.

Banks were blown up. Libraries, cinemas, and temples were destroyed. My family watched as soldiers pointed their guns at people who refused to vacate their homes. They watched as strangers, friends, and neighbors were rounded up and taken away.

Decades later, my mother and father tell me that on that day they fell into a trap. They were not allowed to return to their homes in three days. Instead, they walked. They walked for days and nights into the jungle, into the new Cambodia, Year Zero. They crossed into new lives that would be shattered and remade again and again over the next four decades.

3

———

Cripping the Kapok Tree and
the Cambodian Genocide

When I was growing up, and still to this day, I noticed something peculiar every time my mother would tell someone that our family had come to Canada as refugees from Cambodia. When she said Cambodia, her eyes would drop and her voice would soften, as if she hoped the word would not be heard. She knew that for most people, Cambodia was known only as a place where horrible things had happened. There was no other way of relating her experience except through this narrow script of how tragic her life had been in Cambodia and how lucky she felt to be in Canada. Over time, I came to see my mother's difficulty speaking about Cambodia (beyond the repetition of a familiar set of sound bites) as a kind of debilitating silence, or perhaps aphasia, shaped by the lack of space for her story to genuinely move within the world, by the complications of intergenerational dialogue, and by the precarity of everyday life in Canada that required her to work around the clock, by day on a factory line and by night picking worms in the fields. Along with her pain, Cambodia burrowed inward, into the depths of her being. This burden of silence manifested in her anguished screams, fits of rage, and lifelong addictions. It filled our entire household when I was growing up, covering every aspect of our lives like a thin layer of dust that would settle again moments after being brushed away.

As I got older and began asking more questions about the past, new stories or new versions of the same stories would begin to flow out of my mother. As we were standing in my kitchen in Vancouver washing dishes one day, she suddenly started recounting a memory from the past that I had never heard before. She described a scene of walking through the forest by herself one day in 1976, one year into Pol Pot time. In just one short year, she had lost her mother and two older brothers. Not knowing the exact details of how they had been killed, she could only imagine the gruesome scenes over and over again in her mind. As she gazed up at the tall trees, she felt overwhelmed by grief and despair. She wanted to end her life in this moment. But then she thought of her two young children (my brothers). She wondered who would take care of them if she were dead, how little chance they would have of surviving without her. She reminded herself that they needed a mother to carry them through this world turned upside down, even as the end of the nightmare seemed nowhere in sight. She looked ahead and kept walking through the forest.

Decades later, as we were washing dishes in my kitchen, my mother described this will to continue living using the Khmer expression *kamleang chet* (strength of the heart). She explained this concept to me as emotional survival, turning inward, mental willpower, not giving up. The will to survive in Pol Pot time involved knowing when to remain silent, how to take one's mind elsewhere, how to disappear within oneself. It also involved knowing what to do and what to say at the right time. *Kamleang chet*, my mother explained, was the feeling that propelled other kinds of everyday acts of survival as well: foraging for food, planting vegetables, crossing checkpoints, sharing food, sleeping in the jungle, singing a song, writing a letter, and mourning a death. For her, *kamleang chet* meant the refusal of death or, sometimes, the refusal of the state's refusal to let die.

These scenes from my mother's memories help frame this chapter's exploration of the Khmer proverb of *dam-doeun-kor* (to plant a kapok tree) as a Khmer epistemology of disability and emotional resistance. As discussed at length in the Introduction, the Khmer proverb "to plant a kapok tree" carries similar meaning with "see nothing, hear nothing, say nothing," and can address the disabling legacies of the Cambodian Genocide by making visible the situated practices of emotional resistance and performative disability adopted by Cambodian people during the genocide, which continue to remain illegible within Western paradigms of resistance and subversion. The kapok tree comes up again and again in the Cambodian refugee archive, but there are two works—Vaddey Ratner's novel *In the Shadow of the Banyan* and Rithy Panh's *The Missing Picture*—that illuminate the subtleties and nuances of this Khmer epistemology particularly well, even as they do not make reference to the kapok tree explicitly. In these texts, the kapok tree materializes a Khmer vernacular of suffering, pain, and resistance that has been disqualified as authoritative knowledge within Western liberal humanist ways of knowing. As Rithy Panh puts it, this is the view that "the crime against humanity committed in Cambodia was *specific* to it, partly explicable by a certain quietism connected with Buddhism, and also by a tradition of peasant violence. As if the genocide was cultural, even foreseeable."[1] Time and again in the dominant discourse, Panh has faced the interpretation of Cambodian people as passive, submissive, and docile in the face of Khmer Rouge violence.[2] Conveying his indignation, the narrator of *The Missing Picture* asks: "How do you revolt when all you've got are black clothes and a spoon? When you are lost, when you are hungry? Some say now that it's because of Buddhism and the acceptance of destiny. Where were those fine minds then? In their books? In their lofty ideas?"[3] Such interpretations, Panh suggests, could only originate from the abstract spaces of privilege far removed from Cambodia and the Global South. To interpret a genocide as culturally motivated is to deny its reality at the very core; it is to dismiss the calculated damage of empire as well as the complex and differently legible ways in which Cambodian people confronted and defied the Khmer Rouge.

As Youk Chhang, the director of the Documentation Center of Cambodia has asked, "Has any article [about the Cambodian Genocide] ever been written about a laugh? Or about a couple that had a child and was happy? Or about the sight of a flower during the winter time that is beautiful, despite being surrounded by suffering? Maybe scholars do not see this."[4] Chhang's questions here point to an epistemic injustice that has had implications not only for survivors but for their children born after the war. As a generation, we are haunted by the question of *why our parents and grandparents and aunts and uncles did not resist the Khmer Rouge?* When we seek out answers to this question in the dominant discourse, we discover a narrative of passivity, violence, and shame that does not square with the knowledge that we have inherited from our parents and ancestors. To crip the kapok tree, then, means a different way of attending to the site of resistance across the Cambodian refugee archive, one that illuminates the force of muteness, the amplitude of silence, and the force of performative blindness and deafness in order to safeguard one's self and loved ones against further death and debilitation. It might, at first, seem unfitting to be bringing cripistemology—a theory that emerges out of U.S.-based critical disability studies—to an analysis of the Cambodian refugee archive. But, as I show, crip theory's emphasis on the disabled body in pain, and the systemic structures of domination that have produced it as such, lends itself to a discussion of the needs of the Cambodian community, who continue to suffer from "crippling" rates of physical and mental health impairment extending from the Cold War.

Derived from the word "cripple" that undeniably carries a painful history of stigma for disabled people, the word crip in disabled communities in recent decades has come to take on new meanings: "as a marker of in-your-face, or out-and-proud, cultural model of disability."[5] As Robert McRuer writes in his book, *Crip Times*, "'To crip,' like 'to queer,' gets at processes that unsettle, or processes that make strange or twisted. *Cripping* also exposes the ways in which able-bodiedness and able-mindedness get naturalized and the ways that bodies, minds, and impairments that should be at the absolute center of a space or issue or discussion get purged from that space or issue or discussion."[6] McRuer here emphasizes how cripping involves a centering of the disabled body-mind in discussions of social justice and liberation. Crip and cripping, McRuer argues, can "be positioned alongside a range of terms that represent the need for new or multiple languages for thinking about disability," such as the concept of debility, for example.[7] Cripistemology, according to Merri Lisa Johnson and Robert McRuer, is about those "whose experiences can't or won't, for various reasons, materialize as 'disability,'" because the word can often function as a master term that draws a false equivalence among all disability experiences.[8] Masking hierarchical relations of power, the universalizing term "disability" can fail to account for local vernaculars and idioms of suffering and pain, such as those that extend from the afterlife of the Cambodian Genocide. Cripistemology "expands the focus from physical disability to the sometimes-elusive crip subjectivities informed by psychological, emotional, and other invisible or undocumented disabilities."[9] Furthermore, cripistemology "unwinds the spring between debility and capacity, not only by recognizing the ways one population's capacity depends on the debility of others, but also by recognizing the ways capacity depends on debility within a single individual's body or life."[10] Johnson and McRuer's theory of cripistemology informs this chapter's analysis of the kapok tree as a crip site of meaning in the spirit and tradition of disability movements that "have always desired better knowledge about disability: better than the monovocal singularity of the medical model, better than a rehabilitative model seeking a restored identity or sameness, better than eugenic or genocidal dreams of a world without disability, a world incapable of valuing disability or recognizing the value generated by disability."[11] Noting how crip theory has "crossed some [disciplinary] borders relatively easily" and has "moved in and out of various languages," McRuer cites the examples of the term's uptake in contexts such as Norway, Finland, Sweden, Denmark, Iceland, Spain, Germany, Russia, and Czechoslovakia.

What would it mean to bring crip theory to nonwhite sites of disability and impairment in the Global South such as Cambodia, which has yet to be attended to within the Euro-American field of critical disability studies? How might a cripping of the Cambodian kapok tree reveal something about the "making and unmaking [of] disability epistemologies, and the importance of challenging subjects who confidently 'know' about 'disability,' as though it could be a thoroughly comprehended object of knowledge?"[12] Cripping the kapok tree is thus a way of reading disability differently by routing it through Cambodia and the refugee afterlives of war and genocide. It is about remaining open to the possibility of contingent and incomplete knowledge—and to refugee knowledge of injury, impairment, and survival.

Vaddey Ratner's *In the Shadow of the Banyan*: Muted Lives

In an interview about her 2012 novel *In the Shadow of the Banyan*, Vaddey Ratner relates an anecdote about how, in the final months of the Cambodian Genocide, she stopped speaking completely: "I came out of the Khmer Rouge experience mute."[13] A nine-year-old girl at the time she went mute, Ratner only "regained [her] ability to speak" as a refugee resettled in America,[14] though she continued to struggle with speaking throughout her life. Ratner describes how, during a return trip to Cambodia, in 2009, "the silence [she had] known as a child took hold of [her] again."[15] Her starts and stops with silence and speech would be an interminable journey as she continued to remake her life as an adult between America and Cambodia, shaping her work as an artist in ways that continue to unfold.[16] Ratner's recounting of her experiences recalls Jasbir Puar's argument that "disability is not a fixed state or attribute but exists in relation to assemblages of capacity and debility, modulated across historical time, geopolitical space, institutional mandates, and discursive regimes."[17] Even as someone born with infant polio that left her with a weakened leg—a more ostensibly "visible" disability than acquired muteness—Ratner, to my knowledge, has never explicitly claimed the identity of a disabled person.[18] What is notable in Ratner's description of her complicated relationship to language is the regular slippage she enacts between the conditions of silence and muteness. She became mute *during* the Cambodian Genocide, she spoke again *afterward*, and she has gone back and forth between periods of silence and speech throughout her life. Like many Cambodian survivors, the situated and contingent nature of Ratner's multiple vectors of disability—as a person living with polio, a survivor of genocide, a refugee, and a person living with an uncategorizable speech impairment—are largely illegible within what Puar describes as the "capacitating frame" of liberal disability rights "that recognizes some disabilities at the expense of other disabilities that do not fit the respectability and empowerment models of disability progress."[19] Ratner's way of being and knowing her own disability might be more productively framed in relation to cripistemology, as what Johnson and McRuer describe as an umbrella term that includes the "varied, unstable crip positions [that] could be construed as deeply imbricated in, and trying to do justice to, a range of necessary and queer turns in disability studies: phenomenological, transnational, affective."[20] The turns align with Ratner's anecdote in an interview about the incapacitating effect of struggling to resettle in America while watching her mother struggle with the stigma of being "a refugee, an outsider—who spoke only broken English."[21] In such moments, Ratner writes, "our life seemed as broken as the language we adopted."[22] Ratner thus describes her life in America as weighted with feelings of brokenness compounded by racism and discrimination.

Ratner's semifictional novel *In the Shadow of the Banyan* further explores these multiple registers of crip refugee time and embodiment through the eyes of the novel's narrator and protagonist: a seven-year-old girl named Raami who is a princess in the Cambodian royal family (the daughter of Prince Sisowath Ayuravann). When we first meet Raami, she is a precocious child preoccupied with imagining scenes from famous Khmer myths and legends. Over the course of the narrative, however, as Raami is swept up in the terror of the Khmer Rouge revolution, we witness her retreat into the imagination, followed by its gradual quieting. This transformation culminates in her complete "muteness" by the end.

In the Shadow of the Banyan explores how the experiment of Democratic Kampuchea involved both physical violence and complex forms of psychological warfare. In its targeting of people's private sentiments, feelings, and attachments, the Khmer Rouge would spare no cost. Throughout the narrative, the sound of Khmer Rouge slogans reverberate constantly in Raami's ears: "The Organization has eyes and ears like a pineapple! There's no reason to lie, to hide! You must come out! Reveal yourself!"[23] In this invocation of a common slogan that Cambodian survivors often remember most from Pol Pot time (that Angkar has "eyes and ears like a pineapple"), Ratner alludes to what scholars such as Boreth Ly have described as the Khmer Rouge's panoptic system of totalizing surveillance.[24] The goal of this system was to install in Cambodian people a terrorizing fear that they were always being watched and listened to at all times, that anything they did or said could be turned against them. Like in Foucault's discussion of panoptic power, Angkar's control was also dependent on people's internationalization of surveillance as it also sought to transform Cambodian people into extensions of Angkar: to be loyal to the party, people were told they had to become *like the pineapple*, hypersensory and hyperattuned to any signs of suspicious activity.

Seeing, hearing, and speaking thus became the senses that Cambodian people learned to distrust and fear, to rid themselves of if they were to survive Angkar's violence. The advice that Raami gets from her father and her uncle is that "in the end only the deaf, the dumb, and the mute would survive."[25] A variation on the proverb of "to plant a kapok tree," this Khmer saying of "only the deaf, dumb, and mute would survive" situates disability in Ratner's novel as both the *effect* of a disabling and genocidal regime and the *cause* of Cambodian people's survival. It is a source of knowledge—part of a prophecy—passed down to Raami about the need to perform a kind of sensorial detachment to survive the violence of the new regime. This performative disability is apparent in a scene when Raami is forced to attend a Khmer Rouge indoctrination session, where she reflects: "We didn't learn to read or write a single word, and even though I already knew how, I never let on. It was clear we must keep quiet, keep what we knew hidden."[26] In thinking through Raami's muteness as responsive to the constant assembling of power, the novel opens up space for thinking about both ontological violence and agential being.

Planting the kapok tree signals both the closing down of personhood and the possibility of agency, neither fully subsumed by power nor fully resistant to it. We see this in the novel when Raami inadvertently reveals her father's real name (Sisowath Ayuravann) to the Khmer Rouge. Watching in horror as her father is led away, presumably to his death, Raami afterward feels "suspended in numbness, drifting to and fro, as if this sorrow, which was like no other [she'd] known, had weight and mass exceeding [her] body."[27] The language of familial intimacy that has been nurtured in Raami throughout her childhood is now an endangerment to herself and her family as Raami's world is rapidly transforming into something cruel and hardened. As a child, Raami now carries the shame of inadvertently contributing to her father's death. The novel conveys the excruciating psychological effects of the Khmer Rouge's policies of familial separation and systematic eradication of kinship ties, particularly on children like Raami, whose coming-of-age is a rapid maturation into a kind of enforced disability. She learns all to quickly that if she does not become "deaf, dumb, and blind," if she does not plant the kapok tree, more people around her will suffer or die.

As the years of the Khmer Rouge rule go on and violence accumulates, Raami's external quiet shifts into a numb speechlessness. During the monsoon season, at the site of one of the Khmer Rouge's irrigation construction projects, Raami describes the dulling, repetitious cycle of labor in which "day and night seemed caught in a rut, sending us round and round in the same monotonous rotation."[28] In a muted tone that scarcely resembles the expressive voice of her previous self, Raami narrates the death of two children, her little cousins, who drown in one of the embankments during a monsoon storm. After this loss, Raami feels only the eviscerating pain of grief. She has been reduced to a condition of bare life, and, in this living-dead state of exhaustion, hunger, and grief, Raami has all but abandoned the Khmer myths and fables that previously sustained her. The deafening propaganda of the regime becomes all that she hears. In order to drown it out, Raami privately retreats, no longer into the imagination, but, inward, into a void of silence: "Instead, silence took root in my blood. I became deaf. I became mute. I thought only of the work in front of me."[29] Raami's retreat into silence, in this instance, is both an ontology of emotional resistance and debilitating muteness: "I reached only silence. Deep within myself, within the dark, grave-like hole, I lay. They couldn't touch me anymore."[30] Long after Pol Pot time, after Raami and her mother escape from Cambodia as refugees, Raami will continue to struggle to find her way out of this grave-like hole, this void of silence, that was her armor against threat and violence.

The account of Raami's (and, indeed, Ratner's) internalization of the kapok tree proverb is far from exceptional in the Cambodian refugee archive. Indeed, I have yet to meet a Cambodian survivor from my mother and father's generation who is not familiar with the proverb. One of the darkest ironies of the Cambodian Genocide is that those who *did* survive had to become, to some extent, *like the kapok tree*. We could say that this was a population that had been debilitated on a mass scale, both figuratively and literally. Moreover, the bodies and minds of these survivors were indelibly marked by other kinds of acquired disabilities: corporeal amputations, psychological trauma, chronic injury, untreated wounds, and severe malnutrition. As legal scholar Randle DeFalco notes, in the afterlife of Democratic Kampuchea, Khmer Rouge leaders "have claimed that any starvation during the Khmer Rouge period was the product of a combination of bad harvests, drought, foreign interference and/or honest mistakes by Khmer Rouge leaders in providing local officials too much power."[31] An important aspect of the transitional justice redress movement today is research into the nature of the regime's biopolitical tactics of stunting—what Jasbir Puar describes as the targeting of people not for death but for "physical, psychological, and cognitive injuries . . . that seeks to render impotent any future resistance."[32] Based on the testimonies of local-level Khmer Rouge cadres, we know today that "unrealistic rice production quotas and bans on private eating—rendered it impossible to provide for the civilian population."[33] However, the long-term effect of this stunting on the Cambodian population—a population kept barely alive for almost four years—continues to be poorly understood. As critical disability studies scholar Helen Meekosha writes, "In trying to claim the positives of a disability identity it becomes difficult to acknowledge the overwhelming suffering that results from colonisation, war, famine, and poverty."[34] The analysis of a population starved by planned famine during Democratic Kampuchea and by U.S. sanctions during the Vietnamese occupation remains a "constitutive and capacitating absence" in discussions of Cambodian disability and disability studies more generally.[35]

Equally lacking is an adequate understanding of the history of Cambodian "blindness" as it emerged during the years of Khmer Rouge rule and beyond. It is instructive here to turn to the case of 150 Cambodian women in Southern California who reported becoming psychosomatically blind in the late 1980s. As a *New York Times* article recounted, these women, all survivors of the Cambodian Genocide who had come to the United States as refugees in the early 1980s, refused to leave their homes, citing vision problems, even as "advanced brain wave tests show[ed] that they should have perfect, 20/20 eyesight."[36] While the brain scans served to invalidate these women's claims, an electrophysiologist involved in the case offered the alternative diagnosis that "they just don't want to see anymore."[37] The blurring between the ontologies of "can't see" and "won't see" is reminiscent of the unstable binary between the "can't speak" and "won't speak" in the Khmer epistemology of the kapok tree. The case of the Cambodian women who reported going blind in 1989 reflects Puar's notion of the "ontological irreducibilities that transform the fantasy of discreteness of categories not through their disruption but, rather, through their dissolution via multiplicity."[38] In her insightful analysis of the 1989 case and its inspiration of Tran T. Kim-Trang's experimental short film *Ekleipsis* (1998), Fiona I. B. Ngô writes that while these Cambodian women "are witnesses to atrocities and thus indispensable political agents, their political positioning and humanity are rendered incomprehensible given Enlightenment logics."[39] Branded by the U.S. medico-juridical complex as culturally pathological "curiosities that stand in for the entirety of the US Cambodian population," these women "become unrecuperable as citizens because of a medico-legal complex that claims to want to rehabilitate them."[40] Ngô considers how this blindness was produced through the biopolitical assemblage of war, race, gender, and disability.

For Ratner, the impairments that have marked her embodied experience of the afterlife of the Cold War in Cambodia are not simply a matter of individual disability and speech; they are also about the crisis of language in Cambodia writ large. As the first Cambodian person in the diaspora to publish a work of fiction about the Cambodian Genocide, Ratner carries a particularly heavy burden of representation. The fact that it took over thirty years for a work of Cambodian diasporic fiction to emerge is indicative of the challenges the Cambodian community has faced in accessing resources and in cultivating a post–Cold War generation of artists positioned to voice their histories for themselves. In an interview about her novel, Ratner explains that she "wanted [readers] to see Cambodia before it became synonymous with genocide, before it became the 'killing fields.'"[41] Her writing seeks to grapple with Cambodia's Cold War episteme that has constructed Cambodia as *only* and *nothing more than* a place of killing and genocide. Why is it that the world has struggled to generate an ethical response to the Cambodian Genocide without resorting to the vocabularies of gratuitous violence and horror? How can we do more than simply *recount* violence? The conflation of Cambodia with death and brutality has paradoxically resulted in an inability to grieve what was lost. In response to this crisis of language, Ratner's novel seeks to understand the things that can arise from the space of loss.

What arises from this space in *In the Shadow of the Banyan* is a mythic language that melds the registers of the speculative and the biographical into a literary form reminiscent of works such as Maxine Hong Kingston's *The Woman Warrior* and Audre Lorde's *Zami: A New Spelling of My Name.* Evocative of Kingston's form of "talk-story" and Lorde's genre of "biomythography," Ratner turns to myth as a means of working through muteness and resisting the demands of transparent referentiality often required for audiences to "understand" the Cambodian Genocide as an accessible template.[42] In the early parts of the novel, Ratner allows Raami's imagination to filter through, creating a narrative palimpsest effect between the temporality of Democratic Kampuchea and that of classic Khmer literary texts such as the *Reamker* and *Mak Thoeung.* A Khmer adaptation of the Indian epic poem the *Ramayana,* the *Reamker* tells the story of Prince Rama from his fourteen-year exile to the forest, to the abduction and rescue of his wife Sita, and to his eventual return to the throne. In Ratner's novel, the *Reamker* foreshadows the impending upheaval in Raami's world. As her life is increasingly defined by everyday death, hard labor, harsh slogans, and unceasing surveillance, Raami's clinging to the *Reamker* symbolizes a refusal to cede the private landscape of the imagination. Similarly, the classic tale of star-crossed lovers in Khmer mythology, *Mak Thoeung,* serves as a vehicle of refusal for Raami amid the chaos and violence of the Khmer Rouge revolution. In *Mak Thoeung,* the tale of the perfume seller and his wife reminds Raami of her own mother and father's courtship, forged out of a mutual appreciation of Khmer literature and theater during Cambodia's golden era. Known for its critique of sovereignty, class inequality, and injustice, *Mak Thoeung* functions as a narrative device that enables Ratner to reflect on the system of monarchal privilege that Ratner/Raami herself embodies as a princess of the royal family. Such a system, Ratner's novel makes clear, has contributed to the inequalities fueling the Khmer Rouge revolution against feudalism and sovereign power. Any reckoning with the unredressed violence of the Cold War in Cambodia must also seek to account for the role of sovereign power in sowing the seeds of Communist revolution perpetrated in the name of anticolonial revolution.

Ratner's use of myth militates against the ethnographic demands placed on writers of color to establish *what really happened* in Cambodia. This imperative for Cambodian writing to exist primarily within a "corrective" historical mode is evident in the sentiment expressed by a reviewer of Ratner's novel, who remarks that "the liberal references to Cambodian myths and stories do not serve the immediate narrative."[43] Conversely, others have criticized the novel's reliance on historical veracity, asserting that "the novel's fidelity to real life gradually turns out to be a source of weakness. Though rendered in often lovely prose and marked by many emotionally wrenching passages, 'In the Shadow of the Banyan' feels insufficiently imagined, almost like a diary."[44] Such appraisals illuminate the literary expectations that fault the novel for being either too imaginative or not imaginative enough, suggesting that there is little space for Ratner, as a former Cambodian American refugee, to experiment with an aestheticized literary form.

Indeed, Ratner seems self-aware of the need to find a language that affirms the real pain of Cambodian survivors while also refusing the voyeuristic gaze that has locked Cambodia into an image of horror. In Saidiya Hartman's terms, this is the pursuit of a language with which to "revisit the scene of subjection without replicating the grammar of violence."[45] For those who live in such intimate proximity to death, Hartman writes, the reiteration of the spectacle of death does not serve the memory of the dead. Artists living this afterlife are confronted with the persistent problem of struggling with language. In its exploration of mythic language as the vibrant interiority of outward silence and muteness, Ratner's novel reimagines and confabulates new myths about Cambodian people's emotional resistance during Pol Pot time. Ratner has explained in interviews that Raami's turn to myth as a means of emotional resistance in the novel was modeled after Ratner's own experiences as a child: "In Cambodia, under the Khmer Rouge, when I was lost in a forest or abandoned by my work unit among the vast rice fields because I moved too slowly, I would recall the legends my father or nanny had told me or those tales I'd been able to read myself."[46] The regime's targeted elimination of artists and its systematic erasure of Cambodian mythology from the social fabric of everyday life meant that the act of remembering these myths constituted acts of defiance against the regime. The turn to myth, in this sense, signifies much more than an arbitrary aesthetic choice on Ratner's part. The language of myth returns us to the problem of representation that has defined Cambodia's Cold War episteme: Where documentary language has tended to fail, looping the speaker and reader into endless cycles of darkness and brutality, the mythic language offers Ratner an alternative mode of imagining Cambodia otherwise.

Ratner also crafts this alternative imaginary through the language of the kapok tree. At the end of the novel, Raami, her mother, and her sister are the only three members of Raami's family left alive. They are capacitated enough to orchestrate the next chapter of their perilous journey to a refugee camp, yet they remain physically and psychologically incapacitated in ways that can only be hinted at. Even after the Khmer Rouge has fallen from power, Raami explains, "I stayed mute. I could not find the voice to share with Mama what I understood."[47] Muteness is now constitutive of Raami's being, but she is not silent. As she recounts, "I let out a sob. It was not speech. Nevertheless, it was an expression, a voice of my deepest sorrow. I mourned him aloud, even if only with this single sound." In this single sound, Ratner alludes to the seed of regeneration implied within the proverb of planting the kapok tree. What was planted is not permanent damage, but a new *kapok* language—something close to a grunt, stutter, and sob—that embodies the refugee's capacity for remaking speech and selfhood. This sound will later become the basis for the "first note to break [Raami's] silence."[48] This concluding suggestion of Raami's rehabilitation might be read as an example of what David T. Mitchell and Sharon L. Snyder have termed "narrative prosthesis," the use of disability as a narrative device to reinscribe an ableist logic of disability as a problem to be transcended.[49] I suggest, however, that the novel constructs Raami's muteness less as narrative prothesis and more as an articulation of the Khmer cripistemology of the kapok tree—the gain of the new mode of knowing and speaking, a poetic excess that is inextricable from her experiences as a genocide survivor and a refugee.

Rithy Panh's *The Missing Picture*: "Silence Is a Scream"

I shift now from a discussion of the echoes of the kapok tree in the archives of Vaddey Ratner to those of Rithy Panh. While the previous chapter analyzed Panh's 2011 film *Shiiku, the Catch* about the U.S. bombing of Cambodia, the remainder of this chapter considers *The Missing Picture*, Panh's first explicitly autobiographical film about the Cambodian Genocide. The struggle with language is at the center of *The Missing Picture*, a film released in 2013 that is at once lyrical, multilayered, fragmented, and nonlinear in form. Combining autobiography, documentary, and nonrealist elements, *The Missing Picture* represents a noticeable departure from the style of his previous Khmer Rouge era films, such as *Site 2* (1989), *Bophana: A Cambodian Tragedy* (1996), and *S-21: The Khmer Rouge Killing Machine* (2002), which explicitly adopt strategies of cinema verité and social realism. Viet Thanh Nguyen describes *The Elimination* and *The Missing Picture* as "two of the finest works of art and memory to deal with the genocide, powerful partly because they abolish the sentimentality, the aesthetic weaknesses, and the fear of assigning responsibility to Western countries that limit so many [other] works" about Cambodian history.[50] Indeed, if some of Panh's earlier films could be subjected to this critique that Nguyen identifies, then his later works, beginning with *Shiiku, the Catch*, and followed by *The Missing Picture* and *The Elimination*, exhibit a level of aesthetic experimentation and analytic acuity that push the boundaries of the collective conversation about the legacies of the Cold War in Cambodia. The film's title—the concept of missing pictures—references the way the archival record can be made to speak (or not speak) through the silence of survivors. The film deploys multiple registers of speaking (and silence) through a mixing of Khmer Rouge archival propaganda footage, fragments of media from the golden era of Cambodian history (Panh's early childhood), and diorama scenes reconstructed with hand-carved clay figurines. Panh uses this recombination of elements to address the gap in the archive, illustrating how the experiences of Cambodian people under the Khmer Rouge are unspeakable and inarticulable in a more archival sense, as the film grapples with the question: How do we tell a story for which the record has been destroyed or never existed in the first place?

At the end of *The Missing Picture*, viewers are presented with a symbol of this absence in the image of a dirt pit grave (see Fig. 3.1). From above, we see a clay figurine avatar of Rithy Panh's father lying in the grave, and we watch as the film's montage repeats, as if on an endless cycle of partial burial and partial excavation. The tone of this scene is ominous and ambivalent. It signals Panh's return to a dark place in the recesses of his memory. The image of the void links to several earlier scenes in the film: the memory of how Panh "carried the dead down to the pit" of mass graves made by the Khmer Rouge; how his father was carried away on a piece of scrapped "sheet metal" and thrown into a "pit grave"; how, in Cambodia today, these mass graves are being dug out by international organizations, "the bones carried away" and discarded.[51] As Jacques Derrida put it, the work of mourning "consists always

Figure 3.1 The clay figure representing Rithy Panh's father gets buried. (From *The Missing Picture*, directed by Rithy Panh, 2013.)

in attempting to ontologize remains, to make them present, in the first place by *identifying* the bodily remains and by localizing the dead."[52] "Nothing could be worse," Derrida writes, "for the work of mourning, than confusion or doubt" about how or where the dead are buried.[53] "Teeter[ing] on the edge of the void," Panh laments, "as for the dirt, there is never enough. It's me they will kill. Or maybe they already have."[54] Symbolic of both the haunting specter of Panh's father and Panh himself, the burial scene's placement in the film's final minutes defies the linear, progressive teleology that viewers might have been expecting of Rithy Panh's first explicitly autobiographical documentary film.

Panh's quest in *The Missing Picture*, then, is not for what the title at first seems to allude to—a search for the elusive, missing image of an execution committed directly by the Khmer Rouge. "If at last I should find it," the film's voice-over narrator recites, "I could not show it, of course. And anyway, what would a picture of a dead man reveal?"[55] Panh's withholding of *the* documentary image as evidentiary proof is a bold statement to make given the context of genocide denial and state-organized forgetting that has saturated Cambodia's post–Cold War political landscape. Yet, simply displaying images of the dead, even for the purpose of substantiating war crimes, is no longer acceptable in Panh's view. Emphasizing the partiality and incompleteness of representation, *The Missing Picture* reevaluates the film's relationship to traumatic history and disrupts viewers' desire for the illusion of an authentic and unmediated experience. Given the surfeit of circulating atrocity images, Panh wonders about the use of showing images of the dead to "prove" what really happened. This standpoint via the work of archival recovery recalls Saidiya Hartman's questioning of the value of "subject[ing] the dead to new dangers and to a second order of violence."[56] As I discussed earlier, Panh has admitted that, despite his steadfast commitment to producing artistic films about Cambodia throughout his career, some of his own films have inadvertently contributed to the fetishization of the spectacle and grammar of violence. Cut up into pieces and reused without Panh's consent, Panh's films have been folded into the shocking language of what Hartman describes, with respect to the afterlife of chattel slavery, as the "scandal and excess [that] inundate[s] the archive."[57] "If it is no longer sufficient to expose the scandal," Hartman asks, "then how might it be possible to generate a different set of descriptions from this archive?"[58] Like Hartman's wish to undo the endless replay of the "open casket," Panh's pursuit in *The Missing Picture* is the search for a language that might bring him back from the edge of the void.

The film's recurring image of crashing water, like the pit grave, has multiple symbolic valences. These are the waves of Panh's refugee crip time: the time of erasure, violence, and destruction that disrupted Panh's childhood and that cast him into a world of nightmare; the psychic imprint of trauma that comes to the fore, irrepressibly, at various stages in life, drowning Panh in the remembrances of the past; the waves of madness, depression, and obsession. Like many forms of impairment, Panh's waves of pain are, in the words of crip theorists Johnson and McRuer, "episodic, not linear, a matter of intensities, sensations, and situations, not illness and cure."[59] As the camera's suspended perspective creates the impression of drowning and resurfacing, we hear the narrator's first words in the film: "In the middle of life, childhood returns. The water is sweet and bitter. I seek my childhood, like a lost picture, or rather it seeks me."[60] In search of a lifeline, Panh seeks a place of stable grounding where he can reach out and grab the hands of his childhood self, "this child, who says he's alive and who tells the tale—that's me."[61] Panh—the adult, the filmmaker, and the intellectual—searches for a way, a viable language, to console the thirteen-year-old Panh who flounders. The image of water thus alludes to the psychological and spiritual debilitation of the Cambodian Genocide as well as to the burden of silence and language that Panh has carried with him for decades. The scene works with other parts of the film to disrupt the idea of remembering and speaking past violation as an unquestionable good. Near the end of the film, the narrator says, "They say talking helps. You understand you get over it. For me, this wisdom will never come."[62] For Panh, simply talking—as is prescribed by Western psychoanalytic models of the talking cure—offers no solution to his pain.

Figure 3.2 A close-up of the clay figure representing Rithy Panh. Behind him, the archival footage of a Khmer Rouge labor commune. (From *The Missing Picture*, directed by Rithy Panh, 2013.)

In this way, Panh's film calls attention to how silence, muteness, quiet, screaming, and other modes of subjugated knowledge constituted a Khmer cripistemology of resistance during the Cambodian Genocide. Like in Vaddey Ratner's novel, this is an impaired condition embodied in the image of the kapok tree that is difficult to pinpoint precisely to one side or the other of the disabled/nondisabled binary. As Panh's film demonstrates, the degree of deprivation endured during the Cambodian Genocide is challenging to express in a conventional lexicon. We see this in one scene where the camera zooms in on an enlarged close-up of Panh's figurine superimposed against the backdrop of a Khmer Rouge labor commune (displayed as archival propaganda footage). We see the figurine's distressed facial expression, the dark shadows that contour his figure, and the blurred smudging of his image. At the same time, we hear a loud, high-pitched mechanical score that reinforces the scene's discomforting visuals. Reminiscent of Edvard Munch's *The Scream*, this expressionistic composition functions as a transition into a sequence depicting the surreal necropolitical conditions of Democratic Kampuchea in which Cambodians were subjected to systematic starvation, depletion, psychological reformation, surveillance, disorientation, familial separation of parents and children, and the perpetual fear of being taken away to be killed. Yet, Panh remarks: "Many resisted. Many. In silence, in a word, in a smile. Sometimes, a small gesture is all it takes to say no. I think of my father who announced his choice. Sometimes, silence is a scream"[63] (see Fig. 3.2). There is a dual figuring of the kapok tree here: on the one hand, speaking alone is insufficient to alleviate the weight of the past, assuming that one has the capacity to speak in the first place; some experiences are deeply inexpressible. On the other hand, there is also resistance in silence, especially during the Khmer Rouge years when people's capacity for overt resistance was stunted and almost entirely foreclosed by the biopolitical tactics of the regime. Moreover, this notion that silence is a "scream" (a variation on the kapok tree proverb) pushes the boundaries of disability studies by asking, as cripistemology seeks to do, "questions about remote locations, styles, and modes of transmission for prohibited knowledge about disability."[64] This screaming style extends beyond people's resistance during the Khmer Rouge years proper, for *The Missing Picture*, in the end, raises the overarching question of how the kapok tree might be reconceptualized to acknowledge the act of forceful (emotional) resistance through silence. As the narrator says, "To hang on, you must hide within yourself. A memory, an idea that no one can take from you, for a picture can be stolen; a thought cannot."[65] Planting the kapok tree exists as a Khmer cripistemology of emotional survival, then and now.

Though not explicitly named, the kapok tree, as a symbol of emotional resistance, pervades the narrative of *The Missing Picture*. Panh remembers the multiple ways that his father and mother defied the Khmer Rouge regime. In one scene, Panh's father decides to reject the brutal food rationing system implemented by the Khmer Rouge, declaring to his family, "I will no longer eat animal food. I am a man."[66] Panh's father dies of starvation in a final act of defiance against the Khmer Rouge, though Panh, a child of thirteen at the time, struggles to comprehend his father's actions. Naomi Paik in her book *Rightlessness* has written about hunger strikes as a means by which those in captivity refuse to "be disregarded as bodies left to waste away."[67] The refusal to eat as a modality of resistance can assert agency in a way that exposes the very structure of rightlessness that casts subjects into the impossible choice of death-in-life or life-in-death. *The Missing Picture* inscribes the memory of Panh's father's refusal of food as a final act of emotional opposition wielded against the regime's systematic dehumanization of Cambodian people through severe food rationing, exhaustive labor, and stunting. A body thoroughly depleted, yet kept barely alive, Panh's father elects in the end to exit from this system of endemic debilitation. This scene reveals how the emotional resistance during Pol Pot time consisted of both the refusal to die and, as in Panh's father's case, the calculated choice to die.

As Jasbir Puar argues about the Israeli state's use of stunting as a tactic of warfare, it is a "biopolitical fantasy, that resistance can be located, stripped, and emptied. 'Resistance itself' becomes an implicit target of computational metrics: How to measure, calculate, and capture resistance? But not only is biopolitical control a fundamentally productive assemblage; the ontological irreducibility of 'resistance itself' is fundamentally elusive."[68] What I take Puar to mean here is that while resistance itself becomes the target of biopower, this targeting generates its own ontologies of being—a resistance to the targeting of resistance, we could say, one that is neither fully subsumed nor totally outside of the assemblage of power. In the film, Panh's mother also finds ways to resist the regime's subjection of Cambodian people to the three vectors of debility that Puar identifies as "when to let die, when to maim, and when to 'will not let die.'"[69] "My mother fights for us," the narrator recounts: "She builds a shack of branches, leaves, and vines. Each day she walks two hours so we may drink clean water. She gets permission to take my father a half-ration."[70] The scene emphasizes Panh's mother's determination to keep her children alive through her own private subversion of the Khmer Rouge's water-rationing system. In a related scene, she refuses the Khmer Rouge's prohibition on funerary rites. At night, in the privacy of their hut, Panh's mother performs a "funeral in words" for her deceased husband, painting a picture of a dignified service in the imagination for her son.[71] As the film cuts to a panning shot of a line of silhouetted clay figurines walking in soft light, as if in the afterlife, the narrator declares, "It was an act of resistance."[72]

In *The Missing Picture*, Rithy Panh, like Vaddey Ratner, seems especially concerned with shifting the narrative about Cambodia away from a monolithic image of trauma toward an alternative imaginary linked to the nation's forgotten artistic legacies. Although a film consistently marketed as one that re-creates "the atrocities Cambodia's Khmer Rouge committed between 1975 and 1979,"[73] *The Missing Picture* opens, somewhat unexpectedly, with an image of a dilapidated room filled with hundreds of celluloid reels. Located at Cambodia's National Film Archive, the room embodies a lost domain, an inert and forgotten pathway into the golden era of Cambodia's past. From the piles of decomposing material, the camera zooms in on a pair of hands we assume to be those of Panh, the filmmaker, immersed in the material process of archival excavation and restoration. He pulls and closely examines a celluloid reel that becomes animated in the next shot in the form of an apsara dancer (see Fig. 3.3). Dressed in glittering gold traditional attire, she performs the formations of the apsara dance in front of a Cambodian audience seated on the floor. As viewers, we enter the time of Panh's childhood. While the images of horror and killing have proliferated, it is this image of Khmer creativity that has been rendered absent in the world's picture of Cambodia.

Beyond the issues of archival excavation and restoration, Panh faces another challenge: how to integrate the remnants of the perpetrator's archive—

Figure 3.3 Excavated footage of a Khmer apsara dancer from the pile of deteriorating film reels at Cambodia's National Film Archive. (From *The Missing Picture*, directed by Rithy Panh, 2013.)

the Khmer Rouge's black-and-white propaganda footage—in a manner that serves the filmmaker's political and aesthetic ends? Like in Saidiya Hartman's account of the "libidinal investment in violence [that] is everywhere apparent in" the slaveholders' records of chattel slavery,[74] Panh explains that "we understand the Khmer Rouge by watching their footage. Pol Pot forges a reality conformant with his desire. Even nature must conform."[75] This footage was once used to glorify Pol Pot's Communist revolution.[76] In Panh's versatile hands, however, this perpetrator's archive becomes porous and transparent, with the traces of the regime's violence seeping through the exposures as uncontainable and irrepressible excess. Panh's camera captures Pol Pot giving a speech to a vast stadium of cadres. As the camera pans, the narrator probes what lies off-screen. Panh wonders if the Khmer Rouge cameraman had actually intended to show "the children in rags . . . the true state of the nation,"[77] to secretly call into question Pol Pot's facade of "a model society, unique in the world, without class division."[78] Inspired by this hint of subversion within the ranks of the Khmer Rouge, Panh turns to the art of montage and Claymation, establishing a collision between two filmic registers: the Khmer Rouge's propaganda footage and Panh's own filmic language rooted in the spirit of Khmer creativity and in the labor of working through the kapok tree.

In *The Missing Picture*, this relationship between art and the kapok tree is seen in a close-up of a pair of hands carving a single clay figurine—the avatar of Panh's deceased father. The silent craft of carving constitutes an example of working through the difficulty with language that does not actually privilege the physical act of speech itself. Drawn from the earth and soil that contains the remains of the dead lost during Pol Pot time, clay represents the sediments of this era as well as the raw material for reinvention. The craftsman handling the figurine is not Panh, but rather Sarith Mang, an assistant at Panh's Bophana Audiovisual Center who spent many years in a Thai refugee camp after 1979.[79] Mang, like the film's English-language voice-over narrator Randal Douc, is one of the film's multiple authorial figures, participating in the construction of a collaborative narrative that is Panh's personal autobiography but also a collective story. The "voice" of the film belongs simultaneously to Panh and to a broader community of Cambodian survivors and refugees as the identities of the sculptor, voice-over narrator, and filmmaker do not perfectly align. The labor of working through the kapok tree is collaborative, relational, and material, for the narrator states, "With clay and with water, with the dead, with rice fields, with living hands, a man is made."[80] As we see the figurine of Panh's father take on shape, form, and color in white, Panh enacts a kind of symbolic eulogy for his father. For Cambodian people, Panh explains, "statues are more than simply pieces of stone."[81] It is believed that "the statue of the Buddha has a kind of soul and *is* the Buddha in some sense."[82] The act of carving represents a symbolic eulogy to the unidentified dead, for whom Cambodian survivors were prohibited from mourning during the years of the genocide (see Fig. 3.4).

The Missing Picture dramatizes the labor of working through silence while resisting the spectacularizing of the dead. As Nguyen-Vo Thu-Huong asks about the ethics of representing the dead, "How shall we remember rather than just appropriate the dead for our own agendas, precluding what the dead can tell us?"[83] While I take this point, *The Missing Picture* seems to push back against the implication that Cambodian lives only have value in their deaths. Cultivating an ethics of remembering *life* and *lifeworlds* over and above trauma and death, Panh devotes considerable screen time to representations of "the old days in Phnom Penh," which he recollects with fondness.[84] As the camera pans over a static tableau of Panh's childhood home, the film shifts into a nostalgic register. We see a Cambodian family engaged in the act of everyday domestic life: cooking, eating, conversing, playing with pets and children, dancing, and reading. The theme of Cambodian pleasure and joy is reinforced by a soundtrack of 1960s Cambodian *cha-cha-cha* music as well as

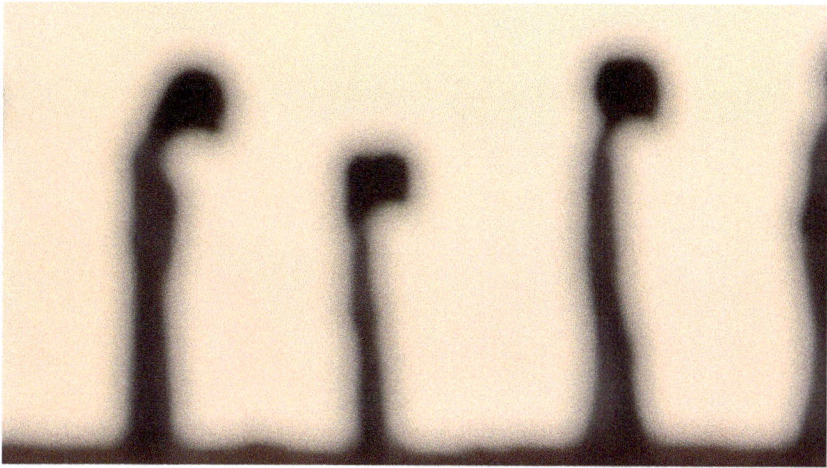

Figure 3.4 A eulogy of clay figures for the missing and the dead during Pol Pot time. (From *The Missing Picture*, directed by Rithy Panh, 2013.)

snippets of laughter and conversation: There was "laughter and singing, the smell of caramel, fish, spices, mango."[85] There is also an abundance of books and a valuing of education, as Panh recalls how his father, a teacher, read him poetry at night.[86] Conveying the sensorial richness of Panh's childhood, *The Missing Picture* accesses the vibrancy and diversity of Cambodian lifeworlds that are missing pictures in the monochrome palette of the Khmer Rouge's black-and-white propaganda films as well as in the reductive global image of Cambodia as a uniform site of horror and killing.

    The Missing Picture affirms the absence in the archive as an opportunity for re-creation. In one scene, Panh's clay avatar sits under a tree, alone and destitute, after years of living under the rule of the Khmer Rouge (see Fig. 3.5). I read this scene as an instantiation of the kapok tree proverb as Panh begins to retreat into the refuge of the imagination. Sitting under the tree as a figurine dressed in black who looks up at the sky in despair, Panh's figurine goes silent. At this moment of psychological transition, the omnipotent hand of the artistic creator swoops into the frame and switches the figurine for a different avatar of Panh dressed in a pink polka-dotted T-shirt (see Fig. 3.6). This figurine is Panh, who has planted the kapok tree. He sits with his eyes closed and reflects: "I have no more name, no more family, no more hope. But I still have a human heart."[87] A quick fade to black cues the beginning of a childhood flashback. We see Panh's brother performing in a 1960s Khmer rock band as the narrator recounts, "I think of the old days, of my brother who disappeared in Phnom Penh on April 17th, 1975, with his guitar."[88] On the soundtrack, we hear the music of Cambodian rock and roll singer Chum

Figure 3.5 The clay figure representing Rithy Panh, exhausted after working under the Khmer Rouge, has retreated into silence. (From *The Missing Picture*, directed by Rithy Panh, 2013.)

Figure 3.6 Another clay figure representing Rithy Panh, switched from his previous avatar, as silence breaks into the music of 1960s Khmer rock. (From *The Missing Picture*, directed by Rithy Panh, 2013.)

Kem, who first wrote and popularized a Khmer version of Chubby Checker's "The Twist," known as the "Kampuchea Twist" in the 1960s.[89] As Chum Kem's music plays, the camera pans across a diorama of clay figure musicians dressed in 1960s-style bell-bottoms and suspenders. A quick montage sequence then captures the exhilarating styles and movements of this period.

The Cambodian female rock star Pan Ron is shown performing onstage in a glittering minidress and Cambodian youths are shown dancing the twist. When the Khmer Rouge came to power, a vibrant and cosmopolitan community of Cambodian musicians was eliminated. Panh's clay figures who dance to this lost music inscribe a missing picture of Cambodian modernity rooted in musical self-expression and pleasure seeking.

Another sequence takes place in *The Missing Picture* when the narrator recounts: "I spent my own childhood in film studios with a director neighbor. I loved the wonderful world of wigs and costumes, colors and gold. The land of giants and fairy tales."[90] A sweeping panoramic shot of this scene shows Panh's clay avatar on the set of a fairy-tale film, where a group of mythical apsara dancers in ancient times sit in formation in front of a king and queen. Here, as in other childhood flashback scenes, we see the unique expressions of each figurine, the vibrancy of the scene's color palette, and the fluidity of kinetic as well as camera movement. The scene returns the viewer to the celluloid strip of the apsara dancers from the film's opening. Suddenly, an archival projection of the apsara dancer is superimposed onto the diorama scene itself. Panh's clay figurine, dressed in the pink shirt, watches in childlike wonder at the seemingly magical image of the dancer. The scene represents the film's effort to forge an image of the creative zeitgeist that once defined Cambodia.

The Missing Picture's final scene reasserts the need for a collective and relational ethics of remembering the past. As the narrator says, "I make this picture . . . this missing picture I now hand over to you, so that it never ceases to seek us out."[91] The image of crashing waves reappears on the screen again, now in black and white. The fading of color suggests that the responsibility to reckon with the legacies of the Cold War in Cambodia is passed on to the viewer, distributing the burden of silence. The silences that pursue the filmmaker, and all Cambodian survivors, will never cease, but perhaps they can weigh less heavily on the community as our works of art and scholarship begin to circulate throughout the world.

Conclusion: Kapok Futures

In 1993, the French-educated Cambodian scholar Vandy Kaonn wrote an influential essay titled "Cambodge ou la Politique sans les Cambodgiens" (Cambodia or Politics without Cambodians) lamenting the absence of the voices of Cambodian people in the debate about the country's "recovery" at the end of the Cold War.[92] Kaonn argued that Cambodia had transitioned into a post-colony (to draw on Achille Mbembe's term) wherein a corrupt Cambodian elite battled for power against imperial foreign powers. It was vital, Kaonn asserted, that mechanisms be put in place to enable Cambodian people to become actors in directing their country's future. In a similar vein, Rithy Panh's 1998 film *One Evening after the War*, set in Phnom Penh in 1992, dramatizes the dark state of affairs in so-called "post-conflict" Cambodia.[93] The narrative begins as Cambodian soldiers are returning home from war in Cambodia's northern front, where they have been enlisted by the Vietnamese army to fight against the Khmer Rouge. Cambodia is being occupied by UNTAC, the supranational humanitarian body charged with repatriating Cambodian refugees from the border camps, running the country's first "democratic" elections in 1993, and assisting in Cambodia's economic reconstruction.

In *One Evening after the War*, the Cold War is supposedly over, yet a Cambodian elder in the film remarks that "these years of war and suffering have driven us mad. The world forgot us for much too long. And now we're willing to accept anything on just a promise. Freedom's like a race through a minefield. It demands sacrifices and we look at it through the eyes of a battered child." Cambodian people harbor the raw and heavy wounds of the recent past while being ushered into a new era of market liberalization spearheaded by the new authoritarian government in power. The elder likens the hardships of the post–Cold War era in Cambodia to the act of navigating a minefield, filled with unpredictable peril, horrific irruptions of violence, and the making of more deaths, injuries, and maiming through *actual minefields*. This suffering is disproportionately shouldered by the most vulnerable citizens of Cambodian society—poor women and children. Panh's *One Evening after the War* examines the nation's passage from Khmer Rouge Communism to neoliberal authoritarianism, where Cambodia's fragile recovery, embodied in the main love story plot between a Cambodian man and woman, is perpetually foreclosed by the structural conditions of entrenched militarized heteropatriarchy, vast socioeconomic inequality, destabilizing resource shortages caused by Western sanctions, a debilitating mental health crisis, and ongoing war. Panh's film represents this historical period of overwhelming Western humanitarian presence and economic liberalization in Cambodia as another state of permanent war, albeit one unfolding, this time, under the guise of humanitarian rescue and capitalist development.

The challenges and absurdity of the post–Cold War era in Cambodia, as captured in Panh's *One Evening after the War*, has led other Cambodian artists, such as Svay Sareth, to turn to the kapok tree in his artistic practice as a means of illuminating the contradictions of the current political order in Cambodia. Illustrative of the syncretic style of the Khmer renaissance movement, Svay Sareth's 2018 art sculpture, *Head & Power*, draws on the iconography of the temples of Angkor (in particular, the stone faces carved into the

Figure 3.7 Svay Sareth's "Head & Power." The head is stuffed with kapok fibers symbolizing the muting effects of authoritarianism, 2018. (Svay Sareth, "Head & Power 2," 2018.)

stupas of Bayon Temple) and combines this kbach style with the aesthetics of the contemporary Cambodian military (specifically, the camouflage pattern of Cambodian army fatigues).[94] In *Head & Power*, one of the heads of Bayon Temple is rendered as a toylike stuffed animal: Its skin is made of soft camouflage print and its interior is stuffed with kapok fibers (see Fig. 3.7). With a godlike headdress on its head and a cigar hanging out of its mouth, the sculpture is evocative of both the mythical power of the ancient Khmer gods and the surveillance and corruption of the current government. Through an unmistakable irreverence toward the traditional authority accorded to both religion and government in Cambodian society, Svay Sareth's *Head & Power* emphasizes the hypocrisy and political masquerading of Hun Sen's government since the end of the Cold War, as many everyday Cambodian people continue to live in a state of mistrust and fear of their government. All of Svay Sareth's sculptures are also filled with kapok fibers to symbolize the ongoing effect of living in a thoroughly militarized state. Like in the Khmer Rouge era, the people are coerced into silence and muteness. Only through the ongoing work of radical art, critique, and political risk can Cambodian society begin to tap into the power of the kapok tree that lays dormant within.

Today, the kapok tree has become one of Cambodia's most valuable commodities as the world begins to feel the effects of dwindling global resources for textile production. Petroleum-based fibers, like spandex, acrylic, polyester, and nylon, are increasingly being criticized for being unsustainable, and natural fibers like cotton are seen as too resource-intensive to manufacture. Suddenly, the kapok tree, once seen as a relatively worthless fiber crop by comparison to, say, bamboo, in terms of monetization potential, has become one of the most sought-after resources of the global textile industry. As the website of the Shanghai-based textile brand Flocus explains, "Kapok is the most sustainable fibre in the market today, leaving no human footprint behind. Combine this with numerous properties like being silky soft, and dry to the touch, as well as antimoth, antimite and insulation properties comparable to down and one has a useful, sustainable fibre."[95] Traditionally, like in other parts of Southeast Asia, the knowledge of how to spin kapok into a usable textile was held only within Cambodian families, passed down generationally, as in the case of my grandfather's business in Kampong Thom. Today, the race to mobilize kapok on an industrial scale has begun and companies like Flocus believe "that monetising the kapok tree in this way can leave behind a positive social impact on communities" and "can provide an additional revenue stream for farmers cultivating the fruit."[96]

Like the art of Svay Sareth, the art of Cambodian artist Sopheap Pich probes the contradictions of economic development in Cambodia and what is at stake for Cambodian people as they face a worsening state of ecological crisis at multiple scales—deforestation, pollution, drought, and many other calamities accelerated by climate change and global capitalist development. Living through the Cambodian Genocide as a young child, Sopheap Pich left Cambodia in 1979 as a refugee along with his family. First resettling in refugee camps in Thailand and the Philippines, his family arrived in the United States in 1984 when Sopheap was thirteen years old. At this age, Sopheap Pich began his formal education and his path toward becoming a sculpture artist using primarily rattan and bamboo, two of Cambodia's most important natural materials. In 2021, Sopheap Pich and his team completed "Kapok," a 170 cm length sculpture in the shape of a fully ripened kapok tree pod (see Fig. 3.8).[97] "Kapok," along with a series of other sculptures on the theme of trees, came to Pich at the beginning of the 2019 pandemic when he "began planting a lot of trees around [his] studio," many were large and mature, and most "did not survive."[98] When the seller would come to take away the dead trees, Sopheap realized that these dead trees were just being discarded. He then set out to buy up the scrap aluminum material from pots and pans and other items in used shops around Phnom Penh in order to make the "skin of a tree"—sculptures in the shape of these trees, just without the trees. He saw these sculptures as capturing the "spirit of the tree" or standing in as a "ghost of the tree."[99]

What is most striking about Pich's wood, bamboo, metal, and rattan "Kapok" sculpture is its fluid integration of a canoe boat into the kapok pod.

Figure 3.8 "Kapok," 2021, sculpture by Sopheap Pich in the shape of a kapok tree pod, made with bamboo, metal, rattan, and a salvaged canoe. (Courtesy of Sopheap Pich.)

In a podcast interview with art critic Brainard Carey, Sopheap Pich explains that the canoe comes from personal memories of his childhood in Cambodia where his family always lived near a body of water so they could fish and trap for food—snails, turtles, crabs, frogs.[100] He always grew up around boats and right before he left Cambodia in 1979 as a refugee, his family built a large boat that he was never able to use. The boat became an image lodged in his memory, and he wanted to go back to "finish that boat."[101] Invited to contribute to a group exhibition at the French Institute in Phnom Penh on the theme of fabric, Sopheap Pich created "Kapok" as a means of capturing the image of the boat as well as a means of going back to "where fabric comes from."[102] To Pich, the kapok pod, shaped like a boat, links Cambodian traditions of fabric and fishing, while also bridging Pich's personal experiences of wanting to "finish that boat" with the refugee migrant experience that is often associated with the movements of boats. The kapok, once a discarded material, was the creative seed from which the "Kapok" sculpture was planted. Created during the pandemic lockdowns of 2020, Pich's "Kapok" stands as a melding of the living, the reclaimed, the spectral, and the future. Describing his process as completely "anti-modern," based completely on manual and artisanal labor, Sopheap Pich's craft counters the accelerated rate of capitalist development in Cambodia and the impact of these processes on art and creativity.

My father and mother often tell stories of the old days in Cambodia, the time before the war. They call this period *ros ne yang sok sabai*, the years of happy living, when the country was relatively peaceful. It is a time full of color, sound, smell, and touch. My parents were young and in love. At my mother's home, the smell of grilled fish, mangoes, coconut, and sour fish soup wafted through the air. My father's home was filled with books, an entire library upstairs. Music played constantly in the background: the Taiwanese love ballads of Teresa Teng and Zhang Xiao Ing; the Khmer rock and roll of Sinn Sisamouth, Ros Serey Sothea, Pan Ron, and Chum Kem; and the American music of Elvis Presley. My father remembers the story of how Chum Kem left Cambodia to study abroad: "Chum Kem didn't go away to study music, but when he came back he started to teach people the twist. He wrote 'A Go Go' and young people started doing the twist and the ramvong. Your mother and I, we loved this music."

Not yet married, my parents kept their love an open secret. My father, a free spirit, was not favored by my mother's family. She had many suitors but was drawn to my father's passion for the arts. To escape the watchful eyes of others, they took the bus from Kampong Thom to Phnom Penh on the weekends. In the capital, they were truly free. They went to the Central Market for *Kuay Teo* and Khmer iced coffee with condensed milk, they wandered the Riverside Park and gazed at the other lovers, and they saw all the new movies playing at the theaters.

My parents describe these old movies as arriving in Phnom Penh in different cultural waves: first came the Shaw brothers films from Hong Kong starring *kung fu* stars Wang Yu (王羽), Chiang Da-wei (姜偉年), Ti Lung (譚富榮), and Lee Xiao Long (李小龙); then came the epic movies from India—tales of the gods such as *Preah Vishnu* and *Preah Hanuman*; after a while, Cambodians started to make their own movies—adaptations of famous legends such as *Mak Thoeung, Moranak Meada*, and *Puos Keng Kang*—starring the great Cambodian actors Dy Saveth, Kem Nova, Kong Som Eun, and Saksi Sbong.

On these date nights, my mother wore bell-bottom pants and long flower-print shirts, or sometimes jean shorts and a white cut-off top. Her hair was cut in the chic Omega style. My father wore blue jeans and a Montague striped shirt imported from France. He carried his Kodak SLR camera everywhere and snapped photos of their adventures all over Phnom Penh. His friend in Kampong Thom owned a photography studio and helped them develop hundreds of photos that they stored in large albums. When the Khmer Rouge arrived in 1975, they hid these photo albums under a mattress and never saw them again. "A record of the happy times," my father says. "But one day, suddenly, it was all gone."

4

Aphasia and the Nervous
Condition of Refugee Asylum

When we arrived as refugees, my extended family was scattered all across Canada. One node of the Troeung family (my family) went to live in a small town, in Southwestern Ontario, sponsored by a private church group; another node went to Hull, Quebec, and then later settled in Montreal. As a family, we made frequent summer excursions to Montreal, where there seemed to be a boundless number of cousins and aunties and uncles to whom I was told I was related, though I could never figure out exactly how.

I remember asking my father about one of my uncles in Montreal who always fascinated me with his gangsterlike swagger and his dark sunglasses. This uncle was blind in one eye. His eye had been damaged during Pol Pot time when he was sent out to a Khmer Rouge labor camp. One day, when he was chopping wood at this camp, a sharp wood chip flew up and pierced his eye. As there was no medicine or treatment available to people during this time, his maimed eye became infected, and he subsequently lost vision in that eye. Though he managed to survive the genocide and resettle in Canada as a refugee, his health remained fragile throughout his life. He suffered from diabetes, frequent bouts of fainting, mental disorientation, and mobility impairment. He was often misdiagnosed by doctors and prescribed the wrong kind of medication. At times, he spoke in hallucinatory fragments, confused about where he was and who he was with. After one particularly bad collapse in his home, an fMRI brain scan in a Montreal hospital revealed that he had suffered a stroke at some point in his life. He had been living for years, maybe even decades, in a state of "postrupture," to use the language of stroke medicine, that had gone undetected and untreated. He passed in October 2021, as I was finishing the final rewrites for this book. Postmortem, his diagnosis was changed to pancreatic cancer.

The story of this uncle (Montreal Uncle, as we always called him) has captivated me for many reasons besides his health, as I knew he was the father of another uncle of mine, who we always refer to today as Texas Uncle. This uncle was a son of Montreal Uncle from a first marriage to a Vietnamese woman in Cambodia in the late 1960s. When the Vietnamese ethnic community started becoming targets of the Lon Nol dictatorship in the early 1970s, Texas Uncle's mother packed up her baby son and fled to Vietnam, where they lived until she suddenly died from a poisonous snakebite while working in the fields one day. When the border to Cambodia reopened in 1979, Texas Uncle, now a teenager on his own, wandered back to a destroyed Cambodia in search of his biological father. By this time, however, his father was already in Montreal. Their separation would continue for a few more years until Montreal Uncle, a highly resourceful man, managed to secure his son's sponsorship to Canada. Texas Uncle arrived in Canada as a young man in his twenties, along with a family of his own (a wife and two "paper daughters") that had been reconstructed in the refugee camp.

For years after their reunion in Canada, father and son found some semblance of peace and normalcy in their lives, despite Montreal Uncle's frequent health problems. They opened up a small convenience store in a rough neighborhood of Montreal. The convenience store was a frequent target for robberies, to the point where everyone in the family (including the kids, my cousins, who sometimes helped in the store) got used to robberies and violence in the store as a banal reality of their everyday lives. But one day, tragedy struck: An armed robber entered the convenience store and fired his gun at Texas Uncle, shooting him in the stomach before fleeing with the contents of the cash register. Although Texas Uncle recovered from his wounds, he no longer felt at ease in Montreal. He felt nervous and anxious at every turn while walking the streets. Montreal was no longer his home, if it had ever been. Hearing rumors about Cambodian American refugees who were making it big by opening doughnut shops and franchises in Houston, Texas Uncle crossed the forty-ninth parallel and once again transitioned into a new life.

When neuroscientists look at fMRI or CT scans of an aphasia patient's brain, they look for the presence of *lacunae*. These are variously called "lacunar infarcts," cerebrospinal fluid–filled cavities, or "black holes" in the Broca's or Wernicke's regions (see Fig. 4.1). The lacunae indicate the presence

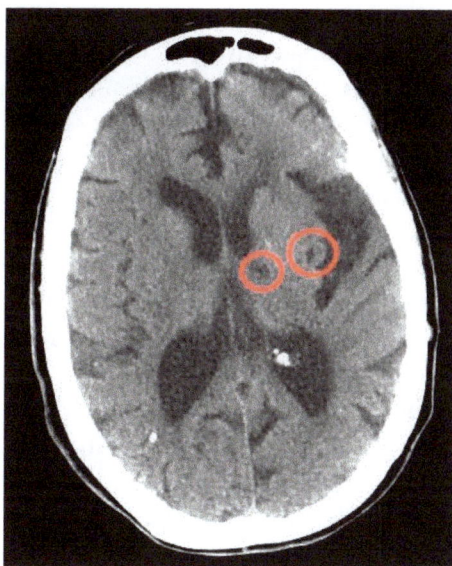

Figure 4.1 CT scan of two lacunae formed after a stroke. Image of an aphasia patient's brain, August 6, 2012. (Prashanthsaddala, CC BY-SA 3.0, via Wikimedia Commons.)

of something else—the brain's destruction, neuronal loss, or degeneration. In philosophy, however, it is common to speak of a lacuna in knowledge, a gap or a void in what we know about a given subject. What we see is a tension between the scientific meaning of a lacuna as medical proof and the philosophical understanding of a lacuna as the absence of certainty.

In this chapter, I elaborate on my theory of refugee lifeworlds as a method of critical refugee and critical disability critique through attention to the specific disability known as *aphasia*. I turn my attention to aphasia, in particular, not to minimize the prevalence of other kinds of impairments that are pervasive in the Cambodian community but because aphasia, in many ways, cuts across, correlates, and intersects with so many categories of disability while problematizing the category of disability itself. Cambodian people's durational experience of colonialism, war, genocide, racism, and differential health vulnerability reinforces the important point that, within Cambodian communities, aphasia—and all disability—has never been a question of mere metaphor. As Susan Sontag famously put it, "Illness is *not* a metaphor. . . . The most truthful way of regarding illness—and the healthiest way of being ill—is one most purified of, most resistant to, metaphoric thinking."[1] In her writing about the curious case of 150 Cambodian refugee women in Southern California in the late 1980s, who were collectively diagnosed as suffering from psychosomatic blindness (a case I take up in Chapter 3 of this book), critical ethnic studies scholar Fiona Ngô asks, "How can we read these inscriptions and their histories without performing the work of transforming the body's wounds into narrative devices?"[2] When actual disabilities are mobilized as metaphors to describe a social ill, Ngô argues, we fall into an analytic trap that effaces the bodies marked by *actual* disability (emphasis mine).[3] On the antiwar slogan, "An eye for an eye makes the whole world blind," Eli Clare comments that this is one of the many slogans that "turns disability into a metaphor, reinforces that disability means broken and is fundamentally undesirable, and ignores the multitude of actual lived disability experiences connected to war."[4] What we need instead, Clare asserts, is "an anti-war politics that doesn't transform disability into a symbol of either patriotism or tragedy, a politics that thinks hard about disability."[5] While I take these points about the need to resist the reduction of disability to mere metaphor, I also agree with critical disability studies scholar Sami Schalk's argument that disability can "symbolize something other than disability while still being about disability."[6] Metaphors of disability, Schalk writes, "allow us to explore the historical and material connections between disability and other social systems of privilege and oppression."[7] Schalk's work highlights the specific analogical possibilities of reading race and disability together as sociomaterial constructs that inform each other.

Drawing on these insights about the need both to *not abstract* and to *abstract* our thinking about disability, in this chapter I discuss the concept of *refugee aphasia* as a critical hermeneutic (coextensive with the other concepts developed in this book) for reading the afterlife of the Cold War in Cambodia. In theorizing refugee aphasia, I draw on the full lexical range of the word aphasia (such as speechlessness, impermissible speech, difficulty speaking, language loss, and silence). I go beyond the *disability* of medical aphasia to touch on aphasia's social and cultural dimensions, yet I do not lose sight of the fact that aphasia is a lived disability that affects millions of people. An effect of brain injury or a symptom of progressive dementia, aphasia is often inseparable from forms of emotional dysphoria: loss of identity; depression, frustration, isolation, blunted feelings, and social stigma. For those who perform the intimate work of caretaking for people living with aphasia, the psychological toll can also be devastating. Aphasia deeply affects the lives of those who suffer from it as well as the lives of caregivers and loved ones.[8] Writer and former mental health practitioner Kai Cheng Thom reminds us that a focus on the social determinants of disability is not to discount the lived and embodied pain of this disability.[9] Focusing on cognitive and psychological disability, Thom asks, "What if, instead of asking how mental illness can be contained or eradicated, we asked instead how it can help show us what kind of healing we really need?"[10] Building on Thom, here, what would it mean to listen to what our aphasias are trying to say? Such a mode of listening would require a different kind of ethical engagement and labor of radical care—a practice of refugee and disability justice that honors the need for access and treatment while refusing the criminalization, pathologizing, and stigmatizing of the "deficient" brain.

With a focus on aphasia, I turn to two works by Malaysian-Chinese Canadian writer Madeleine Thien—the 2011 novel *Dogs at the Perimeter* and the 2014 short story "Alice Munro Country"—that explore the ruptures of the Cambodian refugee's personhood, language, and speech in the afterlife of war and genocide. Thien's novel *Dogs at the Perimeter* probes the generative spaces of incommensurability between medical aphasia and refugee aphasia, illuminating the porous ontological borders between these two categories. The novel also shows refugee aphasia to be grounds for the remaking of new affinities and intimacies through, not in spite of, difficulty in speaking. Thien's short story, "Alice Munro Country," inspired by the true story of a Cambodian refugee family that resettled in Goderich, Ontario, in 1980, opens up discussions about refugee aphasia and the violence of benevolence in the state of asylum wherein the structures of assimilation, charity, and rural remoteness work to generate a perpetual state of racialized aphasia for the refugee. In this condition of racialized aphasia, the refugee does not ascend to an emancipatory discovery of "voice" and "the power of speech" but rather finds herself reincorporated into the structures of silence and captivity.

What Is Aphasia?

First off, what exactly is aphasia? Neurologist Antonio Damasio defines aphasia as "a disturbance of the comprehension and formulation of language caused by dysfunction in specific brain regions."[11] Whereas receptive aphasia (Wernicke's aphasia) is associated with difficulties comprehending spoken or written language, expressive aphasia (Broca's aphasia) is characterized by a person's struggle with speaking and communication. Aphasia is a language impairment that ranges from having trouble retrieving desired words, to not being able to comprehend or receive language, to not being able to speak at all. Linked primarily to the aftermath of a stroke, aphasia can also correlate with dementia, seizures, intense migraines, concussions, or many other conditions. With aphasia, communication may become strained with varying degrees of intensity: speech may come and go; words may go missing; the ability to comprehend the meaning of a question may suddenly vanish; the words on a page may suddenly become incomprehensible; speech may become halting, nervous, and stuttering; language may fall away gradually and then completely.

Aphasia is thus about those moments when language (conceptualized in a normative and capacitated sense) breaks down and fails the speaker.

What is interesting about aphasia, however, is that the patient's cognitive function may remain intact while language function is impaired, making the process of communication all the more frustrating and painful. As neurologist Oliver Sacks explains in his book *The Mind's Eye*, "Even if [aphasia patients] are totally unable to speak or understand speech, there may be perfect preservation of intellectual powers—the power to think logically and systematically, to plan, to recollect, to anticipate, to conjecture."[12] This experience of having a word at the "tip of one's tongue" is especially frustrating for the aphasic speaker since they are often self-aware of their communication difficulties. The disparity between the interior thoughts and the expressive ability of the speaker can be the source of significant emotional pain since the memories and ideas that circulate intensely within the aphasia patient's mind can feel trapped there. According to Sacks, as a consequence of their struggles with communication, "patients with aphasia face special dangers in chronic hospitals or nursing homes. They may have therapy of every sort, but a vital social dimension of their lives is missing, and they frequently feel intensely isolated and cut off."[13] Even for those aphasia patients who recover the ability to speak and write, many will live with an intangible feeling of missing words or words missing for the rest of their lives, with the former referring to the repeated omission of words in a sentence (written or spoken) and the latter to the struggle of finding the desired word. English writer Samuel Johnson, for example, experienced aphasia after a stroke at the age of seventy-three. Though he recovered his language capacity, he continued to struggle with "uncharacteristic mistakes, sometimes omitting a word or writing the wrong word."[14] For this reason, aphasia is sometimes referred to as a language of missing words or a *perforated* language. It is indicated by a texture of brokenness or unevenness, full of cracks, omissions, and unpredictable substitutions.

The study of aphasia dates back to French physician Paul Broca's work on the brain in 1861. Broca discovered that difficulties in the expressive use of speech "consistently followed damage to a particular portion of the left hemisphere of the brain."[15] Broca's work inaugurated the modern conception of brain mapping that ascribes "specific powers—linguistic, intellectual, perceptual, etc.—to equally specific 'centers' in the brain."[16] Sigmund Freud, in his 1891 book *On Aphasia: A Critical Study*, later charged that this model of cortical mapping was too simple as it overlooked complex psychoanalytic processes at play in disorders of speech, cognition, and perception.[17] Freud's critique was followed by Michel Foucault who argued in his lectures on psychiatric power that, before Broca, there was little "differentiation between someone who [did] not want to speak and someone suffering from aphasia."[18] After Broca, neurologists more readily embraced the concept of absolute diagnosis, distinguishing conditions such as "voluntary mutism" and "aphasia."[19] Today, the limits of conceptualizing aphasia simply in medical terms have been widely discussed by scholars in a wide range of disciplines and fields, from neuroscience to linguistics to critical theory. As Oliver Sacks writes, "Neurology's favorite word is 'deficit,' denoting an impairment or incapacity of neurological function."[20] For every deficit, Sacks argues, there is a corollary medical diagnostic that exists: "Aphonia, Aphemia, Aphasia, Alexia, Apraxia, Agnosia, Amnesia, Ataxia"—and the list goes on.[21] With the ceaseless advance of neuroimaging technology, it is now possible to order, name, and rank these conditions with ever more precision. In short, the study of aphasia across a range of disciplines has been linked to and critiqued by a "biopolitics of plasticity" that encompasses the ranking of human life and brains as more or less deficient.[22]

In her book *The New Wounded*, philosopher Catherine Malabou warns of the dangers of scientific reductionism in trying to "locate" or "pinpoint" our traumas precisely at the neurological and cellular level. "The plasticity of the brain," Malabou writes, "has today become the model for the new spirit of capitalism . . . this plasticity is recuperated at all levels to affix new labels and fashion new categories."[23] The designation of the "deficient" brain or the brain in need of "correction" works in the service of all manner of biopolitical regulation and discipline. A refusal of the logics of cure might involve an alternative mode of engaging aphasia—one that recognizes, in Malabou's terms, how in aphasia, we actually "encounter a form of 'compensation' or a 'sharpening of the compensatory function' through 'energetic excess.'"[24] The aphasic person's perforated language—full of silences, pauses, hesitations, and inventive substitutions—enacts an embodied, sensorial, and relational way of speaking through a shared vulnerability that interrupts normative hierarchies of valued or respectable speech.

I am not the first scholar of colonization to be interested in aphasia. Ann Laura Stoler argues that "colonial aphasia" is a "political disorder and a troubled psychic space."[25] It is suggestive of "the political, personal and scholarly dispositions that have made the *racial* coordinates of empire and the racial epistemics of governance so faintly legible to French histories of the present."[26] Stoler argues that the absence of France's colonial past in the nation's public discourse is not an effect of historical forgetting or amnesia. At issue, rather, "is the *irretrievability* of a vocabulary, a limited access to it, a simultaneous presence of a thing and its absence, a presence and the misrecognition of it."[27] Stoler's thinking about colonial aphasia draws on Foucault's earlier writings on aphasia as a "critical metaphor with which to think how categories are formed and dispersed, how aphasiacs disassociate resemblances and reject categories that are viable."[28] For Stoler, Foucault's discussion of aphasia as a dissociation of viable connections is useful for thinking about the operations of empire. Colonial aphasia proceeds by splitting and dispersing the contemporary from the colonial, making "histories appear as History," and thriving "on the capacity to assign to their systems of demarcation innocuous intentions and appellations."[29] In her book *Not Like a Native Speaker*, Rey Chow posits a relation between medical aphasia and what she calls "racialized aphasia," between the struggles of aphasic people and racialized peoples. For Chow, "aphasia (as the limit of having voice or being able to speak) [must] be understood simultaneously in relation to racialization."[30] Chow's analysis of "racialized aphasias" in the writings of Frantz Fanon, Jacques Derrida, Leung Ping-Kwan, and others, shifts the focus away from aphasia as a condition of *failed* speech to aphasia as a making of speechless subjects in destabilizing moments of racial violence and interpellation.[31] Like Malabou, Chow argues that aphasia "can be conceptualized anew as forms of unveiling, as what expose[s] the untenability of 'proper' (and proprietary) speech as such."[32] These theories of aphasia, as generative as they are, tend to rest at the level of abstraction, treating aphasia as a metaphor for a social ill.[33]

While aphasia and amnesia, as impairments of the brain and speech, may share many similarities, they are not synonymous conditions. In her landmark book, *War, Genocide, and Justice*, Cathy J. Schlund-Vials theorizes the world's collective amnesia on Cambodia, defining the "Cambodian syndrome" as "a transnational set of amnesiac politics revealed through hegemonic modes of public policy and memory."[34] The Cambodian syndrome encompasses the ongoing selective amnesia of the Khmer Rouge authoritarianism and the U.S. government, both of which participate in the erasure of their respective culpabilities in the Cold War formation in Cambodia. Schlund-Vials goes on to argue that, in response to the "amnesiac politics that resemble in form—but not in function—neoconservative and neoliberal cooptations of the catastrophic aftermath of the Khmer Rouge regime," Cambodian American creative cultural production, what she terms "Cambodian American memory work," labors to reimagine "alternative sites for justice, healing, and reclamation."[35]

Shifting away from the paradigms of trauma, memory work, and amnesia/forgetting in relation to the afterlife of the Cold War in Cambodia, this chapter tracks the circulation of "refugee aphasia"—which I treat as the refugee's breakdown of language or actual diagnosed condition of medical aphasia—within Cambodian refugee lifeworlds. In her book, *Unspoken: A Rhetoric of Silence*, the literary scholar Cheryl Glenn writes of aphasia as a "silencing of words" and a "loss of nouns" that can affect anyone no matter their "language capacity" and is often intensified by stress, "the stress of the social moment to external stresses."[36] As an example, Glenn considers how Pat Shipman, an associate dean of medicine at Johns Hopkins, became silent through two "stress" events: first, her "house burned to the ground," and second, soon after the fire, she was inundated with a "deluge of insurance forms, with their insistence on lists, infinite description, and replacement-cost analyses."[37] For Glenn, it was not merely *the event* of the house fire that intensified Shipman's aphasia, but the insurance company's demand that she continually retell the event and account for every object involved in it. Likewise, *refugee aphasia* tells us about not merely the events that caused the refugee subject to seek and accept asylum but also the constant demand to retell these stories, to relive these events, and to do so in ways that are recognized and encouraged by the host nation.

I am interested in how we can care for the pain of refugee aphasia while also holding space for its potential as an alternative way of knowing and being. My thinking about refugee aphasia is influenced by a genealogy of anticolonial writing about what Frantz Fanon termed the "nervous condition" of colonialism. As Fanon argued, colonial medical "experts" have a long history of attributing the nature of the Black colonized subject's "criminal" behavior to "a given arrangement of the nervous system."[38] Integral to the propagation of colonial violence, this myth elides the reality of the nervous condition of colonialism—the fact that "in the colonial world, the emotional sensitivity of the native is kept on the surface of his skin like an open sore which flinches from the caustic agent."[39] Instead of being channeled externally, toward decolonial revolution, the colonized subject's unease and anger are directed inward: toward interclan violence and suicidal ideation. In Fanon's writing, the transition from colonialism also engenders a raft of "mental disorders" as perpetrators and victims alike are psychologically wounded in spirals of violence and revolutionary wars.[40] These wars represented triggering situations that would have long-standing impacts on the psyche of African peoples. As Achille Mbembe writes, the more direct the experience Fanon had of the colonial system in Algeria, "the more it appeared to him a leprosy that spared the body of no one, whether settlers or colonized."[41] While leprosy was useful to Fanon as a metaphor for suggesting how colonization attacked and deformed the body, he also understood that colonialism's "essential target [was] the brain and, incidentally, also the nervous system."[42] Fanon referred to this colonial power as the act of "decerebralizing"—"an amputation" or "sterilization" of the brain in order to neutralize the colonized subject's imaginative capacities for dissent.[43] Colonialism's ultimate goal was to induce in the colonized a dissociated self.

In homage to Fanon, Zimbabwean writer Tsitsi Dangarembga wrote her novel *Nervous Conditions* in 1988 about 1960s Rhodesia, twenty years before Zimbabwe won independence. For Dangarembga, many African women in Rhodesia have been made mad by the "double colonialization" of British colonialism and African patriarchy. *Nervous Conditions* follows Tambudzai, a young woman living in a state of inner exile as a consequence of her colonial education. As Dangarembga explains in an interview with Madeleine Thien, "The big problem for Tambudzai is that Rhodesian society is asking her to come to terms with a system that negates her as an African woman, and the sad thing is that she does not, cannot, or will not see that the system has nothing but contempt for her. So she tries to adjust until she becomes contemptible herself."[44] Tambudzai's anger is propelled inward rather than at the patriarchal-colonial system that demands her ceaseless adjustment to its violences. Likewise, in Han Kang's novel *The Vegetarian*, a South Korean woman feels the everydayness of human and animal suffering so acutely that she attempts to transform herself into a plant.[45] Kang cites her inspiration as a line from the work of Korean modernist poet Yi Sang who viewed "catatonic withdrawal as a symptom of oppression."[46] A *New York Times* op-ed essay by Kang opens up another allegorical reading of the novel in relation to the unending temporality of the Korean War. Describing the experience of living in proximity to North Korea, under constant threat of attack, Kang writes that South Korean people's outward appearance of calm and indifference to geopolitics masks the deeper reality that "the tension and terror that have accumulated for decades have burrowed deep inside us and show themselves in brief flashes even in humdrum conversation."[47] This sense of madness as a lodging of something deep within the skin and the nerves has also been expressed by Madeleine Thien, who writes of a "closing down of personhood" in response to life at the margins.[48] Thien writes, those "who are dismissed in our media and our culture, or used as the scapegoats in our political campaigns, whose countries are bombed, and then forgotten, whose genocides are considered minor. They become aware of another reality that is hidden. To see something that the rest of society denies is devastating. It can make you crazy."[49] Going "crazy" involves an acute sensitivity to suffering, both to one's own pain and to the pain of others, coupled with a feeling of helplessness to enact change. This nervous condition also extends from inhabiting a reality of pervasive suffering that seems invisible or merely dismissed by the dominant society.

Madeleine Thien's *Dogs at the Perimeter*:
"A Wordless Sadness"

If we situate Madeleine Thien's novel *Dogs at the Perimeter* within the geneal-ogy of writers of colonial psychological suffering described above, we can ask how Thien's novel explores the refugee's aphasia as a symptom of "the nervous condition" of refugee asylum. Structured as a series of "fragments," Thien's novel adopts a disorienting and nonlinear style. These fragments are at once "medi-cal aphasia case files" and "refugee aphasia case files," the former consisting of medical patient profiles and the latter of refugee stories. As the plot unravels, these two narrative strands begin to spiral together, taking the reader deeper and deeper into a speechless abyss buried in the narrator's consciousness: This is "a space in which there were no doors, no light or darkness, no landmarks. No future, no past."[50] *Dogs at the Perimeter* thus begins with an image of what Eli Clare describes as "lives reduced to case files."[51] This is the medical-in-dustrial complex's reduction of people's lives to medical records: "that scramble of charts, letters, clinical notes, diagnoses, photographs, birth and death cer-tificates, and court orders used to track people's lives through medical care and confinement."[52] As Clare writes, "These files, whatever form they take, possess power. They document, prove, and defend treatment and cure. They transform people into diagnoses and 'expert opinions.' Tellingly they are called case files, not personal files, personhood itself receding. Thousands of stories vanish be-neath their authority."[53] Thien's novel seeks to peel back the layers of the case file form, probing what lies beneath the fragments left in the aftermath of violence.

One case file in the novel is that of a medical patient named Elie who sud-denly begins to "lose language" at the age of fifty-eight.[54] It is described not as a loss of memory but rather as an inability to materialize memory through language. The text figures the alteration in Elie's state of being as a barrier between what she knows—her memories and her thoughts—and her physical ability to communicate this knowledge in speech and writing. This barrier is at once a "blotting out people's names," "a stopper in her throat," and "a black hole in her mind."[55] For Elie, the past has not been erased, but it has become irretrievable, inaccessible, or occluded from view. As her condition progresses, Elie increasingly finds "speaking effortful"[56] and later becomes "almost com-pletely mute."[57] Words begin to go missing and then speech in its entirety. Elie's MRI brain scan reveals that one side of her brain has deteriorated, ex-plaining the progressive impediments to her "speech, movement, and finally breathing itself."[58] She is "at war" with herself.[59]

Although *Dogs at the Perimeter* does not explicitly name Elie's medical condition, the novel's paratextual information explains that the character of

Figure 4.2 *Unravelling Boléro,* by Anne Theresa Adams, painted in the early stages of Adams's primary progressive aphasia. (Courtesy of UCSF Weill Institute for Neurosciences.)

"Elie is inspired by the work and life of Vancouver artist Anne Adams."[60] Best known for her painting *Unravelling Boléro,* a bar-by-bar visualization of the classical music composition *Boléro,* by Maurice Ravel, Adams suffered from a neurodegenerative condition called primary progressive aphasia[61] (see Fig. 4.2). Adams completed her painting *Unravelling Boléro* in 1994 during the early stages of her aphasia, a period of the disease when the degeneration of one part of her brain, her doctors believed, may have "unleash[ed] a flowering of neural development" in the other part of the brain responsible for creativity.[62] As many scientists have observed, an initial flourishing of creative production is a symptom seen in some patients of aphasia.[63] Like Anne Adams, Elie in *Dogs at the Perimeter* turns to art as her ability to speak deteriorates: "In her paintings, she turned music into images, the musical phrases playing out like words, the words breaking into geometric shapes, her paintings grasping all the broken, brilliant fragments."[64] For Elie, painting enables her to traverse the "barriers between herself and reality" since "the image could say everything that she could not."[65] Aphasia creates a condition of verbal silence for Elie, a quieting in which her inner life remains unheard by the outside world, but her silence is not absolute. Painting offers Elie a different mode of expression that allows for the aestheticizing and externalization of her inner world. To understand what Elie is trying to say, those around her, like Elie's doctor Hiroji, must reorient themselves and their ways of listening.

Further in the novel, we come to see Elie as a mirror and a foil to another character, Janie, a neurologist living in Montreal who first came to Canada as a refugee from Cambodia in the aftermath of the Cambodian Genocide. Like Elie, Janie is fighting a war within, but hers is a battle with an unspeakable grief that Janie has carried silently for decades. While Elie suffers from a form of neurological aphasia that leaves her grasping for words, Janie finds herself searching for language as well but has no firm diagnosis, and readers can only speculate that her aphasia-like symptoms likely stem from her traumatic past. More certainly, we could say that she has lived in a world marked by a collective kind of *speechlessness* about Cambodia's Cold War history. Janie's experiences of this history as a child survivor of war, genocide, rape, refugee displacement, and transnational adoption are not known to those around her, even to her husband Navin. Her agitated state of body and mind, accretive over time, brings her to an eventual state of mental collapse—a nervous condition—that leaves the reader with questions about the historical, social, racial, gendered, and medical underpinnings of her mental illness.

Existing somewhere between the genre of the (anti–)case file and the refugee narrative, Thien's *Dogs at the Perimeter* invokes the genre of the "neuronovel," a term coined by Marco Roth, in 2009, to characterize a new strain of the Anglo-American novel focused on the "workings of a mind."[66] As a way of reflecting on the rise of neuroscience as a discipline and the cultural shifts "away from environmental and relational theories of personalities back to the study of brains themselves," the neuronovel's emergence reflects social anxiety's about the increasing prevalence of neuroreductionism: that we "can or will soon describe all human behaviour, from warfare to soul-making," in terms of what can be measured and scanned in the brain.[67] Genre conventions of the neuronovel include a central plot concerning a neurological disorder, a protagonist (who is often a neuroscientist) tasked with understanding or diagnosing the disorder, and a "cognitively anomalous or abnormal person" who solicits the reader's sympathy.[68] Neuronovels are wide ranging in mood and plot, expressing at times a skeptical caution about the dangers of "the new reductionism of mind to brain."[69] With *Dogs at the Perimeter*, Thien offers us an atypical neuronovel—one populated not by white American middle-class doctors and patients but by a cast of Cambodian refugees and other non-Cambodian people (such as Japanese Canadian doctors) whose lives are entangled in the transpacific formation of the Cold War in Cambodia.

The neurological "disorder" at the center of the novel's plot is Janie's aphasia. Since arriving in Canada alone as an orphaned Cambodian refugee, Janie appears to the world as a high-achieving and upwardly mobile "model minority"— a refugee-turned-neurologist, a married woman, and a successful mother of one child. As Eric Tang explains, "Model-minority representations cast Asian immigrants and Asian Americans as self-sufficient and industrious subjects who, unlike Blacks in particular, found ways to make ends meet even under the most difficult conditions without calling for redress or support from external parties."[70] The model minority figure overlaps with what Yến Lê Espiritu describes as the figure of the "good refugee," "the successful, assimilated, and anticommunist" Southeast Asian refugee who plays a key role "in enabling the United States to turn the Vietnam War into a 'good war'" of liberation and rescue.[71] In Thien's novel, Janie presents as a model minority/good refugee, but we soon discover that Janie's composed exterior masks a deep inner turmoil. Janie lives with a number of psychological and physical impairments that she is not even aware of, even as a scientist herself. Janie's case unsettles the disabled/nondisabled binary, highlighting Jasbir Puar's point that "while some bodies may not be recognized as or identify as disabled, they may well be debilitated."[72] Janie's pain has been concealed within an ableist/sanist society that forecloses, for many marginalized groups such as refugees, access to being recognized, supported, and cared for as disabled people.

In *Dogs at the Perimeter*, readers are invited to see how Janie's invisible debilitation exists in contrast to the visible, yet (relatively) capacitated, disability of Elie, a white upper-middle-class woman living in Vancouver, British Columbia, who has the privilege of access to extensive medical care, diagnosis, and support for her deteriorating condition of primary progressive aphasia. Like Elie who "becomes almost completely mute" in the later stages of her aphasia, Janie finds herself increasingly struggling to speak.[73] For Janie, even thirty years after her arrival in Canada, "silence eats into every corner of the room" as she sits alone in her apartment.[74] Whereas Elie's aphasia is "degenerative, a quickening loss of neurons and glia in the other parts of her brain,"[75] Janie, at the outset of the novel, also seems to be transforming into someone else, someone unrecognizable to her son Kiri and husband Navin: "Something has turned over in me, broken, and come undone."[76] As her mental state deteriorates, Janie begins to lose control of her body, finding herself in a state of incapacity that results, in one scene, in Janie unwittingly hitting her son. In this scene, the fragile boundary between the interior chaos of her mind and the conscious control of her physical body begins to dissolve: "I didn't know anymore, I couldn't explain, how this could have happened, why could I not control my hands, my own body. We went through the motions, going to school, going to work, but something inside me, inside Navin, was dying. The broken world finally fell apart."[77] The frantic rhythm of this passage—rendered through the frequent use of commas and disjointed language—conveys Janie's state of embodied dissociation. Recalling the image of Elie's trembling hands as her aphasia progresses, the depiction of Janie's loss of motor control in this scene illustrates the blurred boundaries between mental and physical impairment. Janie's disability is no less impairing than Elie's condition, yet Janie's has not been accommodated or recognized by a society that tends to regard refugees, especially Asian women refugees, as respectable upwardly mobile "success stories" not in need of support.

For Janie, the subjection she endured within the necropolitical system of the Khmer Rouge bled into the debilitating violence she suffered during the exodus from Cambodia onboard a refugee boat. When pirates attack the boat, the crossing becomes a shattering experience of such visceral and bodily suffering that Janie had "no words for what was done."[78] Janie's speechlessness here is linked to the violation of her rape, though Thien elects not to represent such violence directly. Some reviewers have regarded this scene of transpacific crossing as a narrative failure, citing that "it is dangerous for a narrator in a novel to confess to a loss of language."[79] Such a reading fails to grasp the significance of the space of silence itself: that aphasia—the absence of "words for what was done"—is a central part of Thien's aesthetic and ethical project. In the novel, the depiction of violence is eschewed in favor of fragmented and disjointed language that expresses instead the mental and physical aftereffects of sexual violation: "I fell, I kept falling, and then my body rose to the surface. Still they were behind me, holding me, crossing oceans and continents. Coming into every room, every place, preceding me into my life. I no longer wanted to breathe the air."[80] Janie, an eleven-year-old girl who survives such a harrowing experience, is haunted for the rest of her life by the memories of what transpired during the passage at sea. Her speechlessness pertains to multiple traumas: the experience of genocide in Cambodia, the drowning of her brother at sea, and her rape by pirates. For years afterward, these memories are submerged in her consciousness, coming back to her later in life as barely perceptible flashes and fragments of memory: "There was a memory at the edges of my consciousness, but with a great force of will I managed to avert my eyes from it."[81] Indeed, the novel's title itself is a metaphor for aphasia. Janie lives with the difficulty of retrieving the words and language with which to make meaning out of her life's experiences. The landscape of her mind is a landscape in fragments.

Arriving in Canada as "a separated child," Janie's experience of resettlement is marked by an acute sense of cultural isolation and assimilation.[82]

Janie is adopted by a Canadian woman named Lena, a scholar of the history and philosophy of science, who vacationed in Cambodia in the 1960s and keeps film reels from this trip in her basement. At night, Janie secretly sneaks down to the basement to watch these reels and the spectral image of Cambodia on the projector is described as "the wordless sadness of a lost time."[83] Janie becomes transfixed on the film reel images of "a place [she] recognized, and now not."[84] The film reel is another symbol of Janie's aphasia: the absence of a Cambodian community with whom to share the burden of silence. As an adopted child, there is little space for Janie to voice the "numbing grief" that she carries inside her.[85] In his analysis of Korean American adoption narratives, David Eng argues that we often witness in transracial adoption contexts "an emotional cleaving of great consequence in the intimate space of the family."[86] There is a "failure of recognition [that] serves to redouble the effects of racial melancholia, severing [the adoptee] from her family unit, affectively segregating her, and ultimately forcing her to negotiate her losses in silence and isolation."[87] Absented from Janie's life in Canada is what Eng calls "the feeling of kinship—the psychic life of race and the racialization of intimacy" wherein "an *intergenerational* and *intersubjective* negotiation of loss is transformed into an *intrasubjective* negotiation of loss in its inexorable singularity."[88] Janie's aphasia is shaped by her intense isolation as well as the demands of indebtedness placed on her as an adopted refugee. As Janie describes her "desire to be of use to [Lena], to repay her somehow,"[89] the novel explores the silencing structures of refugee and adoptee debt. Commenting on a news story about a woman named Vesna who rebuked the media's characterization of her as "lucky" because she survived a plane crash, Janie narrates: "She sounded ungrateful, but she was not. I understood. I remembered arriving in Canada, my stomach clenched, ashamed that I had lived yet terrified of disappearing. Chance had favoured us, but chance had denied so many others."[90] Janie's enduring feelings of survivor's guilt and shame cannot be accommodated by the national narrative of the grateful refugee. Her aphasia is a nervous condition in which the violence of benevolence works to perpetuate the refugee's physical and mental incapacitation.

If the pairing of Elie's/Janie's aphasia case files interrogates how and why certain bodies are seen or not seen as debilitated or capacitated, there are other paired aphasia case files through which the novel asks: Who is allowed or not allowed to speak about their pain? Who has the right to pain? Aphasia, in this sense, is the impermissibility of speaking about one's pain or loss as a consequence of being deemed an unrecognizable, inauthentic, or unworthy victim. In *Dogs at the Perimeter*, Thien places emphasis on the *entanglement* of pain in the afterlife of the Cold War in Cambodia that intimately, yet unevenly, enfolds the lives of both Cambodian and non-Cambodian people. As Judith Butler reminds us, "For populations to become grievable does not require that we come to know the singularity of every person who is at risk or who has, indeed, already been risked. Rather, it means that policy needs to understand precariousness as a shared condition."[91] Jasbir Puar frames this idea of shared vulnerability in terms of a de-emphasis on individual griev-ance, arguing that "there is no pure debility or pure capacity."[92] Debility is less about a disabled individual's identity or grievances and more about "how disability is *produced*, how certain bodies and populations come into biopo-litical being through having greater risk to become disabled than others."[93] Butler's notion of grievability and Puar's notion of debility thus do not seek to flatten out the pain of all survivors as equivalent; rather they underscore the intertwined lives of injured populations precisely to upend the notion that injury/disability is simply an attribute of a discrete and knowable identity.

Depicted in a visual form, debility as a concept might be illustrated in-stead as the three vectors of biopolitical power that Jasbir Puar describes as "capacity, debility, and disability," which "exist in a mutually reinforcing constellation."[94] In many ways, the "network form" of Thien's novel lends itself to this understanding of debility as a distributed assemblage of power. In her book *Forms: Whole, Rhythm, Hierarchy, and Network*, Caroline Levine makes the case for "expanding our usual definition of form in literary studies to include patterns of sociopolitical experience."[95] In so doing, Levine argues, we can focus less on reading texts as "reflections or expressions of prior social forms" to think more multidirectionally about how "some forms move surpris-ingly easily across social and literary contexts."[96] Network forms, for example, can be found in both literature and the real world, and our methods for ana-lyzing the former can be brought to bear on the latter rather than solely the other way around. For Levine, when we broaden our definition of form in this way, "the traditionally troubling gap between the form of the literary text and its content and context dissolves. Formalist analysis turns out to be as valuable to understanding sociopolitical institutions as it is to reading literature."[97] In his book *Network Aesthetics*, Patrick Jagoda similarly argues that "while network visualizations offer a stable representation or *a map* of elements configured as nodes and links, the novel makes possible *processes of mapping* networks across space and time."[98] Constituted by "interactions between various nodes and links," networks are dynamic structures characterized by "openness, flex-ibility, extensibility, complexity, internal asymmetry, and an interdependence of individual parts."[99] As a descriptor, the network has been "applied to ev-erything from the human brain to the global economy to geopolitics to even the Earth itself as an interconnected totality."[100] Literary and artistic works have picked up on the ubiquity of networks in our everyday lives, adapting the network form to suit a myriad of political and aesthetic ends. Jagoda's work explores how contemporary texts make perceptible the materiality of network structures while also privileging the "affective experiences of networks."[101] In *Dogs at the Perimeter*, the network form reinforces the nervous condition of refugee asylum as a pressure on the brain that is both social and biological. It also reinforces the globality of the Cold War in Cambodia as a geopolitical formation, wherein the "there" of Cambodia is always connected with the "here" of the West in a web of Cold War relations, both debilitating and connective.

As a globe-spanning geopolitical constellation, the Cold War in Cambodia becomes, in Thien's narrative, an imperial formation that deeply implicates the lives of two Japanese Canadian brothers, Hiroji and James Matsui, who form the second set of "aphasia case files" in the novel. In the novel's opening pages, we discover that Hiroji, a neurologist living in Montreal, has suddenly gone missing. His case file is presented to the reader in the form of a fragment from a police investigation report. Narrated in the first person by Janie, Hiroji's colleague and longtime friend, the opening fragment introduces a mystery: Why would Hiroji, who showed no overt signs of depression or suicidal ideation, just suddenly disappear from his life? We later find out that Hiroji's disappearance is related to his three decades' long search for his brother James, who vanished in Southeast Asia in 1975, while working as a Red Cross doctor in Cambodia. When Hiroji discovers that James is actually alive and has been living in Laos since 1979, Hiroji interprets his brother's actions as a kind of neurological anomaly not yet discovered by researchers. Unlike the files of numerous patients that Hiroji has worked on over the years, including that of Elie's primary progressive aphasia, James's case remains open and unresolved, both a medical enigma and a site of personal grief for Hiroji. As a doctor and the symbolic embodiment of medical authority in the novel, Hiroji initially believes that neuroscience will help diagnose James's "illness" and provide a logical and satisfactory medical explanation. Hiroji hoped to "explain [James's] disappearance as a fugue state, an amnesia that carries a person away for weeks, even months. He would return and throw himself into his work, already new ideas and research projects were taking root in his mind."[102] In Laos, Hiroji is shocked to discover that his brother has not been afflicted with amnesia at all; rather, James had elected to completely "abandon the past and become someone else."[103] James now goes by the name "Kwan," the name his former torturer gave him in a Khmer Rouge prison where he was held captive for a number of years during the 1970s.

James's transformation cannot be readily diagnosed through the medicalized epistemes that have structured Hiroji's life's work as a neurologist.

To unravel the layers of James's perplexing transformation, Thien's narrative takes us back in time, to the days of the Cambodian Civil War, when James signs up with the International Red Cross in Southeast Asia. Enlisting as a humanitarian doctor the same year "Nixon's bombs were falling on Cambodia,"[104] James goes specifically to the Cambodian town of Neak Luong to "treat the people hurt by American bombs."[105] Here, James encounters a "Cambodia in disrepair," ravaged by the U.S. bombs that had targeted the region's schools, roads, and reservoirs.[106] The choice of Neak Luong is significant as it was historically one of the most bombed locations during the Cold War in Cambodia. Claiming nearly four hundred casualties and destroying the town's infrastructure, the bombing of Neak Luong was described in one 1973 *New York Times* article as "the worst *accidental* bombing of the Indochina war" (italics mine).[107] Thien's narrative reconstructs the massacre at Neak Luong not as an accidental event at all but as a part of the landscape of endemic debilitation that, in Achille Mbembe's words, renders "great swaths of humanity adjudged worthless and superfluous, whose every organ must be specifically incapacitated in a way that affects generations to come."[108] This attention to corporeal incapacitation is conveyed through Thien's vivid descriptions of the bombings as experienced by the people on the ground, as one survivor of the bombings says, "The light, it breaks. It breaks people open as if they're dogs or dirt. I looked up and there were no houses, no people. Just this hole."[109] James sees thousands of refugees "crawling into the city with missing limbs and missing children, people mutilated by the Khmer Rouge or bombed into hysteria by the Americans."[110] As Gilles Deleuze and Félix Guattari argue, while war has always been a part of human history, it is a rare instance when "the loss of an arm or a leg is reported" as a part of the accounting of the toll of war.[111] In Thien's novel, James stands as a helpless witness to the Cambodian people's protracted subjection to what Jasbir Puar calls the logics of the "right to maim"—"a right expressive of sovereign power that is linked to, but not the same as, 'the right to kill.'"[112] Out of the ruins of this landscape scattered with the bodies of the dead and the mutilated, James becomes more and more speechless.

If James, as a foreign doctor, finds himself speechless in the face of the ruination of the U.S. war machine, Thien shows how his subsequent captivity by the Khmer Rouge produces in James a new kind of ontological selfhood linked to the intensity of physical and psychological torture. Scholars of the Cambodian Genocide have discussed the uniquely *psychological* component of the Khmer Rouge's regime of terror in which "the intensity and length of the persecution experienced by Cambodians has few parallels in the twentieth century."[113] Under Pol Pot, the mass psychology of the Cambodian people became a target for the regime since the goal of the Khmer Rouge was to restart society anew "through calculated targeting of deeply-rooted principles of the Khmer culture and society."[114] In order to transform an entire society, "it was necessary to change the fundamentals of a civilization's psychology. Cambodia's psychology was thus altered in damaging and enduring ways."[115] In their effort to ensure the supremacy of the regime, the Khmer Rouge "rusticated the cities, banned Buddhism, and splintered families, who were often separated for long periods of time while they labored, sometimes day and night, on starvation rations. Spies crept about at night searching for signs of subversion. Meanwhile, the Khmer Rouge established a security apparatus that targeted suspect groups."[116] Nightly indoctrination sessions were held where people had to self-confess their crimes or implicate one another. Suspected enemies of the people were frequently taken away in the middle of the night to be killed or tortured, never to be seen again by family members. In *Dogs at the Perimeter*, James is depicted as someone who undergoes a complete ontological transformation as a consequence of living through perhaps the most violent dimension of Democratic Kampuchea: capture and torture at one of the Khmer Rouge's security centers. Mistaken for a "Chinese-Khmer," James is held as a prisoner at one of these centers (evocative of the S-21 Tuol Sleng in Phnom Penh) and accused of being a CIA spy.[117] While in captivity, James realizes that his Cambodian wife, Sorya, has also been arrested and that her relationship to him, a foreigner deemed an imperialist spy, has contributed to her persecution by the Khmer Rouge.[118] After the fall of the Khmer Rouge, James has survived the genocide but emerges from captivity with a new identity and a new name and chooses never to return to his past: "James, now known as Kwan [has become] a mute, a smuggler, and a solitary man."[119] James's aphasia has been produced in and through the Cold War constellation of U.S. imperial violence and Khmer Rouge Communism.

In *Dogs at the Perimeter*, we see how this geopolitical constellation is itself a part of the broader transpacific formation of the Cold War in Asia that began in the aftermath of World War II. Expecting a conventional account of the horrors of the Cambodian Killing Fields, readers of Thien's novel may be puzzled by the amount of narrative attention given to the case files of the Japanese Canadian characters Hiroji and James. Far from ancillary, they perform an important function in the novel, linking Cambodia to another important node in the post–World War II Cold War formation: Japan, and specifically Tokyo, as a site of unredressed U.S. military violence against a civilian population. Migrating from Japan to Canada at some point in the 1950s,[120] James is not a "refugee" by legal definition, but, like Janie, he carries the lived memory of bombing, war, and displacement in his homeland. James remembers "how the air burned in his throat in Tokyo when he was small, how he was terrified of fire, and then the long journey by boat and plane and bus that took them to Vancouver. . . . Japan was finished, his father said, even the ground was poisoned."[121] James's memories here index a historical trauma that, as one source explains, "has long been overshadowed by the U.S. atomic attacks on Hiroshima and Nagasaki which preceded the Japanese surrender that ended World War II the following August. But the burning of the cap ital, which resulted in more immediate deaths than either of the nuclear bomb-ings, stands as a horrifying landmark in the history of warfare on noncomba-tants."[122] During this firebombing, American "B29 bombers dropped nearly 500,000 cylinders of napalm and petroleum jelly on the most densely popu-lated areas of Tokyo."[123] The firebombing killed an estimated one hundred thousand civilians. As one critic asserts, "To argue that Japanese *civilians* deserved to die—that *children* deserved to die—at the hands of the US mili-tary because their government killed civilians in other Asian countries is an indefensible position, in any moral or ethical framework" [italics mine].[124]

James's case file in the novel thus links two significant nodes in the coor-dinates of U.S. empire in Asia in the twentieth century: Japan and Cambodia as sites of U.S. war crimes for which no reparations or redress have been made. James's nervous condition is a result of multiple traumatic experiences, first as a child in Tokyo hiding from U.S. bombs and then as an adult in Cambodia captured by the Khmer Rouge. It is suggested in the narrative that James's motivation for enlisting as a humanitarian doctor in Southeast Asia in the first place is in part motivated by his experience as a survivor of the Tokyo firebombing. The historical patterning enabled through the novel's network form functions as a device that powerfully assists the novel's act of what Lisa Lowe describes as a "reckoning for an American public engaged for much of the twentieth century in wars in Asia."[125] James's aphasia encodes the history of U.S. transpacific military involvement, wherein hot war sites in Japan and Cambodia, among many other sites, were bombed, forgotten, and never redressed.

In *Dogs at the Perimeter*, aphasia also points to the structures of anti-Asian racism, both banal and violent, that reproduce the nervous condition of refu-gee asylum. On the streets of Montreal one day, Hiroji randomly sees a man that elicits in Hiroji "a shock of recognition."[126] Knowing instantly that this stranger "was his brother" and "that it could not be he his brother," Hiroji eventually realizes that the man is not James but a former medical patient whom Hiroji once treated for a brain injury.[127] Encountering this patient so many years later outside a café in Montreal, Hiroji observes that the man seems to exhibit symptoms of aphasia, amnesia, and confabulation.[128] Upon meeting Hiroji, "the man began to ramble. He was soft-spoken, and Hiroji had to lean forward to catch all the words. The man described waking, suddenly, on the wet ground, his entire body convulsed with pain. Things were broken, blood was sticky on his fingers, but he couldn't remember why, he didn't know how this had happened."[129] The man's description of his suicide attempt suddenly triggers Hiroji's memory of a former patient of his known as "Johnny Doe": "He remembered now, how the patient—Johnny, James—had been persuaded to come down from the railing of the Pattullo Bridge. He had been thirty-five years old at the time, older maybe. Someone had whacked him hard at the back of the head, so violently that his brain had crushed up against the front part of his skull."[130] Equally vivid in Hiroji's memory is the recollection of the anti-Asian sentiments of this time period in Vancouver, for, after the man's hospitalization, "someone had joked, carelessly, that the two young men, Hiroji Matsui and Johnny Doe, the two Japs, looked like brothers."[131] In the man's case file, his suicide attempt is decoupled from the racist and debilitating violence of the attack on the bridge, inscribed in the psychiatric archive as the impaired behavior of a deranged individual.

The processes of racialization and disablement are intimately entangled, though this entanglement often disappears beneath the medical gaze of scientific authority. As Tanja Aho, Liat Ben-Moshe, and Leon J. Hilton argue in their essay on "Mad Futures": "Discourses across the political spectrum continue to uncritically make recourse to the vocabulary of madness and mental illness to explain and 'make sense of' individual acts and modes of behavior."[132] As a neurologist and a Japanese man, Hiroji's awareness of this entanglement is impressed on his psyche. Thien's narrative lends a historicity to the case file of the Japanese man attacked in Vancouver, part of the province of British Columbia that in 2021 is known for having "the most reported incidents [of hate crimes against Asian people] per capita of any sub-national region in North America."[133] The attack on Johnny Doe also has resonances with the 1982 murder of Vincent Chin in Michigan. A Chinese American man, Vincent Chin was attacked on the street and beaten to death by two white male auto factory workers who were angry at the perceived success of Japan's auto industry. Witnesses say the men uttered racial slurs while beating him. Neither served time in prison. Chin's case later became a flashpoint for the Asian American civil rights movement.[134] Thien's mirroring of these cases of targeted anti-Asian violence, specifically anti-Japanese racism, calls attention to structures of violence that underlie the so-called "accident" of racialized debilitation.

A question with which readers of Thien's novel frequently struggle is whether Johnny Doe is actually James. Deploying aphasia as analytic, we can say that Johnny Doe *is and is not James at the same time*. In Canada, Johnny Doe is a victim of a white supremacist ideology that homogenizes and violently targets Asian people as perpetual foreigners and threats to be eliminated from the body politic; in Cambodia, James is targeted by Communist state violence. A Japanese man, James is mistaken by the Khmer Rouge for being an ethnic Chinese Cambodian who is working in collaboration with the CIA. The Khmer Rouge's racist ideology dictated the purging of all "nonpure" Khmers from the new Democratic Kampuchea, especially people of Vietnamese, Cham, and Chinese ethnic ancestry.[135] James's nervous condition is not fully explicable as a neurological anomaly separate from the racial and social contexts that produced it. Linking these two aphasia case files—that of James and of the man on the bridge—reinforces the blurring of boundaries between sociopolitical and biological trauma. The novel's framing of the production of disability through racial, political, and genocidal violence calls to mind some of the questions that guide the impulses of critical disability studies. As Aho, Ben-Moshe, and Hilton ask, "How might we think about not only the specific *acts* of violence inflicted on [disabled people and people of color] . . . while also attending to the state-sanctioned and other *structural* forms of violence that preceded and surround this event?"[136] The nervous condition of refugee asylum, *Dogs at the Perimeter* demonstrates, does not solely refer to the singular experience of a refugee with "mental illness" but rather to the disabling structures of war, genocide, and white supremacy that generate nervous conditions at the interlinked levels of the biological, the psychological, and the linguistic.

Madeleine Thien's "Alice Munro Country": Aphasia and the Violence of Benevolence

In her 1943 essay "We Refugees," Hannah Arendt wrote that newly arrived refugees are compelled to act as if "their whole former life had been passed in a kind of unconscious exile and only their new country now taught them what a home really looks like."[137] Reliant on the charity of the new country, refugees must distance themselves from their pasts as quickly as possible to project a sense of "confidence in the new homeland."[138] This demand that the refugee strip away her past self in order to be granted social acceptance in the asylum country produces a kind of break in the refugee's psyche as she is confronted, day after day, with the demands to be optimistic. As Arendt writes, "We were expelled from Germany because we were Jews. But having hardly crossed the French borderline, we were changed into *boches*. . . . It is the same story all over the world, repeated again and again."[139] Refugees come to asylum states with long, complicated personal histories that find no place in the public discourse, a burden of silence that simply compounds and reiterates in a new context, propelling the refugee toward a "quiet and modest way of vanishing."[140]

This burden of silence touches every aspect of one Cambodian refugee family's life in Madeleine Thien's short story "Alice Munro Country," published in the *Globe and Mail* in October 2017 as a part of a series of stories commissioned for Canada 150, the nation's official sesquicentennial. The story is accompanied by an Author's Note about a "Cambodian family [who in 1980] became the last of sixty thousand Southeast Asian refugees, displaced by war and genocide, to arrive in Canada as part of the Trudeau government's two-year refugee resettlement program. The family was resettled in Goderich, a small town on Lake Huron, in a region often referred to as Alice Munro Country."[141] In "Alice Munro Country," this family is singled out for welcome by the Canadian state and paraded in front of the media in 1980. In a spare and detached tone that invokes the sardonic female narrators of Alice Munro's fiction, the third-person narrator of Thien's story recounts how the story's protagonist, a thirteen-year-old girl named Mina, arrives in Canada and is immediately ushered to meet "the Prime Minister himself, the one with the bright red rose in his lapel, famous for his boyish pirouettes."[142] Suited up perfectly for her photo op, Mina is "presented with a coat, scarf and woollen hat; also, a fuzzy blue sweater, soft as a kitten."[143] In this tale of refugee resettlement in "the clichéd land of wilderness," snow symbolizes multiple things, among them—the blanketing of the past, the demands of gratitude, and the violence of benevolence.[144] The snow is also the aphasia—the loss of language—that envelopes Mina's being as she resettles in the remote rural setting of Alice Munro country in Southwestern Ontario, where not a single other Asian person—or person of color at all for that matter—can be found in sight.

Mina feels "the weight of winter clothing" inside a car where "all the windows were rolled up, which made it harder to breathe."[145] The winter clothing and the car are given to the family by their sponsors, framed as gifts for surviving in the harsh rural climate. In time, the refugee family adapts. First, the children begin throwing snow and playing games, while the Khmer language begins to fade from rote memory and the parents begin to discourage its use. In Mina's household, "the word Cambodia was, if not forbidden, very seldom used."[146] Forgetting the traumatic past becomes normalized and expected in order to manage the challenges of surviving in the new land. In time, snow provides a clean slate, a pallid whiteness for Mina's family to re-create themselves; as Thien writes, "Her parents don't want to return to Cambodia. Her father rushes out to shovel the snow, sometimes he shovels the whole block."[147] Like their own names and official dates of birth that have been changed and altered over time (for example, Mina's name was "Sothea" before arriving in Canada), the refugee family transforms snow from a threatening burden into a gesture of gratitude. Shoveling the snow for the neighbors becomes an act of keeping the community's tacit racism and violence at a distance. By the time Mina grows up and gets her Ph.D., the smell of snow and ice beckons a familiarity for the place she once lived, the town in which she will always feel simultaneously at home and foreign.

As Tobago-born Canadian poet M. NourbeSe Philip writes about the space of the Canadian rural, "There appears to be some sort of psychic border which prohibits or limits our entry, as 'Others,' into this particularly Canadian aspect of life."[148] Life in the rural for people of color is a constant state of precarious survival like "a tree about to fall."[149] As Dionne Brand writes in *Map to the Door of No Return*, to survive in such an unpredictable climate, there is a need for women of color to build up a psychological armor. Brand describes "always taking refuge in the armour of [her] car in these small northern Ontario towns."[150] In the unremitting sameness of these small towns that she travels through, Brand, as a Black woman, feels that she does "not share the same consciousness. There is some other rhythm these people grew up in, speech and gait and probably sensibility."[151] Like Brand, Thien's Mina feels out of sync with the rhythm of her small town, a community that has little space for the sensibilities of grief and anger that mark Mina's being. Mina wears the term "lucky" to survive the cultural norms of the rural, as she knows the townspeople expect this of her. The language of luck becomes a new language Mina quickly learns, one that pleases her hosts and sponsors. For all the years Mina has named Goderich as the town she and her "parents come from," she is never allowed to truly claim the Canadian rural as her home.[152] After "reading and re-reading the words" of the famous author whose stories are set in Mina's hometown, she feels not a calm recognition but a "rushing in her ears"—an aphasia that makes hearing and speaking suddenly difficult.[153]

The snow in "Alice Munro Country" expresses the unyielding need to acclimatize, to assimilate, to put one's hopes for survival on those who brought us here. Snow signifies a barrage of new needs: the need to strip away the heavy past, to forget those left behind, to make oneself invisible, as if to become a part of the landscape itself. Snow is the new climate that the refugee is expected to adjust to with unrestrained optimism. In the story, this is a *crippling* kind of optimism that demands Mina set aside all the pain and loss to put on a happy face. It is the kind of performative optimism Hannah Arendt once described, with reference to expectations placed on the Jewish refugee community in New York in the 1940s, as their "vain attempt to keep head above water."[154] Beneath the veneer of cheerfulness, Arendt argued, these refugees struggled constantly "with despair of themselves."[155] In Thien's story, snow represents the omnipresent demand for the refugee to embrace the optimistic future. As a metaphor for whiteness, the snow is blameless; it merely exists. Its attacks are subtle, invisible, producing headaches for Mina rather than bruises, as on "bright winter days when the snow is blinding."[156] Mina's family, the pitiable refugees rescued by the small town with no other Asian bodies, must change for the snow, for to remain in their own clothes is not an option. But Thien's story probes beneath the refugee's bright glossiness, asking what rages on inside the refugee suited up for success? Is there a space for ingratitude, pain, and loss while cloaked in the nation's fortune?

Growing up in the "Alice Munro Country" of endless gravel, small-town idiom, religious discipline, gossip circles, and secret adulterers, Mina takes to learning English "as naturally as shading her eyes, as blinking against the sun."[157] Not yet acclimatized to the weather, Mina instead learns the language. The word "benighted" gives her the means to rationally "banish" her own nightmares of drowning in the Mekong River.[158] Words become treasures to her, a means to make sense of the climate of her past and to comprehend the snow-laden future ahead. The word "lucky" does not carry the same treasured ease as other words. Being called "lucky" for having survived the Cambodian Genocide, for having come to Canada, for having sponsors who care for her and her family, feels just as blinding to Mina as the new snow. Alone, Mina fits the word into her new family, as Thien writes: "All of them—adopted parents, uncles, the four boys, Mina—are lucky. Together they have created a new kind of family, and no greater fortune is really imaginable to her."[159] "Lucky" denotes community and family, those who are lucky to have each other. Like the climate, luck is blameless, casting fortune on some and wrong on others.

It is with the appearance of Miss Murray, one of the refugee sponsors, that "luck" transforms from a communal fortune to a gift provided by the Canadian people, one conditioned upon the refugee's relationship to the sponsor: "Miss Murray's attachment brought the family luck. She gave them an old Ford. She took Mina's father for driving lessons across the railway tracks and into the surrounding land where things like sugar beets and tobacco lay in wait. She arranged piano lessons for Mina."[160] Miss Murray represents the charity model of white benevolence toward refugees. As Eli Clare writes, the disability community has long contended with the charity regime's "impulse to do away with disability."[161] Just as disabled people have been "charity's favorite object," refugees have often been forced to survive and depend on the charity of their refugee sponsors. In Thien's story, Miss Murray is a figure reminiscent of the white female protagonist of so many Alice Munro stories, the "kind of woman the writer had observed, decade after decade, never quite knowing what would make her free."[162] For Miss Murray, her work as a sponsor becomes a new project that will infuse new meaning and life into the sterile and limited parameters of her rural existence. Miss Murray's struggles with the judgmental gaze of the community are displaced onto Mina, who becomes Miss Murray's sponsored refugee "daughter."[163] As Mina's sponsor mother, Miss Murray promises to acculturate Mina, her favorite charity object, into all the ways of becoming Canadian. Mina's Cambodian identity and traumatic memories, a past ebbing and flowing within her like a "rush of noise," remain invisible to Miss Murray. She recognizes only Mina's fortune as a girl gifted with the opportunities of a new generation, imploring Mina to feel "lucky to be here. To have choices as a young woman."[164] As Eli Clare writes, "People who adopt or foster disabled children—the world treats them as martyrs engaged in charity work."[165] The act of choosing disability, by contrast, is "pathologized, shamed, or sensationalized."[166] Mina's desire to hold on to her refugee memories, to cling to her past life and identity in Cambodia, is incomprehensible to Miss Murray, who thinks of Mina only as a subject of Miss Murray's own altruism.

Juxtaposing the disparate lives of Miss Murray, Mina, and Mina's mother, Thien's "Alice Munro Country" speaks back to the conflation of *all* women's experiences within liberal white feminist paradigms of personhood: "It is not fair, not possible, to compare the luck—of Ma, of Mina, of her mother, of Miss Murray—and the lives of all these women, because the word *luck* can never mean the same thing to all of them."[167] What is the place of the refugee woman within this field of luck? While Miss Murray's sponsorship of Mina and her family turns out to be a fleeting commitment—one that Miss Murray walks away from when the attachment becomes an inconvenient obstacle to the pursuit of her other passions—Mina remains haunted by all the parts of herself that she has "had to pare away" in order to survive in Canadian society.[168] For Mina, this loss includes the memory of those who were not so lucky—her original father was an architect and her mother a schoolteacher, yet they had not made it out of Cambodia alive: "They had endless ingenuity but no miracles."[169] Mina has come to Canada as a refugee and "paper daughter" in a reconstructed family pieced together in the aftermath of the genocide.[170] In Canada, her family's ability to weather the hardships of rural poverty is the result of ingenuity and labor, not of the fortune bestowed on them by the benevolent nation or their capricious sponsor. At night, Mina and her family roam the cemetery fields picking worms to supplement the family income. As Mina sits alone among the graves, "the idea that the dead have a separate parcel of land, that you can know exactly where to find them, somehow the idea makes her first sad, and then angry."[171] Mina has no land, no body, no ashes, to help her grieve all those lost in Cambodia.

To be lucky is not a state of being but a routine—it is the heavy clothing one must change into every day to keep the elements at bay. For Mina, this "clothing" comes in the form of the English language. It gives her the means to survive the climate of whiteness, suspicion, and racism. But the weight of language comes in those words that she cannot lift—the "luck" granted to the refugee. Being "lucky" must be produced and reproduced, worked at, until it reflects one's unconscious self.

Conclusion: Dwelling in/with Aphasia

Survivors of stroke and aphasia know that where aphasia exists, so, too, does the capacity for regeneration and that this capacity to "heal" is inextricable from broader issues of care and disability justice. In stroke rehabilitation labs, doctors may refer to the desired regeneration or plasticity of brain cells over time. In time, aphasia patients may recover partial or full language abilities through access to quality care, including speech therapy and other forms of rehabilitation. Recovery of language, which takes place long after the return of motor function, if at all, is thus linked to structural accessibility to health resources and being in a community of care. What is striking about the fMRI brain scans of these "recovered" patients is that the lacunae (black holes) in their brains have not healed or changed. In aphasia patients, it is the *web of cells* surrounding the lacunae—the penumbra—that have *taken over* to regenerate language function.[172]

Like the work of Madeleine Thien, the art of Los Angeles–based artist Kerry Tribe explores aphasia and regeneration. I end this chapter on aphasia and the nervous condition of refugee asylum with a discussion of Tribe's exhibition *Aphasia Book Club* because, like Thien's writing, Tribe's art makes connections between aphasia and the afterlife of the Cold War in Cambodia. Tribe's art features her collaboration with Christopher Riley who developed aphasia after having two strokes as an adult. In 1993, Riley visited Cambodia for the country's historic national election that would later come to signal the end of the Cold War in Cambodia. While in Phnom Penh at the Tuol Sleng Genocide Museum, Riley, along with photojournalist Douglas Niven, discovered the original negatives of the infamous Tuol Sleng mug shot photos. Riley and Niven secured permission from the Cambodian government to restore these negatives for the museum's archives; later, they used the mug shots in their 1996 photobook, *The Killing Fields*.[173] In Kerry Tribe's 2015 video piece, *The Aphasia Poetry Club*, Riley is no longer the photographer assembling a montage of Cambodian victims at Tuol Sleng. He is now the survivor of aphasia and the object of the camera's lens.

Filmed speaking with great difficulty, in ungrammatical fragments, Riley describes his experience of visiting Cambodia, followed by commentary on how his photographic practice has now been completely altered: "Now I turn and capture negatives upside down," Riley comments in the video.[174] Riley's photography now captures how he sees the world from new angles and perspectives. Discussing her aesthetic choices, Tribe explains that Riley's "1996 photo project about the Killing Fields in Cambodia settled into place as a kind of climax of his narrative."[175] Her project began as an exploration of aphasia but inevitably veered toward Cambodia's history as it became impossible to think about one without the other. Tribe explains that, like Riley, she wanted to examine the question, "What happens if you focus on that loss of language and see what can start to percolate up into its space?"[176] Tribe's attention to what "percolate[s] up" in the absence of verbal language is compelling in its recalibration of commonplace notions of aphasia as a condition of language loss.

Tribe's *Aphasia Book Club* has been described by critics as a work that "disrupts ableist conceits about the human capacity for memory and language."[177] In the case of aphasic Christopher Riley, what Tribe describes as "the 'epic' nature of his distinct elocution" underscores the reality that aphasia does not equate with intellectual or creative deficit, or even with loss of language.[178] Aphasia generates its own creative language, like the refugee condition. Aphasic lifeworlds might be better thought of as an "excess of poetry"—a way of being that is "indicative of a new aesthetic arising from disability experience."[179] As cognitive difference or neurodiversity, aphasia exists in the realm of creativity and translation that affirms the personhood and creative vitality of living the afterlife of loss. This is the art we see when we dwell in/with the Cambodian refugee archive. This is the art, in Madeleine Thien's words, of "grasping all the broken, brilliant fragments."

My mother often tells me the story about how her mother, a superstitious woman and devout Buddhist, was once visited by a fortune-teller in the years before wartime. The fortune-teller foretold of a gap, a dark time in Cambodia, that would take place when my grandmother was sixty years old. If she could cross this gap, her life would be spared. She would go on to live for many more years.

In 1976, during the "dark time" that the fortune-teller had foretold, my grandmother was sent to work in the forest with a group of three other elderly people. As my parents often explained to me, during Pol Pot time, people were grouped according to their age and gender: men, women, children, and the elderly worked separately. My brothers were sent out to work in the children's brigades; my mother primarily worked in rice planting; my father was usually sent out to construct dikes, dams, and canals. On some occasions, he was sent to destroy Buddhist temples.

One day, my grandmother's mobile unit was ordered to go into a forest to cut grass that would be used for roofing. All the locals knew that this forest was under the domain of *Lok Ta*, a powerful guardian spirit that no one dared offend. Everyone knew Lok Ta protected the area, but he could also be a dangerous spirit. All Neak Ta and Lok Ta are this way in Cambodia. You had to ask permission from him before you could pick anything. You had to say something at least. If you did not believe, you just did not go in.

After this day, my grandmother became critically ill, as did the three other people in her work unit. The villagers whispered that they had made Lok Ta angry, that the Khmer Rouge had sent them there on purpose. My mother remembered the fortune-teller's omen.

My mother's last image of her mother was while she was being taken away by the Khmer Rouge. Because she was elderly, she was of no use to the regime. They did not entertain the idea of taking her to the hospital in the city of Kampong Thom. The cadres said she was being taken to the village hospital, but she was never seen again. My mother wept. She could not see her mother's body. And because my mother could not perform a proper Buddhist cremation ritual, she believed that her mother's ghost would remain alone, restlessly wandering the earth.

Coda

Boneyards of the Cold War

On April 17, 1975, the capital city of Phnom Penh in Cambodia fell to the Communist Khmer Rouge regime. I was not yet born but my mother, father, and two brothers remember this day all too well. A year earlier, the Cambodian Civil War had reached a lull. The U.S. B-52 bombs were no longer decimating the Cambodian countryside. The war seemed to be coming to an end, and there was an eerie sense of calm. My parents reopened their convenience supply store in their hometown of Kampong Thom. The store was frequently visited by soldiers and generals of the U.S.-backed Lon Nol army, who accumulated a large tab every month buying food, liquor, and cigarettes. But, then, my mother and father began to notice a change in the air once again. The Cambodian currency—the riel—started to depreciate. Inflation was out of control. People began hoarding food and medicine, paying more for the same item with each passing day. Within a few short days, all the shelves of my mother and father's supply store were completely emptied, as were those of all the jewelry stores and pharmacies in the city.

Fearful of what this could all mean, my parents began to prepare for the family's evacuation. They buried their valuables and money, over 5 million riel, in the ground and waited for further news of the war. People whispered that after years of illegally bombing Cambodia, the Americans were about to withdraw from Southeast Asia. Two days before April 17, 1975, during the Khmer New Year celebrations, a captain in the Lon Nol army came to my parents' store to pay off his tab. He urged my parents to leave Cambodia immediately and told them about a planned U.S. evacuation that was scheduled to take place in twenty-four hours. Those who had some connections to the U.S.-backed regime had the opportunity to leave and become refugees in America, he told them. The general assured my mother and father that he could get the family out on the next helicopter, if they wanted to go. When my mother remembers this pivotal moment—the choice to stay or to go—her eyes glaze over with tears. She said to me once, "We didn't know. We never imagined what Cambodia would become. That the world would change overnight. We thought the war was over. This is the biggest regret of my life. What we went through after, what your brothers went through—I'll never forgive myself." My mother remembers how at 8:00 A.M. the next day, the skies above the city were filled with black helicopters, circling like a spiral of birds. She watched as at least ten of them swooped down and lifted away those who were on the evacuation list.

While these moments at the threshold of wartime transition are seared into the memories of my family and most Cambodian people who lived through the war, audiences outside Cambodia likely remember experiencing the last days of the Vietnam War from a distance, as they watched the scenes of helicopter refugee evacuations on the news. As I write this Coda, these scenes of war are with us again—not from Cambodia, Vietnam, or Laos, but from Afghanistan. *Refugee Lifeworlds* has sought to explore the complex entanglements between war, disability, and refugee life in the afterlife of the Cold War in Cambodia, insisting on an afterlife of war that, as many other scholars have noted, turns out to be no afterlife at all. As I have argued in this book, over twenty years since its official conclusion in 1998, the Cold War in Cambodia endures as an imperial knowledge formation, a system of endemic debilitation, and a cripistemological way of knowing and living the afterlife of war and displacement. I thus wish to conclude *Refugee Lifeworlds* with a brief comment on the place of the Cold War in Cambodia in what Lisa Yoneyama describes as the "longer Cold War trajectory of U.S. transpacific involvement."[1]

Cambodia in the Genealogy of U.S. Permanent War

What happened in Cambodia was not exceptional but was rather one site of wreckage in the long genealogy of U.S. hot wars that stretches backward in time to the wars in Korea, Vietnam, and Laos and forward to the wars in Iraq, Afghanistan, Syria, and Yemen.[2] Contrary to received wisdom, the wars in the Pacific were not fought to liberate Asia and the rest of the world from the

perils of Communism. Rather, they represented imperial wars fought to secure Asia's extractive economies for U.S.-led global capitalism—in the words
of Simeon Man, they were "the start of a permanent war in U.S. culture that
set into motion a range of military and economic activities across the Pacific
including offshore procurement, the building of infrastructure, the training
of armed forces, and the mobilization of civilian workers."[3] Indeed, since the
end of World War II, peacetime and wartime have coexisted along a blurred
global spectrum. When we consider the full continuum of American military
conflicts, Mary Dudziak writes, "including the 'small wars' and the so-called
forgotten wars, there are not many years of peacetime."[4] Nikhil Pal Singh
likewise asserts that the Cold War was "an epoch in which the United States
engaged in continuous and accretive wars all over the world—some named,
almost all formally undeclared."[5] Like in Cambodia, the crisis of permanent
war has been made possible through what Viet Thanh Nguyen describes as
the myth of "perpetual American innocence." This myth "requires forgetting all the previous history of killing civilians and sets the stage for the next
round of killing civilians."[6] With reference to the Taliban takeover of Kabul
in August 2021, Nguyen writes, "perpetual innocence allows the USA to
blame the bad guys for making the good guys kill the innocent bystanders."[7]
Whether it is the Khmer Rouge or the Taliban, it is always the Other, never
the system of permanent war itself, to blame for the "accidental" killing of
civilians. What we see today in the so-called U.S. war on terror is simply a
continuation and extension of the coconstitutive U.S. inner and outer wars
of the Cold War era. Since September 11, 2001, the boundaries of these wars
have continued to blur, morphing into a system of endless conflict in the
Greater Middle East and elsewhere that Ronak Kapadia terms "the US forever war."[8] What these scholars make clear is that, far from an exception to
peacetime, war is the United States' enduring condition.

If Cambodia's recent history teaches us anything, Taylor Owen and Ben
Kiernan argue, it should be a lesson about the collateral aftermaths of such
sustained bombardments on radicalizing the local population.[9] Cambodia has
even been likened to a crucial key, a Rosetta Stone, for deciphering the mechanisms of today's U.S. forever war in the Greater Middle East.[10] Historical
parallels between Cambodia and Syria or Afghanistan are evident in the way
that global superpowers turned these nations into sites of proxy wars and
massive human displacement, that led, in turn, to the rise of militia economies.[11] As in Cambodia, what we see in Afghanistan today is the total failure
of international accountability, where the superpowers such as the United
States and Russia bred the conditions for Afghanistan's collapse for decades,
just to walk away as the structures began to crumble. When Kabul fell to

the Taliban in August 2021, many commentators rushed to point out the uncanny parallels to the 1975 fall of Phnom Penh to the Khmer Rouge, who had been galvanized after years of U.S. bombardments.[12]

The never-ending, deterritorialized nature of contemporary wartime, what Derek Gregory calls "the everywhere war," underscores the stakes of attending to past wars for which there has yet to be a proper accounting.[13] The mirroring of the Cold War in Cambodia and many war zones in the Greater Middle East today certainly begs the question: If the world had learned anything about the costs of war from the Cambodian narrative, would we be witnessing the same scenes of violence and refugee displacement unfolding in Iraq, Afghanistan, and Syria today? Cambodian people's history of suffering was an ethical lesson *not* learned by the world, but U.S. leaders certainly *did* learn something from Cambodia about the expendability of human life and the scant consequences of these actions: that wars could be porous, borderless, waged in secrecy, and that civilians could be killed and maimed with complete impunity. Perhaps what the United States (as well as Canada) also learned was that it could actually come out of such conflicts looking even *better* on the world stage—stronger, nobler, and more humane—for having taken in the refugees, like my family, as its charity. Perhaps what Cambodia taught the United States was that it didn't matter if a war was winnable or not, and that the conditions for winning could be flexible insofar as the American people's sympathies were far more aligned with the U.S. soldiers who had died rather than with the people who had been killed, maimed, and traumatized in far higher numbers. Perhaps what the wars in Southeast Asia taught the United States was that even in a war that was "lost," the United States could still gain a cause for decades of U.S. exports, the growth of American nationalism, and an ever-expanding military budget.

While I make these points here about Cambodia's status as a mirror for contemporary catastrophes, *Refugee Lifeworlds* has elected to take a deep dive into the afterlife of the Cold War in Cambodia, resisting the impulse for comparativity that would render Cambodia merely as a cautionary tale for the present. Instrumentalizations of this sort demand that Cambodia be immediately made *useful* in the service of others, even as, to my mind, we have not yet been able to look at Cambodia on its own terms.

It is July 2018. Today is the last day of my visit to Siem Reap. Later this afternoon I have to catch my flight, and the thought of being so far away from Cambodia pains me deeply. I have failed to do so much: six years ago I moved to Asia to take a job as a professor, and to be closer to Cambodia. I longed for proximity to my parents' birthplace—to see with my own eyes the landscapes of their past. I hoped to lay down some kind of record of the war they had survived, to write a book that my mother and father and brothers could see themselves in. But many things in Cambodia have taken me by surprise; it is one thing to inherit the shadows of the past, another to walk among them.

I arrive at the War Museum Cambodia, just outside of Siem Reap, about five kilometers south of the ancient ruins of Angkor Wat. In the sweltering afternoon heat, I take in the arresting sight of the fenced-in outdoor space: dozens of obsolete war machines are interspersed among the banyan and palm trees. At a glance, the rusted brown tanks and aircraft carriers merge seamlessly with the browns of the trees, soil, and pits. The remains of war are starting to be reclaimed by nature. Lifeworlds woven together. Unlike the nearby ruins of the ancient Angkor empire, an attraction that draws millions of tourists each year, this boneyard feels hidden from the world. Inside the museum, I learn that war material in Cambodia used to be scrapped for recycled metal. People salvaged what they could to make a living. I've spent time in graveyards as a child, alone in the car at night as my family members scavenged the ground for earthworms they could sell to farmers. Back then, I felt excitement at watching my parents move among the dead, but today I feel unsure of how to move through such a ghostly area.

In the compound, one caption catches my eye: "Artillery 85 mm made in China, 1946. 4.75 m length, size 85 mm, fighting power approximately 13.10 km, was used in Cambodia by Pol Pot regime (1975–1979) and was finally destroyed in 1998 at Osmach battlefield the West of Siem Reap Province." This retired artillery is a fragment of a missing picture: one of fraternity between China and Cambodia—brothers in arms, some would say. This is an image of Cambodia that most have preferred not to see, drawn instead to the iconic pictures of skulls and bones, of the sunken earth of mass graves. Many tourists have gaped at the horrors of Pol Pot's killing fields, have shook their heads in astonishment at the sheer brutality of this regime, but few have cared to see the horrors committed before and after Pol Pot's time: the military aid that flowed from China to the Khmer Rouge, the bombs that the United States dropped on Cambodia, the refugees that were turned back at the borders.

This boneyard is a cemetery of the *longue durée* of imperial violence in Cambodia. It houses the remnants of one of the hottest laboratories of the Cold War in Asia, wherein the United States secretly dropped more than 2.7 million tons of bombs, more bombs than the allies dropped in all of World War II combined. One exhibit, labeled Bomb House, gives an account of this planned destruction. The wooden hut's walls are lined with deactivated rockets and an information board displays an archival photo of Richard Nixon pointing at a map of Cambodia. Here stands a technician, the man who turned Cambodia into an experiment in "collateral damage." My mother and father's stories about fleeing from the U.S. bombs suddenly come back to me. "To hide from the American bombs, we took shelter under a Buddhist pagoda," my father once told me. After the Khmer Rouge rose to power in the ashes of those bombs, my parents and brothers slept in the fields for almost four years, barely clinging to life. In the hazy, afternoon heat, I feel the familiar emotions of anger and bitterness rise in me.

Winding dirt paths cut around the inert weapons, creating a maze for solo travelers and tour groups looking for their fix of the war-ravaged exotic. Cambodian men dressed in blue army uniforms, likely former Khmer Rouge soldiers, offer tours of the surroundings. Many guides carry the wounds of war—prosthetics, bullet wounds, and scars—visible for all to see. One guide assembles me and a small group of English-speaking visitors. He tells us: "I spent nearly my whole life in the war. I died more than ten times during the war. They called me a cat. I will show you the scar, the shrapnel, the ball bearing. Everywhere there are holes in my body." At one point during his story, a thirty-something American man in the group, on break from his conference in Chiang Mai, leans over and asks me if I know who Pol Pot is. I have no time for explanations today.

Our guide continues: "They took away my family and then they killed them. I ate the crickets, grasshoppers, frog, fish, snake, everything. A hornet's nest dropped down on me. I live thirty miles north from here. About fifty kilometres. My wife died three years ago. Lung cancer from the uranium. On April 16, 2017, my friend stepped on a mine and it took off his legs." He takes us to a large ruined tank and peers over the top to point out something inside: "My friend's bones inside. Bowin. He died." I feel a whirling as I listen to him, wishing he would stop, but I am incapable of extracting myself from the group.

I am jolted out of my daze as our guide ends his monologue to ask our names. I tell him mine, and there is immediate recognition on his part: "You were born in Khao-I-Dang! Khao-I-Dang is the mountain in Thailand. Her name," he says to the group, "is the same as that mountain." The story of my name is a complicated one. KID is the nickname for the refugee camp on the border of Cambodia and Thailand that swelled to the size of a small city back in 1980. Those who made it to this camp were thought to be the most fortunate refugees of the war. Our guide explains: "Some, like your family, when they went to Thailand, were very, very lucky. They got to immigrate, to live in Canada, Australia, New Zealand, the U.S., and Europe, but some were not so lucky. They got repatriated by the United Nations." Then, he says to me, "I see that you are a little bit upset, but you will know how lucky you are."

Figure C.1 Lotus Pond grows in the space of a former bomb crater, either real or fabricated, War Museum Cambodia, Siem Reap, 2018. (Photo by Y-Dang Troeung.)

I don't know how to respond, to express the sadness I feel in this moment, standing before this man whom I should call bou (uncle in Khmer) but do not. Uncle, I want to say, I am sorry your life has been so hard.

An Australian woman, with two bored and indifferent teenage daughters, jumps in: "Yes, we are very lucky to be Australian, but we have a lot of different cultures that like to bring their cultures into Australia"—laughter from the group—"which is actually the dangerous part." Our group passes by Chinese-speaking tourists who pose for photos with old rifles and tanks, as if wishing the equipment could be suddenly reanimated. The captions are all in English. More than once a Chinese-speaking passerby stops me, points at something, and asks me in Putonghua, "Zhè shì shénme (这是什么)"—What is this? I shrug and say, "Wǒ bù zhīdào (我不知道)"—I don't know.

We come to a crater at the edge of the compound that is fenced in by razor wire but curiously unmarked. Our guide tells us it was caused by the U.S. bombing in 1973, but there is noticeable hesitation in his voice. He does not want to linger here, quickly moving us on to the next station. I wonder what in the museum is real and what is fabricated, if it even matters. At the center of the crater, a little ecosystem has formed, with bright pink lotus blossoms sprouting up from a pool of lily pads and murky brown water (see Fig.

C.1). The Cambodian belief is that the lotus flower emerging from the mud symbolizes strength, hope, and faith that a new lifeworld can be reborn from the darkest places. I think of the biology of cellular and organic regrowth—that every species, no matter how damaged, is capable of regeneration.

The blazing sun shines in my eyes, and time has gotten away from me. Something has both paralyzed me and left me ungrounded. When I arrive at Siem Reap airport, I find I have missed my flight.

Notes

PREFACE

1. Scholarly fields such as "genocide studies," "Asian area studies," and "migration studies" tend to focus on one dimension or the other of the war/migration binary.

2. Lisa Yoneyama, *Cold War Ruins: Transpacific Critique of American Justice and Japanese War Crimes* (Durham, NC: Duke University Press, 2016), xi.

3. Yoneyama, *Cold War Ruins*, xi.

4. Christine Hong, *A Violent Peace: Race, U.S. Militarism, and Cultures of Democratization in Cold War Asia and the Pacific* (Stanford, CA: Stanford University Press, 2020), 15.

5. Rithy Panh and Christophe Bataille, *The Elimination: A Survivor of the Khmer Rouge Confronts His Past and the Commandant of the Killing Fields*, trans. John Cullen (New York: Other Press, 2013), 182.

6. Panh and Bataille, *Elimination*, 411.

7. Cambodia as a "laboratory of ideology" is a line taken from *The Missing Picture*, directed by Rithy Panh (Phnom Penh, Cambodia: Arte, 2013), DVD.

8. For more discussion of the legal debate about the use of the term genocide in the case of Cambodia, see page xxv.

9. For more on the *longue durée* as a structure of deep time, see Fernand Braudel, *On History*, trans. Sarah Matthews (Chicago: University of Chicago Press, 1980).

10. For an example of a reference to the "Cambodian self-genocide," see Giorgio Agamben, *Remnants of Auschwitz: The Witness and the Archive*, trans. Daniel Heller-Roazen (New York: Zone Books, 1999), 32.

11. For more on Foucault's notion of "genealogy" and "subjugated knowledges," see Michel Foucault, "Two Lectures," in *Power/Knowledge: Selected Interviews and Other Writings 1972–1977*, ed. Colin Gordon (New York: Pantheon Books, 1980).

12. Foucault, "Two Lectures," 82–83.

13. War Museum Cambodia, accessed March 1, 2021, available at http://www
.warmuseumcambodia.com, site inactive on November 16, 2021.

14. For more on the Cold War as a "hot war" as it played out in Asia, see Jodi Kim,
Ends of Empire: Asian American Critique and the Cold War (Minneapolis: University of
Minnesota Press, 2010), 16.

15. See Taylor Owen and Ben Kiernan, "Bombs over Cambodia," *The Walrus*,
October 16, 2006, accessed March 11, 2022, available at https://thewalrus.ca/2006
-10-history/. Their research shows that the U.S. bombing actually began in 1965, "four
years earlier than is widely believed—not under Nixon, but under Lyndon Johnson."

16. David Chandler, "The Khmer Rouge in a Cold War Context," Documentation Center of Cambodia, July 2011, 12, accessed March 11, 2022, available at http://
www.cambodiatribunal.org/assets/pdf/court-filings/genocide_education.pdf.

17. Owen and Kiernan, "Bombs over Cambodia."

18. Ibid.

19. Ros Kosal, "Tuol Sleng Genocide Museum Audio Guide," accessed and tran-
scribed at Tuol Sleng Genocide Museum, May 1, 2018.

20. Ma Vang, *History on the Run: Secrecy, Fugitivity, and Hmong Refugee Epistemologies* (Durham, NC: Duke University Press, 2020), 33.

21. See Neta C. Crawford, "Targeting Civilians and U.S. Strategic Bombing
Norms: Plus ça change, plus c'est la même chose?" in *The American Way of Bombing:
Changing Ethical and Legal Norms, from Flying Fortresses to Drones*, ed. Matthew Evan-
gelista and Henry Shue (Ithaca, NY: Cornell University Press, 2014), 74, who explains
that during Operation Menu and Operation Freedom Deal, "the military targets, to
the extent that there were any that could be clearly identified, were located in and near
civilian populations, but the bombing apparently occurred with little regard for nearby
civilians. Neither the Johnson nor the Nixon administration felt political pressure to
prevent civilian deaths."

22. For more on the secret war in Laos, see Ma Vang, *History on the Run*.

23. For more on the Kent State shootings, see Howard Ruffner, *Moments of Truth:
A Photographer's Experience of Kent State 1970* (Kent, OH: Kent State University Press,
2019).

24. Domenic Poli, "Reflecting on Kent State Massacre 50 Years Later," *Greenfield
Recorder*, May 3, 2020, accessed March 11, 2022, available at https://www.recorder
.com/Franklin-County-reflects-on-Kent-State-massacre-50-years-later-34088546.

25. Thomas M. Grace, foreword to Ruffner, *Moments of Truth*, xi.

26. James A. Tyner and Mindy Farmer, *Cambodia and Kent State: In the Aftermath of Nixon's Expansion of the Vietnam War* (Kent, OH: Kent State University Press,
2020), ix.

27. For more on this order by Henry Kissinger, see Chapter 1.

28. Sydney Schanberg, "Remembering the Killing Fields," interview by Gregory
Oliver, *Oxonian Globalist*, November 20, 2010, accessed March 24, 2022, available at
http://toglobalist.org/2010/11/remembering-the-killing-fields/.

29. See Taylor Owen and Ben Kiernan, "Roots of U.S. Troubles in Afghanistan:
Civilian Bombing Casualties and the Cambodian Precedent," *Asia Pacific Journal* 8,
no. 26.4 (2010), accessed March 24, 2022, available at https://apjjf.org/-Taylor-Owen
/3380/article.html.

30. Aom Voeun, "I Volunteered to Join the Khmer Rouge," *Khmer Times*, March 17, 2021, accessed March 24, 2022, available at https://www.khmertimeskh .com/50825759/i-volunteered-to-join-the-khmer-rouge/.

31. For more on the work of Sera, see Michelle Vachon, "Graphic Novel Depicts the Years before Zero," *Cambodia Daily*, April 4, 2015, accessed March 24, 2022, available at https://english.cambodiadaily.com/lifestyle/graphic-novel-depicts-the-years-before -zero-81391/.

32. For more on the evacuation of Cambodian orphans from Canada House in 1975, see Eloise Charet-Calles, *Never without Our Children: Cambodia 1975* (Montreal: Éditions Bambou, 2015).

33. The recitation of this phrase of "three years, eight months, and twenty days" to mark the exact duration of the Cambodian Genocide has become something of a mantra among Cambodian people.

34. The official number of people killed during the Cambodian Genocide has varied across time, ranging from 1.7 million to 2.2. million people. For the most recent estimates of the death toll as of 2021, see Youk Chhang, "A History of Democratic Kampuchea (1975–1979)," Documentation Center of Cambodia, accessed January 17, 2021, available at http://dccam.org/a-history-of-democratic-kampuchea-1975-1979.

35. For more on Pol Pot's use of the "wheel of history" metaphor, see David P. Chandler, "S-21, the Wheel of History, and the Pathology of Terror in Democratic Kampuchea," in *Cambodia Emerges from the Past: Eight Essays*, ed. Judy Ledgerwood (DeKalb, IL: Center for Southeast Asian Studies, Northern Illinois University, 2002), 16–37.

36. Henri Locard, *Pol Pot's Little Red Book: The Sayings of Angkar* (Chiang Mai, Thailand: Silkworm, 2004), 213.

37. For more on "forced marriages" during the era of Democratic Kampuchea, see Peg LeVine, *Love and Dread in Cambodia: Weddings, Births, and Ritual Harm under the Khmer Rouge* (Singapore: National University of Singapore Press, 2010).

38. For more on S-21, see James A. Tyner, *The Politics of Lists: Bureaucracy and Genocide under the Khmer Rouge* (Morgantown: West Virginia University Press), 2018.

39. Elizabeth Becker, *Bophana: Love in the Time of the Khmer Rouge* (Phnom Penh: Cambodia Daily, 2010).

40. See *Bophana: A Cambodian Tragedy*, directed by Rithy Panh (1996; Phnom Penh, Cambodia: Catherine Dussart Productions, 2013), DVD.

41. For more on the prisoners at Tuol Sleng, see Meng-Try Ea and Sorya Sim, *Victims and Perpetrators? Testimony of Young Khmer Rouge Comrades* (Phnom Penh: Documentation Center of Cambodia, 2001).

42. Y-Dang Troeung, "The Lucky One Returns," *Outfront* (April 19, 2009; CBC Radio, August 30, 2011), radio.

43. See Seth Mydans, "Cambodians Demand Apology for Khmer Rouge Images with Smiling Faces," *New York Times*, April 13, 2021, accessed March 25, 2022, available at https://www.nytimes.com/2021/04/13/world/asia/cambodia-khmer-rouge.html.

44. For more on the debate about the care of skeletal remains in Cambodia, see Therith Chy, "One Last Measure for the Wandering Souls of Cambodia," *Asia Foundation*, June 29, 2016, accessed March 24, 2022, available at https://asiafoundation .org/2016/06/29/one-last-measure-wandering-souls-cambodia/.

45. Kosal, "Tuol Sleng."

46. For more on "wealthy memory" versus "poor memory" in the memorialization of atrocity, see Viet Thanh Nguyen, *Nothing Ever Dies: Vietnam and the Memory of War* (Cambridge, MA: Harvard University Press, 2016), 259.

47. Maggie Nelson, *The Argonauts* (Minneapolis: Graywolf, 2015), 120–121.

48. Scholars such as Gareth Porter, George Hildebrand, Malcolm Caldwell, Noam Chomsky, and Edward S. Herman were among those who initially discredited or minimized Cambodian refugee testimony throughout the 1980s. Most of these scholars have since stepped back from those views.

49. See Sophal Ear, "The Khmer Rouge Canon 1975–1979: The Standard Total Academic View on Cambodia" (undergrad. thesis, University of California, Berkeley, 1995), accessed March 24, 2022, available at https://jim.com/canon.htm.

50. Gunnar Bergstrom, *Living Hell: Democratic Kampuchea, August 1978* (Phnom Penh: Documentation Center of Cambodia, 2008), 3.

51. Bergstrom, *Living Hell.*

52. See Philip Short, *Pol Pot: Anatomy of a Nightmare* (New York: Owl Books, 2005), 12.

53. See Larry Clinton Thompson, *Refugee Workers in the Indochina Exodus, 1975–1982* (Jefferson, NC: McFarland, 2010), 43.

54. Thompson, *Refugee Workers,* 3.

55. For more on the Chinese engineers sent to Cambodia during Democratic Kampuchea, see Andrew Mertha, *Brothers in Arms: Chinese Aid to the Khmer Rouge, 1975–1979* (Ithaca, NY: Cornell University Press, 2014).

56. Panh, *Missing Picture.*

57. The Gang of Four—Jiang Qing, Zhang Chunqiao, Yao Wenyuan, Wang Hongwen—was the colloquial name for a political faction composed of four Chinese Communist Party officials during the later stages of the Cultural Revolution in China. For more on the Gang of Four and China's military aid to the Khmer Rouge, see Andrew Mertha, *Brothers in Arms.*

58. Dan Levin, "China Is Urged to Confront Its Own History," *New York Times, Sinosphere: Dispatches from China,* March 30, 2015, accessed March 24, 2022, available at https://sinosphere.blogs.nytimes.com/2015/03/30/cambodian-historians-call-for-china-to-confront-its-own-past/.

59. Michel Foucault, "Michel Foucault on Refugees—An Interview from 1979," interview by H. Uno, originally published on August 17, 1979, *Shûkan posuto,* 34–35. Translated from Japanese into French by Ryôji Nakamura, 1994; translated from French into English by Felix de Montety, October 20, 2015, accessed March 24, 2022, available at https://politheor.net/michel-foucault-on-refugees-an-interview-from-1979/.

60. Foucault, "Michel Foucault on Refugees."

61. Ibid.

62. Rithy Panh, "Remembering Cambodian Border Camps," interview by Bophana Center, July 2021, accessed March 24, 2022, video, 13:09, available at https://vimeo.com/536316545.

63. Panh, "Remembering Cambodian Border Camps."

64. Aihwa Ong, *Buddha Is Hiding: Refugees, Citizenship, the New America* (Berkeley: University of California Press, 2003), 53.

65. Panh, "Remembering Cambodian Border Camps."

66. For more on the Cambodian land bridge, see Thompson, *Refugee Workers.*

67. Ibid., xxvii.

68. Seth Mydans, "Cambodian Leader Resists Punishing Top Khmer Rouge," *New York Times,* December 29, 1998, accessed March 24, 2022, available at https://www.nytimes.com/1998/12/29/world/cambodian-leader-resists-punishing-top-khmer -rouge.html.

69. Cathy J. Schlund-Vials, *War, Genocide, and Justice: Cambodian American Memory Work* (Minneapolis: University of Minnesota Press, 2012), 13.

70. Ben Kiernan, *Genocide and Resistance in Southeast Asia: Documentation, Denial, and Justice in Cambodia and East Timor* (New Brunswick, NJ: Transaction, 2009), 221.

71. Tara Urs, "Voices from Cambodia: Imagining Locally-Motivated Accountability for Mass Atrocities," *Sur: International Journal on Human Rights* 4, no. 7 (2007): 62.

72. Craig Etcheson, *After the Killing Fields: Lessons from the Cambodian Genocide* (Westport, CT: Praeger, 2005), 150.

73. Andrew Cayley, quoted in Seth Mydans, "Trial of Former Khmer Rouge Leaders in Turmoil," *New York Times,* June 15, 2011, accessed March 24, 2022, available at https://www.nytimes.com/2011/06/16/world/asia/16iht-cambodia16.html.

74. For more on the debate about the legal recognition of the Cambodian Genocide in international law, see Rithy Panh, "Rithy Panh: Living the Experience of Genocide in Body and Soul," JusticeInfo.Net, November 27, 2018, accessed March 24, 2022, available at https://www.justiceinfo.net/en/justiceinfo-comment-and-debate /in-depth-interviews/39596-rithy-panh-living-the-experience-of-genocide-in-body -and-soul.html.

75. Gayatri Spivak, *Other Asias* (Malden, MA: Blackwell, 2008), 98.

76. Yoneyama, *Cold War Ruins,* xi.

77. Seth Mydans, "11 Years, $300 Million and 3 Convictions. Was the Khmer Rouge Tribunal Worth It?" *New York Times,* April 10, 2017, accessed March 24, 2022, available at https://www.nytimes.com/2017/04/10/world/asia/cambodia-khmer-rouge -united-nations-tribunal.html.

78. Kuan-Hsing Chen, *Asia as Method: Toward Deimperialization* (Durham, NC: Duke University Press, 2010), 243.

79. Chen, *Asia as Method,* 212.

80. Kim, *Ends of Empire,* 4.

81. Yoneyama, *Cold War Ruins,* x.

82. In my assessment, these works are Cathy J. Schlund Vial's *War, Genocide, and Justice: Cambodian American Memory Work*; Eric Tang's *Unsettled: Cambodian Refugees in the New York City Hyperghetto*; Khatharya Um's *From the Land of Shadows: War, Revolution, and the Making of Cambodian Diaspora*; Krisna Uk's, *Salvage: Cultural Resilience among the Jorai of Northeast Cambodia*; and Boreth Ly's *Traces of Trauma: Cambodian Visual Culture and National Identity in the Aftermath of Genocide.* The existence of just five substantive scholarly books by Cambodian/Cambodian-adjacent scholars about the Cold War in Cambodia is a noticeable silence in the existing scholarship.

83. In my assessment, these books include: Jodi Kim's *Ends of Empire* (Japan, China, Korea, Vietnam, and Asian America), Kuan-Hsing Chen's *Asia as Method*

(which attends to Taiwan, South Korea, and Singapore); Josephine Park's *Cold War Friendships* (Korea, Vietnam, and Asian America), Lisa Yoneyama's *Cold War Ruins* (Japan, Okinawa, and Asian America), Simeon Man's *Soldiering through Empire* (Vietnam, Hawaii, Taiwan, South Korea, the Philippines, and Asian America), Lily Wong's *Transpacific Attachments* (China, Hong Kong, Taiwan, and Asian America), Sunny Xian's *Tonal Intelligence* (Japan, South Korea, Vietnam, and Asian America), Christine Hong's *A Violent Peace* (Japan, Korea, the Philippines, the Marshall Islands, and Asian and Black America), David S. Roh's *Minor Transpacific: Triangulating American, Japanese, and Korean Fictions* (Asian America, Japan, and Korea), Jini Kim Watson's *Cold War Reckonings* (South Korea, the Philippines, Singapore, and Indonesia), and many other important scholarly contributions to the field of transpacific Cold War studies.

84. Paul Thomas Chamberlin, *The Cold War's Killing Fields: Rethinking the Long Peace* (New York: Harper Collins, 2018), 11.

85. Khatharya Um, *From the Land of Shadows: War, Revolution, and the Making of the Cambodia Diaspora* (New York: New York University Press, 2015), 113.

86. Alexander G. Weheliye, *Habeas Viscus: Racializing Assemblages, Biopolitics, and Black Feminist Theories of the Human* (Durham, NC: Duke University Press, 2014), 11.

87. Weheliye, *Habeas Viscus*, 11.

88. Denise Ferreira da Silva, "The 'Refugee Crisis' and the Current Predicament of the Liberal State," *L'Internationale Online*, March 8, 2017, accessed November 18, 2021, available at https://www.internationaleonline.org/research/politics_of_life_and_death/88_the_refugee_crisis_and_the_current_predicament_of_the_liberal_state/.

89. Weheliye, *Habeas Viscus*, 14.

90. My use and adaptation of the term "afterlife" throughout this book derives from Walter Benjamin's essay "The Task of the Translator" in which Benjamin theorizes "a stage of continued life" that comes after the original production of the work of art. For more, see Walter Benjamin, "The Task of the Translator," in *Illuminations*, translated by Harry Zohn and edited by Hannah Arendt (New York: Harcourt Brace Javanonich, 1968), 69–82. I am also influenced by Saidiya Hartman's use of the term "the afterlife of slavery" to question whether chattel slavery has really ever ended given the ongoing subjection of Black Americans to racialized impoverishment, disproportionate rates of incarceration, and premature death. For more, see Saidiya Hartman, *Scenes of Subjection: Terror, Slavery, and Self-Making in Nineteenth-Century America* (New York: Oxford University Press, 1997). In the spirit of Benjamin's and Hartman's discussions of social-historical formations that extend far beyond the event of organic materiality and history, the "afterlife" of the Cold War in Cambodia seeks to express the enduring presence of this unfinished history.

INTRODUCTION

1. Monica Sok, "On Fear, Fearlessness, and Intergenerational Trauma," *VIDA: Women in Literary Arts*, January 11, 2016, accessed March 27, 2022, available at https://www.vidaweb.org/on-fear-fearlessness-and-intergenerational-trauma/.

2. Ibid.

3. See Lauren Fournier, *Autotheory as Feminist Practice in Art, Writing, and Criticism* (Cambridge, MA: MIT Press, 2021), 16.

4. Barbara Christian, "The Race for Theory," *Cultural Critique*, no. 6, (Spring 1988): 68.

5. Barbara Christian, "The Race for Theory," *Cultural Critique*, no. 6 (Spring 1987): 51–52.

6. Ocean Vuong, "The 10 Books I Needed to Write My Novel," *Literary Hub*, October 1, 2019, accessed March 27, 2022, available at https://lithub.com/ocean-vuong -the-10-books-i-needed-to-write-my-novel/.

7. Vuong, "10 Books."

8. These writers include: Frantz Fanon, Edward Said, Chinua Achebe, James Baldwin, Audre Lorde, Gloria E. Anzaldúa, Theresa Hak Kyung Cha, Trinh T. Minh-ha, Dionne Brand, Saidiya Hartman, Grace Cho, Leanne Betasamosake Simpson, Claudia Rankine, Viet Thanh Nguyen, Julietta Singh, Madeleine Thien, Christina Sharpe, Leah Lakshmi Piepzna-Samarasinha, Cathy Park Hong, and many others.

9. Cathy Park Hong, *Minor Feelings* (New York: One World, 2020), 173.

10. Frantz Fanon, quoted in Cathy Park Hong, *Minor Feelings*, 64.

11. "The 1951 Convention Relating to the Status of Refugees and Its 1967 Protocol," *UNHCR: The UN Refugee Agency*, 3, accessed May 3, 2021, available at https:// www.unhcr.org/about-us/background/4ec262df9/1951-convention-relating-status -refugees-its-1967-protocol.html.

12. For more on the definition of a refugee, see, for example, Peter Nyers, *Rethinking Refugees: Beyond State of Emergency* (New York: Routledge, 2006); Vinh Nguyen, "Refugeetude: When Does a Refugee Stop Being a Refugee?" *Social Text* 37, no. 2 (2019): 109–131.

13. Anne Penketh, "Snow 'Looks Nice' to Asian Refugees," *Montreal Gazette*, December 4, 1980, accessed March 27, 2022, available at https://news.google.com/ne wspapers?nid=1946&dat=19801204&id=zmUxAAAAIBAJ&sjid=waQFAAAAIBAJ& pg=4281,1294274&hl=en.

14. See Eli Clare, *Brilliant Imperfection* (Durham, NC: Duke University Press, 2017).

15. "Pierre Elliott Trudeau Welcomes Cambodian Refugees in 1980," *CBC News*, December 9, 2015, accessed March 27, 2021, available at https://www.cbc.ca/news /canada/ottawa/archives-1980-trudeau-cambodian-refugees-1.3354888. In one social media thread, this video had been viewed over twenty-seven hundred times since it was first posted in 2015.

16. Belle Puri, "'The Wounds of War Never Go Away': Baby Y-Dang Named after Cambodian Refugee Camp Remembers Canadian Arrival," *CBC News*, December 30, 2019, accessed March 27, 2022, available at https://www.cbc.ca/news/canada/british -columbia/y-dang-troeung-cambodian-refugee-activism-1.5386073.

17. "Nansen Refugee Award," UNHCR, accessed March 29, 2021, available at https://www.unhcr.org/ir/nansen-refugee-award/.

18. Simon Lewsen, "America Is Not a 'Safe Country' for Refugees," *The Walrus*, February 9, 2017, last modified January 25, 2021, accessed March 27, 2022, available at https://thewalrus.ca/america-is-not-a-safe-country-for-refugees/.

19. Sunera Thobani, *Exalted Subjects: Studies in the Making of Race and Nation in Canada* (Toronto: University of Toronto Press, 2007), 20.

20. Thobani, *Exalted Subjects*, 20.

21. Lewsen, "America."

22. "Syrian Refugees are Greeted with Open Arms in Canada," *Mashable*, December 11, 2015, accessed March 28, 2022, video, 00:01:31, available at https://www.dailymotion.com/video/x3i5l66.

23. Justin Trudeau, "Full Text of Justin Trudeau's Remarks ahead of Refugees' Arrival," *CBC News*, December 11, 2015, accessed March 27, 2022, available at https://www.cbc.ca/news/canada/toronto/syrian-refugees-justin-trudeau-remarks-1.3360401.

24. "Pierre Elliot Trudeau."

25. Canada's public image of neutrality and humanitarianism belied the ways in which it "quietly" backed America's wars in Southeast Asia. This included the voluntary enlistment of approximately thirty thousand Canadian soldiers to fight in Vietnam, the Canadian government's collaboration with the CIA's covert espionage missions in Southeast Asia, Canadian industries' production and provision of arms and chemical warfare such as napalm to the Pentagon, and the Canadian military's assistance with the U.S. military's testing of weapons such as Agent Orange on Canadian soil. For more on Canada's complicity in the U.S.-led wars abroad, see Victor Levant's *Quiet Complicity: Canadian Involvement in the Vietnam War* (Toronto: Between the Lines, 1986); Yves Engler's *The Black Book of Canadian Foreign Policy* (Nova Scotia: Fernwood, 2009).

26. Michel Foucault, *The Will to Knowledge: The History of Sexuality* Volume 1, trans. R. Hurley, (New York: Pantheon, 1998), English translation copyright 1978 by Random House.

27. Achille Mbembe, *Necropolitics* (Durham, NC: Duke University Press, 2019), 92.

28. Ibid.

29. Achille Mbembe, *On the Postcolony* (Berkeley: University of California Press, 2001), 15.

30. Ibid.

31. Ibid.

32. Ibid., 8.

33. For more on the critique of the trauma paradigm, see, especially, Lauren Berlant, "Slow Death (Sovereignty, Obesity, Lateral Agency)," *Critical Inquiry* 33, no. 4 (Summer 2007): 760.

34. For more on Sigmund Freud's notion of the "return of the repressed," see the foundational text on trauma theory: Cathy Caruth, *Unclaimed Experience: Trauma, Narrative, and History* (Baltimore, MD: Johns Hopkins University Press, 1996), 13.

35. Veena Das, *Life and Words: Violence and the Descent into the Ordinary* (Berkeley: University of California Press, 2006), 205.

36. Berlant, "Slow Death," 761.

37. "Cambodia Suffers from an Appalling Mental Health Crisis," *GlobalPost*, June 17, 2014, accessed March 27, 2022, available at https://www.pri.org/stories/2014-06-17/cambodia-suffers-appalling-mental-health-crisis.

38. Ingrid Olivia Norrmén-Smith, "Unbroken Courage," *Pulitzer Center*, August 14, 2020, accessed March 27, 2022, available at https://pulitzercenter.org/stories/unbroken-courage.

39. See Beth Van Schaack, Daryn Reicherter, and Youk Chhang, *Cambodia's Hidden Scars: Trauma Psychology in the Wake of the Khmer Rouge* (Phnom Penh: Documentation Center of Cambodia, 2011), accessed November 11, 2020, available at https://

tpocambodia.org/wp-content/uploads/2015/09/DCCAM_Cambodias-Hidden-Scars
.pdf.

40. Norrmén-Smith, "Unbroken Courage."

41. Aihwa Ong, *Buddha Is Hiding: Refugees, Citizenship, the New America* (Berkeley: University of California Press, 2003), 96.

42. For an example of this discourse, see Joel Brinkley, *Cambodia's Curse: The Modern History of a Troubled Land* (New York: PublicAffairs, 2011).

43. Jasbir K. Puar, *The Right to Maim: Debility, Capacity, Disability* (Durham, NC: Duke University Press, 2017), 157.

44. FONKi Yav, quoted in *The Roots Remain*, directed by Jean-Sébastien Francoeur and Andrew Marchand-Boddy, 2015, accessed March 25, 2021, available at https://www.youtube.com/watch?v=HH7_8dXy7fw.

45. Grant N. Marshall, Terry L. Schell, Eunice C. Wong, S. Megan Berthold, Katrin Hambarsoomian, Marc N. Elliott, Barbara H. Bardenheier, and Edward W. Gregg, "Diabetes and Cardiovascular Disease Risk in Cambodian Refugees," *Journal of Immigrant and Minor Health* 18, no. 1 (2016): 113.

46. Ong, *Buddha Is Hiding*, 18.

47. Janet McLelland, *Cambodian Refugees in Ontario: Resettlement, Religion, and Identity* (Toronto: University of Toronto Press, 2009), 222.

48. For more on Cambodian refugees and worm picking, see McLellan, *Cambodian Refugees in Ontario.*

49. Ruth Wilson Gilmore, *Golden Gulag: Prisons, Surplus, Crisis, and Opposition in Globalizing California* (Berkeley: University of California Press, 2007), 28.

50. Nirmala Erevelles, "The Color of Violence: Reflecting on Gender, Race, and Disability in Wartime," in *Feminist Disability Studies*, ed. Kim Q. Hall (Bloomington: Indiana University Press, 2011), 118.

51. Helen Meekosha, "Decolonising Disability: Thinking and Acting Globally," *Disability and Society* 26, no. 6 (2011): 667–668.

52. Puar, *Right to Maim*, 89.

53. Ibid., 16.

54. Ibid., 11.

55. Natalia Duong, "Agent Orange Bodies: Việt, Đức, and Transnational Narratives of Repair," *Canadian Review of American Studies* 48, no. 3 (2018): 387–414, 395.

56. Duong, "Agent Orange Bodies," 396.

57. H-Dirksen L. Bauman and Joseph J. Murray, "Deaf Studies in the 21st Century: 'Deaf-Gain' and the Future of Human Diversity," in *The Disability Studies Reader*, 4th ed., ed. Lennard J. Davis (New York: Routledge, 2013), 246. See also, Michael Davidson, "Cleavings: Critical Losses in the Politics of Gain," *Disability Studies Quarterly* 36, no. 2 (2016), accessed March 27, 2022, available at https://dsq-sds.org/article/view/4287/4307.

58. Rosemarie Garland-Thomson, "Becoming Disabled," *New York Times*, August 19, 2016, accessed March 27, 2022, available at https://www.nytimes.com/2016/08/21/opinion/sunday/becoming-disabled.html.

59. Rosemarie Garland-Thomson, quoted in Dianna Douglas, "Disability Matters Series Creates Dialogue about the Benefit of Differences," *UChicago News*, January 17, 2014, accessed March 27, 2022, available at https://news.uchicago.edu/story/disability-matters-series-creates-dialogue-about-benefit-differences.

60. Puar, *Right to Maim*, xvii.

61. Ibid., 67–68.

62. Liat Ben-Moshe, *Decarcerating Disability: Deinstitutionalization and Prison Abolition* (Minneapolis: University of Minnesota Press, 2020), 31.

63. Puar, *Right to Maim*, 67.

64. Clare, *Brilliant Imperfection*, 8.

65. Ibid., 56.

66. For more on the supercrip figure, see Eli Clare, *Exile and Pride: Disability, Queerness, and Liberation* (Durham, NC: Duke University Press, 2015).

67. Robert McRuer, *Crip Times: Disability, Globalization, and Resistance* (New York: New York University Press, 2018), 128.

68. Gada Mahrouse, "Producing the Figure of the 'Super-Refugee' through Discourses of Success, Exceptionalism, Ableism, and Inspiration," in *Refugee States: Critical Refugee Studies in Canada*, ed. Vinh Nguyen and Thy Phu (Toronto: University of Toronto Press, 2021), 173–193, 182.

69. Yến Lê Espiritu, *Body Counts: The Vietnam War and Militarized Refugees* (Berkeley: University of California Press, 2014), 110.

70. Eric Tang, *Unsettled: Cambodian Refugees in the New York City Hyperghetto* (Philadelphia: Temple University Press, 2015), 21.

71. Vinh Nguyen, "Refugeetude," 121.

72. Hannah Arendt, "We Refugees," in *The Jewish Writings*, ed. Jerome Kohn and Ron H. Feldman (New York: Schocken Books, 2007), 274.

73. Anthony Veasna So, quoted in Jane Hu, "On Anthony Veasna So," *n+1*, September 5, 2018, accessed March 27, 2022, available at https://nplusonemag.com/online-only/online-only/on-anthony-veasna-so/.

74. Thi Bui, *The Best We Could Do: An Illustrated Memoir* (New York: Abrams ComicArts, 2017).

75. Michel Foucault, "Michel Foucault on Refugees—An Interview from 1979," interview by H. Uno, originally published on August 17, 1979, in *Shûkan posuto*, 34–35. Translated from Japanese into French by Ryôji Nakamura, 1994; translated from French into English by Felix de Montety, October 20, 2015, accessed March 27, 2022, available at https://politheor.net/michel-foucault-on-refugees-an-interview-from-1979/.

76. For more on the New Cold War, see Nikhil Pal Singh, "Cold War Redux: On the 'New Totalitarianism,'" *Radical History Review*, no. 85 (2003): 171–181; Chris Chien and Ellie Tse, "'The Hong Kong Card': Against the New Cold War," *The Abusable Past*, October 23, 2019, accessed March 27, 2022, available at https://www.radicalhistoryreview.org/abusablepast/the-hong-kong-card-against-the-new-cold-war/.

77. Ai Weiwei, "The Refugee Crisis Isn't about Refugees. It's about Us," *The Guardian*, February 2, 2018, accessed March 27, 2022, available at https://www.theguardian.com/commentisfree/2018/feb/02/refugee-crisis-human-flow-ai-weiwei-china.

78. Weiwei, "Refugee Crisis."

79. Ibid.

80. The category of "displaced subjects" includes internally displaced peoples, asylum seekers, and those officially recognized as "refugees." See Tina Chen and Cathy J. Schlund-Vials, "Editors' Introduction: On the Subjects of Displacement," *Verge: Studies in Global Asias* 6, no. 1 (2020): vi.

81. David Vine, Cala Coffman, Katalina Khoury, Madison Lovasz, Helen Bush, Rachael Leduc, and Jennifer Walkup, "Creating Refugees: Displacement Caused by the United States' Post-9/11 Wars," September 21, 2020, *Costs of War*, accessed March 27, 2022, available at https://watson.brown.edu/costsofwar/files/cow/imce/papers/2020 /Displacement_Vine%20et%20al_Costs%20of%20War%202020%2009%2008.pdf.

82. David Vine, *The United States of War: A Global History of America's Endless Conflicts, from Columbus to the Islamic State* (Oakland: University of California Press, 2020), 325.

83. For more on the use of suffering as epiphenomenal, see erin Khuê Ninh, "Without Enhancements: Sexual Violence in the Everyday Lives of Asian American Women," in *Asian American Feminisms and Women of Color Politics*, ed. Lynn Fujiwara and Shireen Roshanravan (Seattle: University of Washington Press, 2018), 73.

84. According to Spillers, "It is not customary that a studies protocol discloses either its provenance or its whereabouts. By the time it reaches us, it has already acquired the sanction of repetition, the authority of repression, and the blessings of time and mimesis so that, effectually, such a protocol now belongs to the smooth natural ordering of the cultural." Hortense J. Spillers, *Black, White, and in Color: Essays on American Literature and Culture* (Chicago: University of Chicago Press, 2003), 3.

85. Ben-Moshe, *Decarcerating Disability*, 27.

86. Ibid.

87. Ibid., 116.

88. Ibid., 5. Ben-Moshe explains that whereas "*[a]bleism* is oppression faced due to disability/impairment (perceived or lived) . . . *[s]anism* is oppression faced due to the imperative to be sane, rational, and non-mad/crazy/mentally ill/psychiatrically disabled," 16–17.

89. Gayatri Spivak, "Can the Subaltern Speak?" in *Marxism and the Interpretation of Culture*, ed. Cary Nelson and Lawrence Grossberg (Urbana: University of Illinois Press, 1988), 271–313. More recently, Olúfẹ́mi O. Táíwò, in "Being-in-the-Room Privilege: Elite Capture and Epistemic Deference," *The Philosopher* 108, no. 4 (December 2020), accessed March 27, 2022, available at https://www.thephilosopher1923 .org/essay-taiwo, critiques the notion of "deference epistemology" as a practice grounded in the view that the experience of oppression or trauma is intrinsically "a prep school" for social justice organizing. Táíwò argues instead for a nuanced understanding of "standpoint epistemology" that goes beyond simple calls for deference, that "demands *more* rigour from science and knowledge production processes, not less." More rigor, in the case of the refugee's standpoint, might entail making space for listening and honoring the refugee's story without rushing to accept its legitimacy or radicality.

90. Mimi Thi Nguyen, *The Gift of Freedom: War, Debt, and Other Refugee Passages* (Durham, NC: Duke University Press, 2012), 30.

91. M. Nguyen, *Gift of Freedom*, 30.

92. Thomas Betro, quoted in *Mercury News*, "Life Story Motivates Work of Pentagon's 'Bomb Lady,'" December 1, 2007, accessed March 27, 2022, available at https:// www.mercurynews.com/2007/12/01/life-story-motivates-work-of-pentagons-bomb -lady/.

93. Mbembe, *Necropolitics*, 100.

94. "Life Story Motivates Work."

95. To watch the video ad from New Faces GOP, see "New Faces GOP," September 13, 2019, YouTube video, 0:30, accessed March 27, 2022, available at https://youtu.be/BG0T_hVMqLs.

96. "New Faces GOP," September 13, 2019, video, 0:30.

97. Dean Itsuji Saranillio, "Why Asian Settler Colonialism Matters: A Thought Piece on Critiques, Debates, and Indigenous Difference," *Settler Colonial Studies* 3, nos. 3–4 (2013): 280–294.

98. Laura Madokoro, "Peril and Possibility: A Contemplation of the Current State of Migration History and Settler Colonial Studies in Canada," *History Compass* 17, no. 1 (2018): 1.

99. Madokoro, "Peril and Possibility," 2.

100. Iyko Day, *Alien Capital: Asian Racialization and the Logic of Settler Colonial Capitalism* (Durham, NC: Duke University Press, 2016), 21.

101. Day, *Alien Capital*, 21. For more on Asian-Indigenous and Indigenous-Refugee relations, see also Malissa Phung, "Asian-Indigenous Relationalities: Literary Gestures of Respect and Gratitude," *Canadian Literature* 227 (2015): 56–72; Quynh Nhu Le, *Unsettled Solidarities: Asian and Indigenous Cross-Representations in the Américas* (Philadelphia: Temple University Press, 2019); Ma Vang, *History on the Run: Secrecy, Fugitivity, and Hmong Refugee Epistemologies* (Durham, NC: Duke University Press, 2020).

102. Evyn Lê Espiritu Gandhi, *Archipelago of Resettlement: Vietnamese Refugee Settlers and Decolonization across Guam and Israel-Palestine* (Oakland: University of California Press, 2022).

103. Tang, *Unsettled*, 6.

104. Ibid., 5.

105. Current statistics detailing the high rates of incarceration, poverty, diabetes, and deportation in the Cambodian American community continue to trouble any kind of easy characterization of Cambodian American refugees as settled in the literal sense. For more on this, see Sucheng Chan, *Survivors: Cambodian Refugees in the United States* (Urbana: University of Illinois Press, 2004). Chan explains that "overall, some 40 percent of Cambodian [Americans] still live below the poverty line. Since the 1996 'welfare reform' legislation was enacted, those who can hold any kind of job at all have been pushed into the working-poor segment of the ethnic community," 137.

106. For more on Indigenous peoples in Cambodia, see Jonathan Padwe, *Disturbed Forests, Fragmented Memories: Jarai and Other Lives in the Cambodian Highlands* (Seattle: University of Washington Press, 2020); Krisna Uk, *Salvage: Cultural Resilience among the Jorai of Northeast Cambodia* (Ithaca, NY: Cornell University Press, 2016).

107. Michael Vickery, "Cambodia," *Anthropological Archive Database*, 1961, accessed May 9, 2021, available at https://www.sac.or.th/databases/anthroarchive/en/file.php?collection_name=MV&level_name=File&s_reference=MV_01&ss_reference=&f_reference=MV_01_02&s_id=156&ss_id=&f_id=287.

108. Uk, *Salvage*, xiv.

109. Ibid., xxii.

110. Ibid., xxiii.

111. For more on being wayward, undisciplined, and crip in our scholarship, see Saidiya Hartman, *Wayward Lives, Beautiful Experiments: Intimate Histories of Riotous Black Girls, Troublesome Women and Queer Radicals* (New York: W. W. Norton, 2019);

Christina Sharpe, *In the Wake: On Blackness and Being* (Durham, NC: Duke University Press, 2016); McRuer, *Crip Times*.

112. Merri Lisa Johnson and Robert McRuer, "Cripistemologies: Introduction," *Journal of Literary and Cultural Disability Studies* 8, no. 2 (2014): 136.

113. Vang, *History on the Run*, 24.

114. Ibid.

115. Puar, *Right to Maim*, 65.

116. Viet Thanh Nguyen and Janet Hoskins, "Transpacific Studies: Critical Perspectives on an Emerging Field," in *Transpacific Studies: Framing an Emerging Field*, ed. Viet Thanh Nguyen and Janet Hoskins (Honolulu: University of Hawaii Press, 2014), 2. For more on transpacific studies, see also, Denise Cruz, *Transpacific Femininities: The Making of the Modern Filipina* (Durham, NC: Duke University Press, 2012); Christopher B. Patterson, *Transitive Cultures: Anglophone Literature of the Transpacific* (New Brunswick, NJ: Rutgers University Press, 2018); Lily Wong, *Transpacific Attachments: Sex Work, Media Networks, and Affective Histories of Chineseness* (New York: Columbia University Press, 2018); Erin Suzuki, "Transpacific," in *The Routledge Companion to Asian American and Islander Literature*, ed. Rachel C. Lee (London: Routledge, 2014): 352–364; Aimee Bahng, *Migrant Futures: Decolonizing Speculation in Financial Times* (Durham, NC: Duke University Press, 2017); Aimee Bahng and Erin Suzuki, "The Transpacific Subject in Asian American Culture," in *The Oxford Encyclopedia of Asian American Literature and Culture*, ed. Josephine Lee (Oxford: Oxford University Press, 2020).

117. Nguyen and Hoskins, "Transpacific Studies," 3.

118. Yến Lê Espiritu, Lisa Lowe, and Lisa Yoneyama, "Transpacific Entanglements," in *Flashpoints for Asian American Studies*, ed. Cathy J. Schlund-Vials (New York: Fordham University Press, 2017), 175.

119. Espiritu, Lowe, and Yoneyama, "Transpacific Entanglements," 176.

120. Tiara R. Naʻputi and Michael Lujan Bevacqua, "Militarization and Resistance from Guåhan: Protecting and Defending Pågat," *American Quarterly* 67, no. 3 (2015): 839.

121. Bahng and Suzuki, "Transpacific Subject."

122. Tina Chen, "The Transpacific Turns," *The Oxford Encyclopedia of Asian American Literature and Culture*, January 30, 2020, accessed March 27, 2022, available at https://oxfordre.com/literature/view/10.1093/acrefore/9780190201098.001.0001/acrefore-9780190201098-e-782.

123. T. Chen, "Transpacific Turns."

124. Christine Kim and Helen Hok-Sze Leung, "Minor Transpacific: A Roundtable Discussion," *BC Studies*, no. 198 (Summer 2018): 13–36.

125. C. Kim and Leung, "Minor Transpacific."

126. Ibid., 15.

127. Lisa Yoneyama, "Toward a Decolonial Genealogy of the Transpacific," in *The Chinese Factor: Reorienting Global Imaginaries in American Studies*, ed. Chih-ming Wang and Yu-Fang Cho, special issue, *American Quarterly* 69, no. 3 (September 2017): 472.

128. I use the word "phase" here hesitatingly since I am aware of the problems of suggesting a teleology of progress where the "transpacific" evolves from the "autobiographical" or "national" as a qualifier for a more sophisticated form of cultural pro-

duction. As I suggest in this section, it is important that we appreciate the function of Cambodian testimonial writing in its own time and context.

129. Teri Shaffer Yamada, "Cambodian American Autobiography: Testimonial Discourse," in *Form and Transformation in Asian American Literature*, ed. Zhou Xiaojing and Samina Najmi (Seattle: University of Washington Press, 2005), 146.

130. See Larry Clinton Thompson's *Refugee Workers in the Indochina Exodus, 1975–1982* (Jefferson, NC: McFarland, 2010) in which he writes that "many Western intellectuals were favorable to the KR or regarded reports of its brutality as tall tales told by refugees," 130.

131. Yamada, "Cambodian American Autobiography," 150.

132. Ibid., 147.

133. George Yudice, "Testimonio and Postmodernism," *Latin American Perspectives* 18, no. 3 (Summer 1991): 17.

134. Yudice, "Testimonio and Postmodernism," 17.

135. A. Naomi Paik, *Rightlessness: Testimony and Redress in U.S. Prison Camps since World War II* (Chapel Hill: University of North Carolina Press, 2016), 14.

136. Paik, *Rightlessness*, 15.

137. See Cathy J. Schlund-Vials, "Refugee Aesthetics: Cambodia, Laos, and the Hmong," in *The Cambridge History of Asian American Literature*, ed. Rajini Srikanth and Min Hyoung Song (Cambridge: Cambridge University Press, 2015), 484–500.

138. See Jodi Kim, *Ends of Empire: Asian American Critique and the Cold War* (Minneapolis: University of Minnesota Press, 2010).

139. Chloe Baker, "Cambodia Here and Now," *artpress*, October 21, 2019, accessed March 27, 2022, available at https://www.pressreader.com/france/artpress/20191021/283003991586844.

140. Tian Veasna, *Year of the Rabbit* (Montreal: Drawn and Quarterly, 2020), 86.

141. For more on the Cambodian understanding of "emotional resistance," see Chanrithy Him, quoted in David Hutt, "Revealing Cambodia's Secret Khmer Rouge Resistance," *Southeast Asia Globe*, March 17, 2016, accessed March 27, 2022, available at https://southeastasiaglobe.com/cambodia-khmer-rouge-resistance-cham-uprising/?fbclid=IwAR0-wvzSRJr0G0Ry4-xa5rLbSbzEQbBxVeTmE5LLp2LyWDKZxMa3K1rHxW8.

142. For more on the Khmer Rouge's panoptic system of surveillance, see Boreth Ly, *Traces of Trauma: Cambodian Visual Culture and National Identity in the Aftermath of Genocide* (Honolulu: University of Hawaii Press, 2020), 59–61.

143. Ros Kosal, "Narrowcasters Audio Tour," Choeung Ek Genocidal Center, transcript, September 7, 2011, accessed March 27, 2022, available at http://www.cambodiatribunal.org/assets/pdf/reports/7Sept11%20CECG%20NC%20Audio%20Tour%20Script%20English%20As%20Recorded%20Media%20Version.pdf.

144. In her book, Um explains that the "surrealism" of the Cambodian experience "rendered many first-generation survivors mute, with tongues parched and heavy with pain and rage," (Khatharya Um, *From the Land of Shadows: War, Revolution, and the Making of the Cambodia Diaspora* [New York: New York University Press, 2015], 231). Um, *From the Land of Shadows*, 23.

145. Cheryl Glenn, *Unspoken: A Rhetoric of Silence* (Carbondale: Southern Illinois University Press, 2004), 11.

146. Laura Hyun Yi Kang, "Epistemologies," in *A Companion to Gender Studies*, ed. Philomena Essed, David Theo Goldberg, and Audrey Kobayashi, 1st ed. (Malden, MA: Blackwell Publishing, 2005), 73.

147. Karen Barad, *Meeting the Universe Halfway: Quantum Physics and the Entanglement of Matter and Meaning* (Durham, NC: Duke University Press, 2017), 185. For more on the concept of ontoepistemologies, see Denise Ferreira da Silva, "Notes for a Critique of the 'Metaphysics of Race,'" *Theory, Culture and Society* 28, no. 1 (2011): 138–148; as well as Jasbir Puar's discussion of the shift from "epistemological corrective to ontological irreducibility," *Right to Maim*, 18–21.

148. Puar, *Right to Maim*, 18.

149. Johnson and McRuer, "Cripistemologies," 140.

150. Adania Shibli, "Adania Shibli in Conversation with Madeleine Thien," *Literary Hub*, June 9, 2020, accessed March 27, 2022, available at https://lithub.com/watch-adania-shibli-in-conversation-with-madeleine-thien/.

151. Shibli, "Adania Shibli in Conversation."

152. Rey Chow, *Not Like a Native Speaker: On Languaging as a Postcolonial Experience* (New York: Columbia University Press, 2014), 15.

153. For a well-known literary depiction of aphasia as resistance in a postcolonial context, see Assia Djebar, *Fantasia: An Algerian Cavalcade* (Portsmouth, NH: Heinemann, 1993).

154. Lee Kuan Yew, "Speech by the Prime Minister, Mr. Kuan Yew, at the state dinner in his honour given by the head of state of Cambodia, Samdech Norodom Sihanouk, in Phnom Penh on December 7th, 1967," National Archives of Singapore, accessed March 30, 2021, available at https://www.nas.gov.sg/archivesonline/data/pdfdoc/lky19671207b.pdf.

155. Yew, "Speech by the Prime Minister."

156. Ibid.

157. Lee Kuan Yew, quoted in Claire Knox, "Cambodia's Affordable Housing Crisis," *Globe*, March 31, 2017, accessed March 27, 2022, available at https://southeastasiaglobe.com/cambodias-affordable-housing-crisis/.

158. Tilman Baumgärtel, *Kon: The Cinema of Cambodia* (Phnom Penh: VS Vann Sophea, 2010), 3, accessed August 13, 2019, available at https://southeastasiancinema.files.wordpress.com/2010/10/kon-the-cinema-of-cambodia.pdf.

159. Baumgärtel, *Kon*, 3.

160. John Pirozzi, quoted in Ben Sisario, "'Don't Think I've Forgotten,' a Documentary, Revives Cambodia's Silenced Sounds," *New York Times*, April 9, 2015, accessed August 20, 2019, available at https://www.nytimes.com/2015/04/12/movies/dont-think-ive-forgotten-a-documentary-revives-cambodias-silenced-sounds.html.

161. Youk Chang, quoted in Sisario, "'Don't Think I've Forgotten.'"

162. Sharon May and Soth Polin, "Beyond Words: An Interview with Soth Polin." *Manoa* 16, no. 1, (2004): 9–20, 17.

163. FONKi Yav, quoted in Mercedes Grundy, "Street Artist FONKi Takes Us on a Journey through Phnom Penh to Share Cambodia's Artistic Renaissance," *CBC Arts*, Janaury 25, 2021, accessed March 28, 2022, available at https://www.cbc.ca/arts/street-artist-fonki-takes-us-on-a-journey-through-phnom-penh-to-share-cambodia-s-artistic-renaissance-1.5882254..

164. FONKi Yav, quoted in Peter Knegt, "Montreal Graffiti Artist FONKi Returns to His 'Roots' in Powerful Documentary," *CBC Arts*, April 5, 2016, accessed March 25, 2022, available at https://www.cbc.ca/arts/montreal-graffiti-artist-fonki -returns-to-his-roots-in-powerful-documentary-1.3521712

165. Rob Nixon, *Slow Violence and the Environmentalism of the Poor* (Cambridge, MA: Harvard University Press, 2011), 31.

166. Nixon, *Slow Violence*, 31.

167. Ibid., 32.

168. See Elda E. Tsou, *Unquiet Tropes: Form, Race, and Asian American Literature* (Philadelphia: Temple University Press, 2015), 3, in which she claims that "the past decade has witnessed a resurgence of scholarly interest in form and aesthetics, which Marjorie Levinson has termed a 'new formalism.' What differentiates this formalism from previous versions is its commitment to yoking the study of form to history and politics."

169. Timothy K. August, *The Refugee Aesthetic: Reimagining Southeast Asian America* (Philadelphia: Temple University Press, 2021), 23.

170. Saidiya Hartman, quoted in Patricia J. Saunders, "Fugitive Dreams of Diaspora: Conversations with Saidiya Hartman," *Anthurium: A Caribbean Studies Journal* 6, no. 1 (2008): 5.

171. Trinh T. Minh-ha, quoted in Nancy N. Chen, "'Speaking Nearby': A Conversation with Trinh T. Minh-ha," *Visual Anthropology Review* 8, no. 1 (Spring 1992): 87.

172. Trinh T. Minh-ha, quoted in Nancy Chen, "Speaking Nearby," 87.

173. Ibid.

174. Madeleine Thien, quoted in Fiona Tinwei Lam, "Madeleine Thien on Making Fragments Whole," *The Tyee*, September 1, 2011, accessed March 25, 2022, available at https://thetyee.ca/Books/2011/09/01/Madeleine-Thien/.

175. Madeleine Thien, quoted in Hsiu-chuan Lee, "Writing, History, and Music in *Do Not Say We Have Nothing*: A Conversation with Madeleine Thien," *Canadian Literature* 238 (2019): 16.

176. Madeleine Thien, quoted in Heather, "Interview with Author Madeleine Thien," *The Unexpected Twists and Turns* (blog), June 27, 2011, accessed March 27, 2022, available at http://www.theunexpectedtnt.com/2011/06/interview-with-madeleine -thien.html.

177. *The Missing Picture*, directed by Rithy Panh (Cannes: Les Acacias, 2013).

178. Rithy Panh and Christophe Bataille, *The Elimination: A Survivor of the Khmer Rouge Confronts His Past and the Commandant of the Killing Fields*, trans. John Cullen (New York: Other Press, 2013), 162.

CHAPTER 1

1. Anne Penketh, "Snow 'Looks Nice' to Asian Refugees," *Montreal Gazette*, December 4, 1980, accessed March 27, 2022, available at https://news.google.com/news papers?nid=1946&dat=19801204&id=zmUxAAAAIBAJ&sjid=waQFAAAAIBAJ&pg =4281,1294274&hl=en.

2. Anne Penketh, "Snow."

3. Ibid.

4. Ibid.

5. Ibid.

6. Ibid.

7. Ibid.

8. Rithy Panh and Christophe Bataille, *The Elimination: A Survivor of the Khmer Rouge Confronts His Past and the Commandant of the Killing Fields*, trans. John Cullen (New York: Other Press, 2013), 258.

9. Panh and Bataille, *The Elimination*, 258.

10. Việt Lê, "What Remains: Returns, Representation, and Traumatic Memory in 'S-21: The Khmer Rouge Killing Machine' and 'Refugee,'" *American Quarterly* 66 no. 2 (June 2014): 301–332, 327.

11. Panh and Bataille, *The Elimination*, 259.

12. Davi Hyder (former refugee camp relief worker), in discussion with the author, March 31, 2021.

13. Colin Grafton (former refugee camp relief worker), in discussion with the author, March 31, 2021.

14. Colin Grafton, "Colin Grafton—Cambodia 1972–75 / Thai border 1980," photo caption, accessed March 27, 2022, available at https://colingrafton.wixsite.com /phnompenh1973/ettap?lightbox=dataItem-jd1dihus.

15. For more on the method of "listening to images," see Tina M. Campt, *Listening to Images* (Durham, NC: Duke University Press, 2017).

16. Paul Thomas Chamberlin, *The Cold War's Killing Fields: Rethinking the Long Peace* (New York: Harper-Collins, 2018), 11.

17. "Anecdote," *Merriam-Webster*, accessed May 10, 2021, available at https:// www.merriam-webster.com/dictionary/anecdote.

18. erin Khuê Ninh, "Without Enhancements: Sexual Violence in the Everyday Lives of Asian American Women," in *Asian American Feminisms and Women of Color Politics*, ed. Lynn Fujiwara and Shireen Roshanravan (Seattle: University of Washington Press, 2018), 71.

19. Ninh, "Without Enhancements," 71.

20. Ibid., 72.

21. Ma Vang, *History on the Run: Secrecy, Fugitivity, and Hmong Refugee Epistemologies* (Durham, NC: Duke University Press, 2020), 9.

22. Vang, *History on the Run*, 9.

23. Ibid.

24. Ibid., 22.

25. "Wayward Bomb Kills about 100," *Tuscaloosa News* (Tuscaloosa, AL), August 6, 1973.

26. Richard Nixon, quoted in Lou Cannon, "Nixon: I Gave Order for Secret Bombing," *St. Petersburg Times* (Saint Petersburg, FL), August 21, 1973, available at https://news.google.com/newspapers?nid=888&dat=19730821&id=BMANAAAAIBA J&sjid=-HIDAAAAIBAJ&pg=6122,8578&hl=en.

27. Nixon, quoted in Cannon, "Nixon."

28. Judith Butler, *Frames of War: When Is Life Grievable?* (London: Verso, 2009), 24.

29. Henry Kissinger, *The White House Years*, (Boston: Little, Brown and Company, 1979), 292.

30. See Henry Kissinger, quoted in "The Kissinger Telecons," *National Security Archive*, December 9, 1970, accessed March 27, 2022, available at https://nsarchive2.gwu .edu/NSAEBB/NSAEBB123/3%20%20Kissinger%20telcon%20with%20Haig.pdf.

31. This information was provided to me by Ian Hill, author of *Advocating Weapons, War, and Terrorism: Technological and Rhetorical Paradox*, email message to the author, September 24, 2021.

32. Kissinger, quoted in "Kissinger Telecons."

33. Nikhil Pal Singh, *Race and America's Long War* (Berkeley: University of California Press, 2017), 8.

34. Taylor Owen and Ben Kiernan, "Bombs over Cambodia," *The Walrus*, October 12, 2006, 63, accessed March 27, 2022, available at https://thewalrus.ca/2006-10-history/. See also Wade C. Roberts, *Landmines in Cambodia: Past, Present, and Future* (Amherst, NY: Cambria, 2011). According to Roberts, "Landmine/UXO incidents in Cambodia have permeated the boundaries of every district, maiming and killing tens of thousands," since the end of the Cold War (31).

35. "The Kissinger Telecons," *National Security Archive.*

36. Joel Brinkley, *Cambodia's Curse: The Modern History of a Troubled Land* (New York: Public-Affairs, 2011), xv.

37. From 2016 to 2018, I organized field study courses in Siem Reap, Cambodia, for senior undergraduate students at my university in Hong Kong. To my dismay, students brought up *Cambodia's Curse* over and over again as the *one* book they had consulted when asked what kind of advanced research they had begun in preparation for their monthlong field study course.

38. For a historical overview of the White Building and efforts by Cambodian artists to combat the government's redevelopment plans, see Vuth Lyno, "Knowledge Sharing and Learning Together: Alternative Art Engagement from Stiev Selapak and Sa Sa Art Projects," *UDAYA: Journal of Khmer Studies* 12 (2014): 253–301.

39. For more on slum tourism, see Malte Steinbrink, "'We Did the Slum!'—Urban Poverty Tourism in Historical Perspective," *Tourism Geographies: An International Journal of Tourism Space, Place, and Environment* 14, no. 2 (2012): 213–234.

40. Achille Mbembe, *On the Postcolony* (Berkeley: University of California Press, 2001), 3.

41. Brinkley, *Cambodia's Curse*, 7–8.

42. Ibid., 31.

43. Ibid., 13.

44. Ibid., 15.

45. The "culture of passivity/violence thesis" can be seen in works such as Sheri Prasso, "Cambodia: A Heritage of Violence," *World Policy Journal* 11, no. 3 (Fall 1994): 71–77; Seanglim Bit, *The Warrior Heritage: A Psychological Perspective of Cambodian Trauma* (Hayward, CA: Seanglim Bit, 1991).

46. Brinkley, *Cambodia's Curse*, 11–12.

47. Ibid., 222.

48. Ibid., 15.

49. Ibid., 9.

50. Mbembe, *On the Postcolony*, 4.

51. Frantz Fanon, *The Wretched of the Earth*, trans. Constance Farrington (New York: Grove, 1963), 43, 37.

52. Fanon, *Wretched of the Earth*, 4.

53. Penny Edwards, *Cambodge: The Cultivation of a Nation, 1860–1945* (Honolulu: University of Hawaii Press, 2007), 9.

54. *L'Illustration*, quoted in Edwards, *Cambodge*, 39.

55. Edward W. Said, *Orientalism* (New York: Vintage Books, 1979), 1.

56. Panivong Norindr, *Phantasmatic Indochina: French Colonial Ideology in Architecture, Film, and Literature* (Durham, NC: Duke University Press, 1996), 1.

57. Edwards, *Cambodge*, 14.

58. Ibid.

59. See Amitav Ghosh, *Dancing in Cambodia and Other Essays* (New York: Penguin, 2002), 37.

60. Anna Blair, "Cambodian Dancers, Auguste Rodin, and the Imperial Imagination," *The Appendix*, December 9, 2014, accessed March 27, 2022, available at http:// theappendix.net/issues/2014/10/cambodian-dancers-auguste-rodin-and-the-imperial -imagination.

61. Blair, "Cambodian Dancers."

62. Ibid.

63. Ibid.

64. Ghosh, *Dancing in Cambodia*, 1.

65. Ibid., 25.

66. Ibid., 24.

67. *Eat, Pray, Love*, directed and written by Ryan Murphy (2010; Culver City, CA: Sony Pictures Releasing, 2010).

68. *Eat, Pray, Love.*

69. Ibid.

70. Elizabeth Gilbert, *Eat, Pray, Love: One Woman's Search for Everything Across Italy, India and Indonesia* (New York: Viking, 2006), 157.

71. Maggie Nelson, *The Argonauts* (Minneapolis: Graywolf, 2015), 120–121.

72. During Pol Pot time, Khmer Rouge soldiers killed women and children before discarding their bodies in a mass grave. As Ros Kosal, the voice of the audio guide at Choeung Ek, says: "Of all the graves here at Choeung Ek, this may well be the most difficult to think about. . . . Why kill children? Why this brutal way? First it was quick and easy. Also, when one member of a family was murdered all the rest were killed too so no one would be left alive to seek revenge. . . . Another Khmer Rouge slogan: 'to dig up the grass, one must remove even the roots,'" "Narrowcasters Audio Tour," Choeung Ek Genocidal Center, transcript, September 7, 2011, accessed March 27, 2022, available at http://www.cambodiatribunal.org/assets/pdf/reports/7Sept11%20 CECG%20NC%20Audio%20Tour%20Script%20English%20As%20Recorded%20 Media%20Version.pdf.

73. Ghosh, *Dancing in Cambodia*, 23.

74. To see a clip of this speech by Westmoreland, see the film *Hearts and Minds*, directed by Peter Davis (Cannes, France: Rainbow Releasing, Warner Bros., 1974), DVD.

75. See Sylvia Shin Huey Chong's discussion of the Cambodian setting of *Apocalypse Now* in *The Oriental Obscene: Violence and Racial Fantasies in the Vietnam Era* (Durham, NC: Duke University Press, 2012), 154–162.

76. Robert McRuer, *Crip Times: Disability, Globalization, and Resistance* (New York: New York University Press, 2018), 22.

77. Liat Ben-Moshe, *Decarcerating Disability: Deinstitutionalization and Prison Abolition* (Minneapolis: University of Minnesota Press, 2020), 23–24.

CHAPTER 2

1. Lisa Yoneyama, *Cold War Ruins: Transpacific Critique of American Justice and Japanese War Crimes* (Durham, NC: Duke University Press, 2016), viii.

2. See *Year Zero: The Silent Death of Cambodia*, directed by David Munro and written by John Pilger (London: Associated Television, 1979), accessed May 31, 2018, available at http://johnpilger.com/videos/year-zero-the-silent-death-of-cambodia.

3. For more on collateral damage, see Eric Tang, "Collateral Damage: Southeast Asian Poverty in the United States," *Social Text* 62, vol. 18, no. 1 (Spring 2000): 59–79.

4. Jasbir K. Puar, *The Right to Maim: Debility, Capacity, Disability* (Durham, NC: Duke University Press, 2017), 128.

5. Puar, *Right to Maim*, 90.

6. Ibid., xix.

7. Ibid., 73.

8. Ibid., xiii–xiv.

9. Ibid., 27.

10. For more on the work of soldiering in U.S. wars in the transpacific, see Simeon Man, *Soldiering through Empire: Race and the Making of the Decolonizing Pacific* (Oakland: University of California Press, 2018).

11. Nikhil Pal Singh, *Race and America's Long War* (Berkeley: University of California Press, 2017), 8–9.

12. William Patterson, *We Charge Genocide: The Historic Petition to the United Nations for Relief from a Crime of the United States Government against the Negro People* (New York: Civil Rights Congress, 1951), 8.

13. Man, *Soldiering through Empire*, 2.

14. *Shiiku, the Catch*, directed by Rithy Panh (Phnom Penh, Cambodia: Arte, 2011), DVD, was shot entirely with a Cambodian team, with the exception of Cyril Guei (the U.S. pilot in the film), who is a French actor of Ivorian descent. Most of the dialogue is spoken in Khmer and translated on the screen with English subtitles. When it was released in 2011, the film screened at major international film festivals such as the Toronto International Film Festival, the Hong Kong International Film Festival, and the Twenty-Fourth Tokyo International Film Festival, where it was nominated for Best Asian–Middle Eastern Film Award.

15. Kenzaburo Oe's *Shiiku* is also the source text of a 1961 film titled *The Catch*, directed by Japanese auteur Nagisa Ōshima, who, like Oe, is known for the antiwar themes that mark his work.

16. Christine Hong, *A Violent Peace: Race, U.S. Militarism, and Cultures of Democratization in Cold War Asia and the Pacific* (Stanford, CA: Stanford University Press, 2020), 59.

17. Christine Hong, *Violent Peace*, 59.

18. Rithy Panh, quoted in James Dingle, "A Completely Cambodian Production— Interview with Rithy Panh," *The Advisor*, no. 4, December 26, 2011, accessed March

27, 2022, available at http://www.expat-advisory.com/articles/southeast-asia/cambodia /completely-cambodian-production-interview-rithy-panh?quicktabs_1=2.

19. For a history of female Khmer Rouge cadres, see Brent Crane, "Female Cadres of the Khmer Rouge," *Phnom Penh Post*, August 1, 2015, accessed March 27, 2022, available at https://www.phnompenhpost.com/post-weekend/female-cadres-khmer -rouge?

20. Achille Mbembe, *Necropolitics* (Durham, NC: Duke University Press, 2019), 86.

21. For more on the Khmer Rouge's recruitment of children as child soldiers, see Chhay Sophal, *Mom and Angkar's Kid* (self-pub., 2012).

22. Khatharya Um, *From the Land of Shadows: War, Revolution, and the Making of the Cambodia Diaspora* (New York: New York University Press, 2015), 113.

23. In this way, Panh's *Shiiku, the Catch* can be read in the context of contemporary discussions of reconciliation in Cambodia that have revisited the previously held rigid distinction between victims and perpetrators. As James A. Tyner has said, in recent decades, there has been a growing "awareness of the brutal means by which children, especially, were recruited to serve the Khmer Rouge" (*Landscape, Memory, and Post-violence in Cambodia* [Lanham, MD: Rowman and Littlefield, 2017], 185); for more on this topic, see also Meng-Try Ea and Sorya Sim, *Victims and Perpetrators? Testimony of Young Khmer Rouge Comrades* (Phnom Penh: Documentation Center of Cambodia, 2001); Burcu Munyas, "Genocide in the Minds of Cambodian Youth: Transmitting (Hi)stories of Genocide to the Second and Third Generation in Cambodia," *Journal of Genocide Research* 10, no. 3 (2008): 417; Khamboly Dy, "Genocide Education in Cambodia: Local Initiatives, Global Connections" (Ph.D. diss., Rutgers University, 2015), 208; Cathy J. Schlund-Vials and Samuel Martinez, "Interrogating the Perpetrator: Violation, Culpability and Human Rights," in *Interrogating the Perpetrator: Violation, Culpability, and Human Rights*, ed. Cathy Schlund-Vials and Samuel Martinez (London: Routledge, 2017): 1–6.

24. Mbembe, *Necropolitics*, 81–82.

25. For more on the U.S. military's "view from above," see Caran Kaplan, *Aerial Aftermaths: Wartime from Above* (Durham, NC: Duke University Press, 2018).

26. The archival footage of the U.S. bombing of Cambodia was shot by U.S. Air Force servicemen and sourced from the U.S. National Archives and Records Administration.

27. *Shiiku, the Catch*, directed by Rithy Panh (Phnom Penh, Cambodia: Arte, 2011).

28. Christine Hong, *Violent Peace*, 59.

29. For an insightful analysis of this aspect of the film, see Cathy J. Schlund-Vials, "Aerial Aftermaths and Reckonings from Below: Reseeing Rithy Panh's *Shiiku, the Catch*," in *The Cinema of Rithy Panh: Everything Has a Soul* (New Brunswick, NJ: Rutgers University Press, 2021), 86–98.

30. Panh, *Shiiku, the Catch*.

31. Tyner, *Landscape, Memory, and Post-violence*, 162.

32. Panh, *Shiiku, the Catch*.

33. See Ian Hill, "Not Quite Bleeding from the Ears: Amplifying Sonic Torture," *Western Journal of Communication* 76, no. 3 (2012): 218, who defines "sonic torture" as the use of "sound reproduction technologies to blast prisoners with a continuous noise at peak loudness in order to coerce cooperation." While, according to this definition, sonic torture is not the same as the incidental sounds of explosions and reverberations

during an airstrike, Hill's arguments about the military's use of sonic torture in prisons can be extrapolated to the psychological damage caused by sound exposure in a bomb zone.

34. Hill, "Not Quite Bleeding," 218.

35. Panh, *Shiiku, the Catch*.

36. Puar, *Right to Maim*, 89.

37. Panh, *Shiiku, the Catch*.

38. Mel Chen, *Animacies: Biopolitics, Racial Mattering, and Queer Affect* (Durham, NC: Duke University Press, 2012), 188.

39. M. Chen, *Animacies*, 192.

40. Panh, *Shiiku, the Catch*.

41. Angela Naimou, *Salvage Work: U.S. and Caribbean Literatures amid the Debris of Legal Personhood* (New York: Fordham University Press, 2015), 8.

42. Taylor Owen and Ben Kiernan, "Bombs over Cambodia," *The Walrus*, October 12, 2006, accessed March 27, 2022, https://thewalrus.ca/2006-10-history/.

43. Mbembe, *Necropolitics*, 87.

44. Alex Catanese, "Painting the Tin Can," *Medium*, January 18, 2016, accessed March 27, 2022, available at https://medium.com/design-and/painting-the-tin-can -485964ddb44.

45. Catanese, "Painting the Tin Can."

46. "Guerrilla Tactics: An Overview," *PBS*, accessed April 19, 2021, available at https://www.pbs.org/battlefieldvietnam/guerrilla/.

47. Panh, *Shiiku, the Catch*.

48. Ibid.

49. Alexander G. Weheliye, *Habeas Viscus: Racializing Assemblages, Biopolitics, and Black Feminist Theories of the Human* (Durham: Duke University Press, 2014), 12.

50. Panh, *Shiiku, the Catch*.

51. Ibid.

52. Ibid.

53. Though the tweet is no longer publicly available, the author was able to confirm this from the author himself.

54. Christine Hong, *Violent Peace*, 15.

55. Viet Thanh Nguyen, "The Americans," *Chicago Tribune*, December 17, 2010, accessed March 27, 2022, available at https://www.chicagotribune.com/entertainment /books/chi-books-algren-the-americans-htmlstory.html.

56. Viet Thanh Nguyen, "The Americans."

57. Ibid.

58. Ibid.

59. Chinua Achebe, *Things Fall Apart* (Toronto: Anchor Canada, 2009); Ralph Ellison, *Flying Home and Other Stories* (New York: Vintage International, 1998); Toni Morrison, *Home* (New York: Alfred A. Knopf, 2012). For more on representations of the Black soldier in U.S. Black independent cinema, see Elizabeth Reich, *Militant Visions: Black Soldiers, Internationalism, and the Transformation of American Cinema* (New Brunswick, NJ: Rutgers University Press, 2016).

60. Viet Thanh Nguyen, "The Americans."

61. Rob Nixon, *Slow Violence and the Environmentalism of the Poor* (Cambridge, MA: Harvard University Press, 2011), 220.

62. Puar, *Right to Maim*, xxi.

63. Viet Thanh Nguyen, "The Americans."

64. Ibid.

65. Ibid.

66. Ibid.

67. Nixon, *Slow Violence*, 226.

68. Puar, *Right to Maim*, 81.

69. Viet Thanh Nguyen, "The Americans."

70. Puar, *Right to Maim*, 145.

71. Merri Lisa Johnson and Robert McRuer, "Cripistemologies: Introduction," *Journal of Literary and Cultural Disability Studies* 8, no. 2 (2014).

72. Viet Thanh Nguyen, "The Americans."

73. Ibid.

74. In her speech, Toni Morrison wrote that she had originally planned to call the paper "cannon fodder" because the term reminded her "of that host of young men—black or 'ethnics' or poor or working-class—who left high school for the war in Vietnam and were perceived by war resisters as 'fodder'" ("Unspeakable Things Unspoken: The Afro-American Presence in American Literature," October 7, 1988, University of Michigan, Ann Arbor, transcript, accessed Dec 28, 2021, available at https://tannerlectures.utah .edu/_resources/documents/a-to-z/m/morrison90.pdf).

75. Reich, *Militant Visions*, 8.

76. Viet Thanh Nguyen, "The Americans."

77. Ibid.

78. Ibid.

79. Ibid.

80. Ibid.

81. For more on the U.S. inner and outer wars, see Nikhil Pal Singh, *Race and America's Long War* (Berkeley: University of California Press, 2017).

82. Viet Thanh Nguyen, "The Americans."

83. Ibid.

84. Ibid.

85. Ibid.

86. Ibid.

87. Puar, *Right to Maim*, 12.

88. Viet Thanh Nguyen, "The Americans."

89. Ibid.

90. Ibid.

91. Ibid.

92. Ibid.

93. Ibid.

94. Eric Tang, *Unsettled: Cambodian Refugees in the New York City Hyperghetto* (Philadelphia: Temple University Press, 2015), 30.

95. Tang, *Unsettled*, 44.

96. See Liat Ben-Moshe, Chris Chapman, and Allison C. Carey, eds. *Disability Incarcerated: Imprisonment and Disability in the United States and Canada* (New York: Palgrave Macmillan, 2014).

97. Puar, *Right to Maim*, 74.

98. Julius Thiemann, "7 Questions with Kosal Khiev," *Phnom Penh Post*, November 23, 2012, accessed March 27, 2022, available at https://www.phnompenhpost.com/7days/7-questions-kosal-khiev?

99. For more on the deportation of Cambodian Americans and the Illegal Immigration Reform and Immigrant Responsibility Act, see Lisa Marie Cacho, *Social Death: Racialized Rightlessness and the Criminalization of the Unprotected* (New York: New York University Press, 2012).

100. See Peter Nyers, *Irregular Citizenship, Immigration, and Deportation* (London: Routledge, 2019), 2, who uses "'irregular citizenship' as an analytic that describes both the processes of control within the political subjectification process, and the lines of flight and movement toward other modes of being political."

101. See Leitner Center for International Law and Justice, 21, "Removing Refugees: U.S. Deportation Policy and the Cambodian-American Community," a report that explains how gang membership for Cambodian American youths "offered some young refugees a surrogate family and a sense of belonging. This activity is responsible for a significant percentage of the deportable offenses committed by Cambodian teens," accessed January 6, 2022, available at http://www.leitnercenter.org/files/2010%20Cambodia%20Report_FINAL.pdf.

102. This data is as of August 14, 2019. See Jonathan W. Rosen, "Deported to Their Parents' Homeland, Cambodian Americans Start Anew," *FP*, August 14, 2019, accessed March 27, 2022, available at https://foreignpolicy.com/2019/08/14/deported-to-their-parents-homeland-cambodian-americans-start-anew/. This article reports that, of the 733 Cambodian Americans deported, 16 are women.

103. Prak Chan Tul, "U.S. Deports 37 Cambodian Refugees after Criminal Convictions," *Reuters*, July 4, 2019, accessed March 27, 2022, available at https://www.reuters.com/article/us-usa-cambodia-deportees/u-s-deports-37-cambodian-refugees-after-criminal-convictions-idUSKCN1TZ0WF.

104. *Cambodian Son,* directed by Masahiro Sugano (2014; Phnom Penh, Cambodia: Studio Revolt, 2014), Vimeo USA.

105. Ibid.

106. Ibid.

107. Ibid.

108. Ibid.

109. Cathy Park Hong, *Minor Feelings*, (New York: One World, 2020), 55.

110. Loan Dao, "Refugee Representations: Southeast Asian American Youth, Hip Hop, and Immigrant Rights," *Amerasia Journal* 40, no. 2 (2014): 90.

111. Thy Phu, *Picturing Model Citizens: Civility in Asian American Visual Culture* (Philadelphia: Temple University Press, 2012), 152.

112. Phu, *Picturing Model Citizens*, 152.

113. Mimi Thi Nguyen, *The Gift of Freedom: War, Debt, and Other Refugee Passages* (Durham, NC: Duke University Press, 2012), 63.

114. M. Nguyen, *Gift of Freedom*.

115. Ibid.

116. Sugano, *Cambodian Son.*

117. Liat Ben-Moshe, *Decarcerating Disability: Deinstitutionalization and Prison Abolition* (Minneapolis: University of Minnesota Press, 2020), 8.

118. Jean Stewart and Marta Russell, "Disablement, Prison, and Historical Segregation," *Monthly Review* 53, no. 3 (2001): 61–75.

119. For more on how the system of racial capitalism in the United States works to collapse the imagination of racialized people, especially Black people, see Charlene Carruthers, *Unapologetic: A Black, Queer, and Feminist Mandate for Radical Movements* (Boston: Beacon, 2018).

120. Sugano, *Cambodian Sun.*

121. Ibid.

122. Ibid.

123. Ibid.

124. Ben-Moshe, *Decarcerating Disability*, 8.

125. Sugano, *Cambodian Son*; Kosal Khiev's chapbook *Finding Home* (Singapore: Red Wheelbarrow, 2013), 17, which explains that the poem "Moments in between the Nights" was written at Corcoran, in C Yard, in 2003.

126. Sugano, *Cambodian Son.*

127. I am referencing the text version of the poem (Khiev, "Moments in Between," in *Finding Home*, 17–20).

128. Ibid.

129. Ibid.

130. Ibid.

131. Ibid.

132. Ibid.

133. Ibid.

134. Ibid.

135. Ibid.

136. Tang, *Unsettled*, 10.

137. Ibid., 13.

138. For more on carceral capitalism, see Jackie Wang, *Carceral Capitalism* (South Pasadena, CA: Semiotext[e], 2018), 69, who examines "the ways in which the carceral techniques of the state are shaped by—and work in tandem with—the imperatives of global capitalism."

139. Robert McRuer, *Crip Times: Disability, Globalization, and Resistance* (New York: New York University Press, 2018), 174.

140. Ibid.

141. Ta-Nehisi Coates, *Between the World and Me* (New York: One World, 2015), 110.

142. Coates, *Between the World and Me*, 110.

143. Ibid., 111.

144. McRuer, *Crip Times*, 133.

145. Sugano, *Cambodian Son.*

146. Ibid.

147. Ibid.

148. Ibid.

149. McRuer, *Crip Times*, 175.

150. Sugano, *Cambodian Son*.

151. Ibid.

152. Kosal Khiev, quoted in Helier Cheung, "Kosal Khiev's Journey from Prison to Poetry," *BBC News*, February 10, 2014, accessed March 27, 2022, available at https://www.bbc.com/news/world-asia-24923096.

153. Sugano, *Cambodian Son*.

154. Khiev, quoted in Cheung, "Kosal Khiev's Journey."

155. Ibid.

156. Vinh Nguyen, *Lived Refuge: Gratitude, Resentment, Resilience*, (unpublished manuscript, January 17, 2022), typescript.

157. Sugano, *Cambodian Son*.

158. Ibid.

159. Puar, *Right to Maim*, 73.

160. Jodi Kim, "Settler Modernity, Debt Imperialism, and the Necropolitics of the Promise," *Social Text* 135, vol. 36, no. 2 (June 2018): 41.

161. William Heidt, quoted in Colin Meyn and Ben Sokhean, "US Hits Back at Government over $500 Million Debt, Democracy," *Cambodia Daily*, February 6, 2017, accessed January 7, 2022, available at https://english.cambodiadaily.com/news/us-hits-back-at-government-over-500m-debt-democracy-124612/.

162. Heidt, quoted in Meyn and Sokhean, "US Hits Back."

163. See Elizabeth Becker, quoted in George Wright, "With War-Era Debt Demands, US on Shaky Moral Ground," *Cambodia Daily*, February 10, 2017, accessed January 7, 2022, available at https://english.cambodiadaily.com/news/with-war-era-debt-demands-us-on-shaky-moral-ground-124912/. According to Becker, the United States' refusal to accept legal responsibility for the U.S. bombings is presumably "out of fear that the U.S. might have to pay war reparations for the destruction and that former American officials might be sued."

CHAPTER 3

1. Rithy Panh and Christophe Bataille, *The Elimination: A Survivor of the Khmer Rouge Confronts His Past and the Commandant of the Killing Fields*, trans. John Cullen (New York: Other Press, 2013), 258.

2. Cambodian American author Chanrithy Him singles out Joel Brinkley's book (*Cambodia's Curse: The Modern History of a Troubled Land* [New York: Public-Affairs, 2011]) as one of the key texts responsible for disseminating the problematic view that "Cambodians were passive and didn't rebel." See Chanrithy Him, quoted in David Hutt, "Revealing Cambodia's Secret Khmer Rouge Resistance," *Southeast Asia Globe*, March 17, 2016, accessed March 27, 2022, available at https://southeastasiaglobe.com/cambodia-khmer-rouge-resistance-cham-uprising/?fbclid=IwAR0-wvzSRJr0G0Ry4-xa5rLbSbzEQbBxVeTmE5LLp2LyWDKZxMa3K1rHxW8.

3. *The Missing Picture*, directed by Rithy Panh (2013; Phnom Penh, Cambodia: ARTE, 2013), DVD.

4. Youk Chhang, quoted in David Hutt, "Revealing Cambodia's Secret Khmer Rouge Resistance," *Southeast Asia Globe*, March 17, 2016, accessed March 27, 2022,

available at https://southeastasiaglobe.com/cambodia-khmer-rouge-resistance-cham
-uprising/?fbclid=IwAR0-wvzSRJr0G0Ry4-xa5rLbSbzEQbBxVeTmE5LLp2LyWDKZ
xMa3K1rHxW8.

5. Robert McRuer, *Crip Times: Disability, Globalization, and Resistance* (New
York: New York University Press, 2018), 23.

6. McRuer, *Crip Times*, 23.

7. Ibid., 22.

8. Merri Lisa Johnson and Robert McRuer, "Cripistemologies: Introduction,"
Journal of Literary and Cultural Disability Studies 8, no. 2 (2014): 142.

9. Johnson and McRuer, "Cripistemologies," 134.

10. Ibid., 135.

11. Ibid., 137.

12. Ibid., 130.

13. Vaddey Ratner, quoted in Jack Smith, "In the Shadow of Terror," *The Writer
Magazine*, May 6, 2013, accessed March 27, 2022, https://www.writermag.com/writing
-inspiration/author-interviews/in-the-shadow-of-terror/.

14. Vaddey Ratner, quoted in "Living to Tell the Tale," *Punch Magazine*, June
30, 2017, accessed March 27, 2022, available at https://thepunchmagazine.com/the
-byword/interviews/living-to-tell-the-tale.

15. Vaddey Ratner, "Author's Note," *In the Shadow of the Banyan* (New York: Simon and Schuster, 2012), 319.

16. Ratner's second novel is *Music of the Ghosts* (New York: Atria Books, 1st ed.,
2017). In many ways a follow-up to Ratner's first novel, *Music of the Ghosts* takes the
reader beyond the Khmer Rouge years to the present day of the novel's protagonist,
Suteera, and her life in America as a Cambodian refugee. Centering on the plot of
Suteera's journey from Minneapolis to Cambodia, ostensibly to scatter the ashes of
her deceased aunt, the narrative then unfolds a story about Suteera's search for long-
awaited answers about her father's disappearance during the Cambodian Genocide.

17. Jasbir K. Puar, *The Right to Maim: Debility, Capacity, Disability* (Durham,
NC: Duke University Press, 2017), xiv.

18. For more on Ratner's polio, see Lynn Neary, "In The 'Shadow' of Death,
Stories Survive," *NPR*, August 14, 2012, accessed March 27, 2022, available at https://
www.npr.org/2012/08/14/158691935/in-the-shadow-of-death-stories-survive.

19. Puar, *Right to Maim*, xvii.

20. Johnson and McRuer, "Cripistemologies," 133.

21. Ratner, quoted in *Punch Magazine*, "Living."

22. Ibid.

23. Ratner, *In the Shadow of the Banyan*, 127.

24. For more about the Khmer Rouge's panoptic system of surveillance, see Boreth Ly, *Traces of Trauma: Cambodian Visual Culture and National Identity in the Aftermath of Genocide* (Honolulu: University of Hawaii Press, 2020), 59–61.

25. Ratner, *In the Shadow of the Banyan*, 227.

26. Ibid., 246.

27. Ibid., 141.

28. Ibid., 277–278.

29. Ibid., 298.

30. Ibid., 296.

31. Randle C. DeFalco, "Justice and Starvation in Cambodia: The Khmer Rouge Famine," *Cambodia Law and Policy Journal* 2 (2014): 48–49.

32. Puar, *Right to Maim*, 152.

33. Defalco, "Justice and Starvation," 49.

34. Helen Meekosha, "Decolonising Disability: Thinking and Acting Globally," *Disability and Society* 26, no. 6 (2011): 677.

35. Puar, *Right to Maim*, 89.

36. Alexandra Smith, "Long Beach Journal: Eyes That Saw Horrors Now See Only Shadows," *New York Times*, September 8, 1989, accessed March 27, 2022, available at https://www.nytimes.com/1989/09/08/us/long-beach-journal-eyes-that-saw-horrors-now-see-only-shadows.html.

37. Smith, "Long Beach Journal"; for more on this case, see Lee Siegel, "Cambodians' Vision Loss Linked to War Trauma," *Los Angeles Times*, October 15, 1989, accessed January 20, 2022, available at https://www.latimes.com/archives/la-xpm-1989-10-15-mn-232-story.html.

38. Puar, *Right to Maim*, 36.

39. *ekleipsis,* directed by Tran, T. Kim-Trang (United States: Tran, T. Kim-Trang, 1998); Fiona I. B. Ngô, "Sense and Subjectivity," *Camera Obscura* 26, no. 1 (2011): 95–129, 117.

40. Ngô, "Sense and Subjectivity," 113–114.

41. Vaddey Ratner, "A Conversation with Vaddey Ratner on *In the Shadow of the Banyan*," *Vaddey Ratner*, accessed August 12, 2019, available at https://vaddeyratner.com/banyan/q-a.

42. For more on Kingston's and Lorde's blending of myth and autobiography, see Maxine Hong Kingston's *The Woman Warrior: Memoirs of a Girlhood among Ghosts* (New York: Knopf, 1976); Audre Lorde, *Zami: A New Spelling of My Name—A Biomythography* (New York: Crossing, 1982).

43. Krys Lee, "*In the Shadow of the Banyan* by Vaddey Ratner—Review," *The Guardian*, September 29, 2012, accessed January 20, 2022, available at https://www.theguardian.com/books/2012/sep/29/in-shadow-banyan-vaddey-ratner-review.

44. Howard W. French, "Coming of Age in Cambodia," *Wall Street Journal*, August 26, 2012, accessed March 27, 2022, available at https://www.wsj.com/articles/SB10000872396390444423704577576060047775918.

45. Saidiya Hartman, "Venus in Two Acts," *Small Axe* 12, no. 2 (2008): 1–14.

46. Ratner, "A Conversation,".

47. Ratner, *In the Shadow of the Banyan*, 310.

48. Ibid., 315.

49. David T. Mitchell and Sharon L. Snyder, *Narrative prosthesis: Disability and the Dependencies of Discourse* (Ann Arbor, MI: University of Michigan Press, 2014), 9.

50. Viet Thanh Nguyen, *Nothing Ever Dies: Vietnam and the Memory of War* (Cambridge, MA: Harvard University Press, 2016), 88.

51. Panh, *The Missing Picture.*

52. Jacques Derrida, *Specters of Marx: The State of the Debt, the Work of Mourning, and the New International,* trans. Peggy Kamuf (New York: Routledge, 1994), 9.

53. Derrida, *Specters of Marx*, 9.

54. Panh, *Missing Picture.*

55. Ibid.

56. Hartman, "Venus in Two Acts," 5.

57. Ibid.

58. Ibid., 7.

59. Merri Lisa Johnson and Robert McRuer, "Cripistemology," 135.

60. Panh, *The Missing Picture*.

61. Ibid.

62. Ibid.

63. Ibid.

64. Johnson and McRuer, "Cripistemology," 130.

65. Panh, *Missing Picture*.

66. Ibid.

67. A. Naomi Paik, *Rightlessness: Testimony and Redress in U.S. Prison Camps since World War II* (Chapel Hill: University of North Carolina Press, 2016), 141.

68. Puar, *The Right to Maim*, 152.

69. Ibid., 147.

70. Panh, *Missing Picture*.

71. Ibid.

72. Ibid.

73. This is the description of the film on the website of IMDb and various others, see "The Missing Picture," *IMDb*, accessed March 30, 2021, available at https://www.imdb.com/title/tt2852470/.

74. Hartman, "Venus in Two Acts," 5.

75. Panh, *Missing Picture*.

76. Ibid.

77. Ibid.

78. Ibid.

79. For more on Sarith Mang, see Tobias Grey, "Cambodia's Oscar Contender," *Wall Street Journal*, February 24, 2014, accessed March 27, 2022, available at https://www.wsj.com/articles/SB10001424052702303945704579391220487019860.

80. Panh, *The Missing Picture*.

81. Rithy Panh, "Busan: Cambodia's Rithy Panh on His Cannes Winner 'The Missing Picture' (Q&A)," interview with the *Hollywood Reporter*, October 6, 2013, accessed January 20, 2022, available at https://www.hollywoodreporter.com/news/busan-cambodias-rithy-panh-his-643788.

82. Panh, "Busan."

83. Nguyên-Vo Thu-Huong, "Forking Paths: How Shall We Mourn the Dead?" *Amerasia Journal* 31, no. 2 (2005): 159.

84. Panh, *Missing Picture*.

85. Ibid.

86. Ibid.

87. Ibid.

88. Ibid.

89. For more on Chum Kem, see Alex Benson, "The Rise and Fall of Cambodian Rock and Roll," *Loop and Replay*, July 30, 2018, accessed January 20, 2022, available at https://medium.com/loopandreplay/the-rise-and-fall-of-cambodian-rock-and-roll-825a09fea07a.

90. Panh, *Missing Picture*.

91. Ibid.

92. Vandy Kaonn, *Cambodge 1940–1991, ou, la politique sans les Cambodgiens: essai* (Paris: L'Harmattan, 1993).

93. Rithy Panh, *One Evening after the War* (Compagnie Méditérranéenne de Cinéma, 1998), film.

94. Svay Sareth, *Head & Power* (Siem Reap, Cambodia: Batia Sarem Art Gallery, 2018), sculpture.

95. "Sustainable Textile Innovations: Flocus™ Kapok Fibres." Flocus.pro, April 2019, accessed March 27, 2022, available at https://www.flocus.pro/post/sustainable-textile-innovations-kapok-fibres.

96. Sally Ho, "This Shanghai Startup Transforms Kapok Trees into Sustainable Textiles." *Green Queen*, August 6, 2021, accessed March 27, 2022, available at https://www.greenqueen.com.hk/flocus-kapok-tree-sustainable-textile/.

97. Sopheap Pich, "Kapok," 2021, sculpture, Phnom Penh, Cambodia, accessed January 20, 2022, 2021, available at https://sopheap-pich.com/work/.

98. Sopheap Pich, "Sopheap Pich," interview by Brainard Carey, *Interviews with Brainard Carey*, Museum of Non-Visible Art, April 19, 2021, accessed March 27, 2022, available at https://museumofnonvisibleart.com/interviews/sopheap-pich/.

99. Ibid.

100. Ibid.

101. Ibid.

102. Ibid.

CHAPTER 4

1. Susan Sontag, *Illness as Metaphor* (New York: Farrar, Straus and Giroux, 1978), 3.

2. Fiona I. B. Ngô, "Sense and Subjectivity," *Camera Obscura* 26, no. 1 (2011): 95–96.

3. Ngô, "Sense and Subjectivity," 99.

4. Eli Clare, *Exile and Pride: Disability, Queerness, and Liberation* (Durham, NC: Duke University Press, 2015).

5. Clare, *Exile and Pride*, xxiv.

6. Sami Schalk, "Interpreting Disability Metaphor and Race in Octavia Butler's 'The Evening and the Morning and the Night,'" *African American Review* 50, no. 2 (2017): 141.

7. Schalk, "Interpreting Disability Metaphor."

8. See Louise Steinman, "The Aphasia Book Club," *LARB Quarterly Journal*, no. 6 (Summer 2015), accessed October 3, 2020, available at http://www.kerrytribe.com/media/2011/03/The-Aphasia-Book-Club-The-Los-Angeles-Review-of-Books.pdf.

9. Kai Cheng Thom, "The Myth of Mental Health." *DSM: Asian American Edition. Asian American Literary Review* 7, no. 2 (Washington, DC: Asian American Literary Review, 2016): 4–12.

10. Thom, "The Myth of Mental Health," 9.

11. Antonio R. Damasio, "Aphasia," *New England Journal of Medicine* 326, no. 8 (1992): 531.

12. Oliver Sacks, *The Mind's Eye* (New York: Knopf, 2010), 57.

13. Sacks, *Mind's Eye*, 58.

14. Ibid., 55.

15. Oliver Sacks, *The Man Who Mistook His Wife for a Hat* (London: Picador, 1986), 3.

16. Sacks, *Man Who Mistook*.

17. Sigmund Freud, *On Aphasia: A Critical Study*, first published in German in 1891, trans. E. Stengal (New York: International University Press, 2011).

18. Michel Foucault, *Psychiatric Power: Lectures at the College de France, 1973–74*, trans. Graham Burchell, ed. Jacques Lagrange, François Ewald, and Alessandro Fontana (London: Palgrave Macmillan, 2006), 304.

19. Foucault, *Psychiatric Power*, 303.

20. Sacks, *Man Who Mistook*, 3.

21. Ibid.

22. For more on the "biopolitics of plasticity," see Kyla Schuller and Jules Gill-Peterson, "Introduction: Race, the State, and the Malleable Body," *Social Text* 38, no. 2 (June 2020): 1–17.

23. Catherine Malabou quoted in Brenna Bhandar and Jonathan Goldberg-Hilliter, "Interview with Catherine Malabou," in *Plastic Materialities: Politics, Legality, and Metamorphosis in the Work of Catherine Malabou*, ed. Brenna Bhandar and Jonathan Goldberg-Hiller (Durham, NC: Duke University Press, 2015), 298–299.

24. Catherine Malabou, *The New Wounded: From Neurosis to Brain Damage*, trans. Steven Miller (New York: Fordham University Press, 2012), 184.

25. Ann Laura Stoler, *Duress: Imperial Durabilities in Our Times* (Durham, NC: Duke University Press, 2016), 166.

26. Stoler, *Duress*, 123.

27. Ibid., 157.

28. Ibid., 167.

29. Ibid., 168.

30. Rey Chow, *Not Like a Native Speaker: On Languaging as a Postcolonial Experience* (New York: Columbia University Press, 2014), 2.

31. Chow, *Not Like a Native Speaker*, 2.

32. Ibid., 15.

33. This tendency is also seen in the work of P. Khalil Saucier and Tryon P. Woods (*Conceptual Aphasia in Black: Displacing Racial Formation* [Lanham, MD: Lexington Books, 2016]), who use the term "conceptual aphasia in black" to describe limitations of academic discourse. They target some strands of contemporary critical race studies, such as racial formation theory, that continue to exhibit an inability to confront the "specter of black historical struggle" (2). Saucier and Woods define "conceptual aphasia in black" as the "silencing of blackness within contemporary thinking on race and how this occlusion is but a manifestation of the larger occlusion of slavery from contemporary analytics and the ongoing trauma of antiblack sexual violence" (5). The inability to address the foundations of slavery constitutes a conceptual aphasia that has marked contemporary critical race studies.

34. Cathy J. Schlund-Vials, *War, Genocide, and Justice: Cambodian American Memory Work* (Minneapolis: University of Minnesota Press, 2012), 13.

35. Schlund-Vials, *War, Genocide, and Justice*, 162, 17.

36. Cheryl Glenn, *Unspoken: A Rhetoric of Silence* (Carbondale: Southern Illinois University Press, 2004), 12.

37. Glenn, *Unspoken*, 12.

38. Frantz Fanon, *The Wretched of the Earth*, trans. Constance Farrington (New York: Grove, 1963), 303.

39. Fanon, *Wretched of the Earth*, 56.

40. Ibid., 249.

41. Achille Mbembe, *Necropolitics* (Durham, NC: Duke University Press, 2019), 146.

42. Mbembe, *Necropolitics*, 146.

43. Ibid.

44. Tsitsi Dangarembga, quoted in Madeleine Thien, "An Interview with Tsitsi Dangarembga," *Brick: A Literary Journal* 91 (August 1, 2013), accessed March 27, 2022, available at https://brickmag.com/an-interview-with-tsitsi-dangarembga/.

45. See Han Kang, *The Vegetarian*, trans. Deborah Smith (London: Hogarth, 2016).

46. Jiayang Fan, "Han Kang and the Complexity of Translation," *New Yorker*, January 18, 2018, accessed March 27, 2022, available at https://www.newyorker.com/magazine/2018/01/15/han-kang-and-the-complexity-of-translation.

47. Han Kang, "While the U.S. Talks of War, South Korea Shudders," *New York Times*, October 7, 2017, accessed January 23, 2022, available at https://www.nytimes.com/2017/10/07/opinion/sunday/south-korea-trump-war.html.

48. Madeleine Thien, "The Closing Down of Personhood," *Walrus Talks*, May 3, 2014, McCord Museum, Montreal, available at https://www.youtube.com/watch?v=JbrSA8jDOlE.

49. Thien, "Closing Down of Personhood."

50. Madeleine Thien, *Dogs at the Perimeter* (Toronto: Vintage Canada, 2011), 121.

51. Eli Clare, *Brilliant Imperfection* (Durham, NC: Duke University Press, 2017), 112.

52. Clare, *Brilliant Imperfection*.

53. Ibid.

54. Thien, *Dogs at the Perimeter*, 10.

55. Ibid., 12.

56. Ibid., 12.

57. Ibid., 15.

58. Ibid., 15.

59. Ibid., 14.

60. Ibid., copyright page.

61. See Peter Aldous, "Boléro: 'Beautiful Symptom of a Terrible Disease,'" *New-Scientist*, April 7, 2008, accessed March 27, 2022, available at https://www.newscientist.com/article/dn13599-bolero-beautiful-symptom-of-a-terrible-disease/.

62. Aldous, "Boléro."

63. Ibid.

64. Thien, *Dogs at the Perimeter*, 12.

65. Ibid.

66. Marco Roth, "The Rise of the Neuronovel," *n+1*, no. 8 (Fall 2009), accessed January 23, 2022, available at https://nplusonemag.com/issue-8/essays/the-rise-of-the-neuronovel/.

67. Roth, "The Rise of the Neuronovel."

68. Ibid.

69. Ibid.

70. Eric Tang, *Unsettled: Cambodian Refugees in the New York City Hyperghetto* (Philadelphia: Temple University Press, 2015), 62–63.

71. Yến Lê Espiritu, *Body Counts: The Vietnam War and Militarized Refugees* (Berkeley: University of California Press, 2014), 22.

72. Jasbir K. Puar, *The Right to Maim: Debility, Capacity, Disability* (Durham, NC: Duke University Press, 2017), xv.

73. Thien, *Dogs at the Perimeter*, 15.

74. Ibid., 18.

75. Ibid., 15.

76. Ibid., 139.

77. Ibid., 153.

78. Ibid., 137.

79. Philip Marchand, "Open Books: *Dogs at the Perimeter* by Madeleine Thien," *National Post*, May 6, 2011, accessed March 27, 2022, available at https://nationalpost .com/afterword/open-book-dogs-at-the-perimete.

80. Thien, *Dogs at the Perimeter*, 137.

81. Ibid., 37.

82. Ibid., 24.

83. Ibid., 23.

84. Ibid., 24.

85. Ibid., 7.

86. David Eng, *The Feeling of Kinship: Queer Liberalism and the Racialization of Intimacy* (Durham, NC: Duke University Press, 2010), 122.

87. Eng, *Feeling of Kinship*.

88. Ibid.

89. Thien, *Dogs at the Perimeter*, 22.

90. Ibid., 21.

91. Judith Butler, *Frames of War: When Is Life Grievable?* (London: Verso, 2009), 28.

92. Puar, *Right to Maim*, 19.

93. Ibid., xix.

94. Ibid., xv.

95. Caroline Levine, *Forms: Whole, Rhythm, Hierarchy, and Network* (Princeton, NJ: Princeton University Press, 2015), 2.

96. Levine, *Forms*, 122.

97. Ibid., 2.

98. Patrick Jagoda, *Network Aesthetics* (Chicago: University of Chicago Press, 2016), 44.

99. Jagoda, *Network Aesthetics*, 41, 8.

100. Ibid., 10.

101. Ibid., 41.

102. Thien, *Dogs at the Perimeter*, 245.

103. Ibid., 170.

104. Ibid., 18.

105. Ibid., 186.

106. Ibid., 80.

107. Sydney H. Schanberg, "Bomb Error Leaves Havoc in Neak Luong," *New York Times*, August 9, 1973, accessed March 27, 2022, available at https://www.nytimes

.com/1973/08/09/archives/bomb-error-leaves-havoc-in-neak-luong-us-bomb-error
-leaves-havoc.html.

108. Mbembe, *Necropolitics*, 100.

109. Thien, *Dogs at the Perimeter*, 93.

110. Ibid., 177.

111. Gilles Deleuze and Félix Guattari, quoted in Puar, *Right to Maim*, 64.

112. Puar, *Right to Maim*, xviii.

113. James K. Boehnlein and J. David Kinzie, "The Effect of the Khmer Rouge on the Mental Health of Cambodia and Cambodians," in *Cambodia's Hidden Scars: Trauma Psychology in the Wake of the Khmer Rouge*, ed. Beth Van Schaak, Daryn Reicherter, and Youk Chhang (Phnom Penh: Documentation Center of Cambodia, 2011), 38.

114. Daryn Reicherter, "Introduction," in *Cambodia's Hidden Scars*, ed. Van Schaak, Reicherter, and Chhang, 2.

115. Reicherter, "Introduction," 8.

116. Devon Hinton, Alexander Hinton, Kok-Thay Eng, and Sophearith Chhoung, "PTSD Severity and Key Idioms of Distress among Rural Cambodians: The Results of a Needs Assessment Survey," in *Cambodia's Hidden Scars*, ed. Van Schaak, Reicherter, and Chhang, 49.

117. Thien, *Dogs at the Perimeter*, 183.

118. Sorya's punishment for writing letters to her husband James in Thien's novel is reminiscent of the historical figure Hout Bophana, the subject of Elizabeth Becker's biography, *Bophana: Love in the Time of the Khmer Rouge* (Phnom Penh: Cambodia Daily Press, 2010).

119. Thien, *Dogs at the Perimeter*, 210.

120. The novel's assumption of the historical plausibility of Japanese Canadian migration to Canada, particularly to Vancouver, British Columbia, in the 1950s, has been the subject of criticism by some commentators, as Japanese citizens were largely barred from emigrating to Canada during this period. Nonetheless, the Canadian government's legal restrictions on Japanese Canadian movement, which had been in place since 1942, were officially lifted on April 1, 1949, meaning some migration from Japan to Canada during the 1950s was historically plausible. For more on this point, see Guy Beauregard, "Interwoven Temporalities: Reading Madeleine Thien's *Dogs at the Perimeter*," *Studies in Canadian Literature / Etudes en literature Canadienne* 39, no. 2 (2014): 181.

121. Thien, *Dogs at the Perimeter*, 182.

122. Earlier examples of the military targeting whole cities and civilians include the bombing of Coventry, England, by the Nazis, in 1940, and the bombing of Dresden, Germany, by the Western Allies, in 1945. While these cities have completed extensive reconciliation processes, critics in Japan and elsewhere continue to decry the U.S. firebombing of Tokyo as war crimes. See Joseph Coleman, "1945 Tokyo Firebombing Left Legacy of Terror, Pain," *Seattle Times*, March 9, 2005, accessed January 23, 2022, available at https://www.seattletimes.com/nation-world/1945-tokyo-firebombing-left -legacy-of-terror-pain/.

123. Matthew Carney, "Tokyo WWII Firebombing, the Single Most Deadly Bombing Raid in History, Remembered 70 Years On," *ABC News*, March 8, 2015, accessed January 23, 2022, available at https://www.abc.net.au/news/2015-03-09/tokyo -wwii-firebombing-remembered-70-years-on/6287486.

124. Rory Fanning, "The Firebombing of Tokyo," *Jacobin*, March 9, 2015, accessed January 23, 2022, available at https://www.jacobinmag.com/2015/03/tokyo-firebombing-world-war-ii/.

125. Lisa Lowe, "Reckoning Nation and Empire: Asian American Critique," in *A Concise Companion to American Studies*, ed. John Carlos Rowe (Malden, MA: Wiley-Blackwell, 2010), 240.

126. Thien, *Dogs at the Perimeter*, 43.

127. Ibid.

128. For more on confabulation, see Edwin A. Weinstein, "Linguistic Aspects of Amnesia and Confabulation," *Principles, Practices, and Positions in Neuropsychiatric Research* (1972), accessed April 29, 2021, available at https://www.sciencedirect.com/topics/neuroscience/confabulation, who defines confabulation as a "fictitious narration of some past event or events and, in brain injured subjects, it is most commonly elicited by questioning the patient about his injury or disability."

129. Thien, *Dogs at the Perimeter*, 45.

130. Ibid., 48.

131. Ibid.

132. Tanja Aho, Liat Ben-Moshe, and Leon J. Hilton, "Mad Futures: Affect/Theory/Violence," *American Quarterly* 69, no. 2 (June 2017): 300.

133. Sophie Liu, "Hidden Hate: Exposing the Roots of anti-Asian Racism in Canada," *Global News*, April 24, 2021, accessed March 27, 2022, available at https://globalnews.ca/news/7784170/hidden-hate-exposing-the-roots-of-anti-asian-racism-in-canada/.

134. Eric Fish, "35 Years after Vincent Chin's Murder, How Has America Changed?" *Asia Society*, June 16, 2017, accessed March 27, 2022, available at https://asiasociety.org/blog/asia/35-years-after-vincent-chins-murder-how-has-america-changed.

135. For more on racism and the persecution of ethnic minorities during the Cambodian Genocide, see Ben Kiernan, *Blood and Soil: A World History of Genocide and Extermination from Sparta to Darfur* (New Haven, CT: Yale University Press, 2009).

136. Aho, Ben-Moshe, and Hilton, "Mad Futures," 292.

137. Hannah Arendt, "We Refugees," in *The Jewish Writings*, ed. Jerome Kohn and Ron H. Feldman (New York: Schocken Books, 2007), 264.

138. Arendt, "We Refugees," 265.

139. Ibid., 270.

140. Ibid., 268.

141. Madeleine Thien, "Alice Munro Country," *Globe and Mail*, October 5, 2017, accessed March 27, 2022, available at https://www.theglobeandmail.com/news/national/canada-150/fiction-story-of-canada-madeleine-thien/article36364937/.

142. Thien, "Alice Munro Country."

143. Ibid.

144. M. NourbeSe Philip, "Black W/Holes: A History of Brief Time," in "Writing Black Canadas," guest ed. Phanuel Antwi and David Chariandy, special issue, *Transition: The Magazine of Africa and the Diaspora* 124 (2017): 133.

145. Thien, "Alice Munro Country."

146. Ibid.

147. Ibid.
148. Philip, "Black W/Holes," 125.
149. Thien, "Alice Munro Country."
150. Dionne Brand, *Map to the Door of No Return: Notes to Belonging* (Toronto: Vintage Canada, 2001), 200.
151. Brand, *Map to the Door*, 201.
152. Thien, "Alice Munro Country."
153. Ibid.
154. Arendt, "We Refugees," 268.
155. Ibid.
156. Thien, "Alice Munro Country."
157. Ibid.
158. Ibid.
159. Ibid.
160. Ibid.
161. Clare, *Brilliant Imperfection*, 13.
162. Thien, "Alice Munro Country."
163. Ibid.
164. Ibid.
165. Clare, *Brilliant Imperfection*, 130.
166. Ibid.
167. Thien, "Alice Munro Country."
168. Ibid.
169. Ibid.
170. For more on "paper daughters" or "paper sons" and the history of Asian immigration to North America, see Estelle T. Lau, *Paper Families: Identity, Immigration Administration, and Chinese Exclusion* (Durham, NC: Duke University Press, 2006). There has been little scholarly research done on this phenomenon in relation to Southeast Asian refugee history, although, anecdotally, I know of many cases of refugee children, including members of my own extended family, that came to Canada or the United States as paper children.
171. Thien, "Alice Munro Country."
172. For more on stroke, aphasia, and the brain penumbra, see Alexandre Croquelois, Max Wintermark, Marc Reichhart, Reto Meuli, and Julien Bogousslavsky, "Aphasia in Hyperacute Stroke: Language follows Brain Penumbra Dynamics," *Annals of Neurology* 54, no. 3 (September 2003).
173. Chris Riley, Douglas Niven, David Chandler, Sara Colm, Choeung Pochin, Moeun and Chhean Narriddh, *The Killing Fields: Photographs from the S-21 Death Camp* (Twin Palms Publishers, 1996).
174. Chris Riley quoted in Kerry Tribe, "The Aphasia Poetry Club," 2015, excerpt from video installation, originally presented at 356 Mission, Los Angeles, CA, accessed January 23, 2022, available at http://www.kerrytribe.com/project/the-loste-note-2/the-aphasia-poetry-club/#video.
175. Kerry Tribe, quoted in Rita Gonzalez, "Artists at Work: Kerry Tribe," *East of Borneo*, July 13, 2015, accessed May 14, 2020, available at https://eastofborneo.org/articles/artists-at-work-kerry-tribe/.
176. Tribe, quoted in Gonzalez, "Artists at Work."

177. Leslie Cozzi, "Metaphor to Métier: Kerry Tribe's 'Aphasia Poetry Club' and the Discourse of Disability in Contemporary Art," *Arts* 9, no. 2 (2020), accessed May 14, 2020, available at https://www.mdpi.com/2076-0752/9/2/49/htm.

178. Cozzi, "Metaphor to Métier."

179. Ibid.

CODA

1. Lisa Yoneyama, *Cold War Ruins: Transpacific Critique of American Justice and Japanese War Crimes* (Durham, NC: Duke University Press, 2016), 152.

2. For more on parallels between the wars in Cambodia and Iraq, see Ben Kiernan, "'Collateral Damage': from Cambodia to Iraq," *Forum on the American Invasion of Iraq*, accessed June 1, 2018, available at https://gsp.yale.edu/sites/default/files/collateral _damage_from_cambodia_to_iraq.pdf.

3. Simeon Man, *Soldiering through Empire: Race and the Making of the Decolonizing Pacific* (Oakland: University of California Press, 2018), 8.

4. Mary Dudziak, *War Time: An Idea, Its History, Its Consequences* (Oxford: Oxford University Press, 2012), 5.

5. Nikhil Pal Singh, *Race and America's Long War* (Berkeley: University of California Press, 2017), 3.

6. Viet Thanh Nguyen, "When I began writing the book I'm working on, the U.S. had just killed Nurto Kusow Omar Abukar, a teenage girl, describing her as a 'terrorist'," Facebook, August 13, 2021, accessed January 23, 2022, https://www.facebook .com/vnguyen1/posts/10109150481623305.

7. Ibid.

8. Ronak Kapadia, *Insurgent Aesthetics: Security and the Queer Life of the Forever War* (Durham, NC: Duke University Press, 2019), 14.

9. Taylor Owen and Ben Kiernan, "Bombs over Cambodia," *The Walrus*, October 12, 2006, accessed March 27, 2022, https://thewalrus.ca/2006-10-history/.

10. See David Corn, "'Vice' Director Adam McKay Talks about Dick Cheney's Love Affair with Power," *Mother Jones*, January 8, 2019, accessed January 23, 2022, available at https://www.motherjones.com/politics/2019/01/adam-mckay-interview -vice-dick-cheney-iraq-george-bush/. In this interview, *Vice* director Adam McKay explains that a scene in the film in which Richard Nixon and Henry Kissinger discuss the U.S. bombing of Cambodia becomes a Rosetta stone for understanding the U.S. war in Iraq.

11. According to Andrew Mumford (*Proxy Warfare* [Malden, MA: Polity, 2013]), a proxy war is "the indirect engagement in a conflict by third parties wishing to influence its strategic outcome" (1). Proxy wars "are the logical replacement for states seeking to further their own strategic goals yet at the same time avoid engaging in direct, costly and bloody warfare" (11).

12. See Elizabeth Becker's interview with *Cambodia Daily* about the parallels between Cambodia and Afghanistan, "កម្មវិធី Idea Talk សម្រាប់រាត្រីថ្ងៃទី ២៨ ខែសីហា ឆ្នាំ២០២១," *The Cambodia Daily TM*, August 24, 2021, accessed January 23, 2022, YouTube video, available at https://www.youtube.com/watch?v=3QI8EwxOzzU&t=727s.

13. Derek Gregory, "The Everywhere War," *Geographical Journal* 177, no. 3 (2011): 238–250.

Index

colonialism/imperialism, (*continued*)
4–10, 17, 19–23; subempires, xxvi; and
the transpacific, 24–26; U.S., x, xxiv,
xxvi, 15, 19–20, 22–25, 43, 53, 73–84,
90–91, 94–95, 105, 154–55, 173n2.
See also anti-imperialism; decoloniality;
neocolonialism; settler colonialism
communism, xxi, 63, 75, 117, 148, 157,
167; Chinese, 176n57; Khmer Rouge
and, xvi, xix, 20, 43, 124, 130, 154,
165; U.S. fear of, xiv, 20, 25, 27, 43, 72;
Vietnamese, 72. *See also* red scare
Communist Party of Kampuchea, xvi
comparative transpacific methodology,
xxvii
confabulation, 117, 156, 207n128
Conrad, Joseph: *Heart of Darkness*, 66
Coppola, Francis Ford: *Apocalypse Now*, 66
cosmopolitanism, 37, 128
Coventry, England, UK, 206n122
Crawford, Neta C., 174n21
crimes against humanity, xxv, 108. *See also*
Cambodian Genocide; war crimes
criminalization, 21, 23, 67, 96–97, 102,
139, 143
crip Cambodian refugee archive, 24
crip displacement, 101–2
crip economy, 89
cripistemologies, 13, 35–36, 42, 44, 109–
11, 118, 121, 123, 166
crip of color critique, 19
crip theory/studies, 35, 43, 109–10, 121
crip willfulness, 23
critical disability studies, 6, 12–13, 16, 23,
114, 157; and methodology of book, 10,
14, 18, 24, 42, 67, 109–10, 137–38
critical refugee studies, 16, 18, 24, 67
critical theory, 4, 141
culture of passivity/violence thesis, 57–58,
108–9, 190n45, 198n2
Czechoslovakia, 110

Damasio, Antonio, 139
dance, 38, 69, 82, 128; apsara, 39, 59–62,
124–**25,** 129
Dangarek Mountains, xxiii
Dangarembga, Tsitsi, 144
Das, Veena, 11
da Silva, Denise Ferreira, xxviii

Day, Iyko, 21
DC-Cam, 38
DDT, xviii
deaf gain, 14
deathworlds, 9–10
debility, xxiii, 12–15, 24, 28, 42, 56, 66, 166;
and aphasia, 4, 107, 148–56; and kapok
trees, 109–11, 114, 121–24, 130; and U.S.
bombing of Cambodia, 43, 71–106
debility dollar, 89
debt, 23; and disability/debility, 100, 104;
and gift of freedom, 19–20, 97, 150; and
imperialism, 26, 60, 105
decerebralizing, 143
decoloniality, xi, 15, 26, 54, 143
DeFalco, Randle, 114
deindustrialization, xvi
Deleuze, Gilles, 153
Democratic Kampuchea, xvi, xix–xx, 49,
58, 79, 106, 112, 114, 116, 122, 154, 157,
176n55
dengue fever, xxi
Denmark, 110
deportation, 12, 67, 196n99; of refugees,
21, 26, 43, 74, 93, 94–104, 184n105
deportation diaspora, 95
depressed Cambodian refugee trope, 11
Derrida, Jacques, 119, 142
detention, 21, 70, 94, 97
development, 67, 73, 100, 130, 132–33,
190n38; under-, 50, 86
disability, 6, 66, 100, 183n88, 207n128;
and aphasia, 35–36, 42, 44, 135–64;
and capitalism, 24, 88, 93, 104; and
colonialism/imperialism, 12–13, 14–15,
23–24, 35, 43, 73, 77, 89, 93–94,
166; and genocide, 12, 35, 43, 72–73,
107–34; and kapok trees, 32, 35, 43,
107–34; and the Khmer Rouge, 43, 75,
111–16, 135; as metaphor, 137–38; and
refugees, 10–15, 18–19, 28, 43, 67, 166;
southern, 13; and trauma, 10–14, 73, 97,
114; and U.S. bombing of Cambodia,
43, 71–106. *See also* ableism; aphasia;
crip Cambodian refugee archive;
crip displacement; crip economy;
cripistemologies; crip of color critique;
crip willfulness; critical disability studies;
madness; sanism

Johnson, Merri Lisa, 35, 89, 110–11, 121
Johnson, Samuel, 140
Jorai People, 22
just war paradigm, 19, 72

K-15, xviii
Kaing Guek Eav (Duch), xvii, xxv
kamleang chet (emotional resistance), xvi, 32, 108, 114, 117, 123
Kampong Thom, Cambodia, 23, 32, 45, 68–69, 71–72, 105, 132, 134, 164–65
Kandal Province, Cambodia, **x**
Kaonn Vandy, 129
Kapadia, Ronak, 167
kapok trees: and aphasia, 28–34; and disability, 32, 35, 43, 107–34
Kbach Khmer graffiti, **39**
Kem, Chum: "Kampuchea Twist," 127
Kem Nova, 134
Kent State University, xiv, 52, 85, 174n23
KGB, xvii
Khao-I-Dang Holding Center (KID), xxi–**xxii**, 1, 1–**3,** 70, 94–95, 170
Khiev, Kosal: *Cambodian Son,* 43, 73–74, 93–**104;** "Love U I," 103; "Moments in between the Nights," 99, 197n125; "Take Me Home," 104
Khmer (language), xiii, xvi, 2, 32, 43, 69, 80, 82, 108, 158, 192n14
Khmer cripistemology, 35, 118, 121, 123
Khmer culture, xxi, 32, 36–42, 58–62, 82, 115–16, 125–28, 130–31, 134, 154
Khmer Exiled American community, 94, 103
Khmer Leu, 22
Khmer people, xxv, 22, 28, 49, 60, 104
Khmer proverbs, 28–36, 43, 107–34. *See also* kapok trees
Khmer renaissance, 36–42, 130
Khmer Rouge, 22, 131, 142, 164, 167, 199n16; attacks on artists, 38, 117; and Cambodian passivity trope, 57–58, 108–9; Chinese support for, 169, 176n57; and communism, 20, 63; and disability/debility, 43, 75, 111–16, 135; in *Dogs at the Perimeter,* 152–57; and genocide, xxii–xxv, xxvii, 12, 26–28, 49, 65–66, 79, 96–97, 118–29, 152–53, 169–71, 191n72; in Kampong Thom, 105–6;

labor camps under, 99, 135; and Lon Nol army, 50–51, 71; in *The Missing Picture,* 118–29; in *One Evening after the War,* 130; in Phnom Penh, xv, 165, 168; recruiting children, 193n21, 193n23; and refugees, xiii, xxiii, 1, 72, 149; resistance to, xxvi, 58, 108–9, 121–24; in *S-21,* 49–50, 119; sexual violence under, xvii; in *In the Shadow of the Banyan,* 111–18; in *Shiiku,* 75–83; and surveillance, 34, 112, 199n24; survival of, 17, 23, 32, 45; tribunal for, xxiii–xxv, 26, 49; and U.S. bombings, xiii, xv, 57, 75, 103, 105–6, 169; and Vietnamese invasion, xx, 68; Western support for, xix–xx, 51. *See also* Angka; Angkar; Cambodian Genocide
Khmer Rouge Tribunal. *See* Extraordinary Chambers in the Courts of Cambodia (ECCC)
Khmer-Soviet Poly Technic Institute, xviii
Khuê Ninh, erin, 52, 183n83
Kiernan, Ben, xii, 79, 167
Killing Fields, xi, xix, 20, 51, 64–66, 97, 100–102, 116, 154, 163, 169
Killing Tree, xix, 65–66. *See also* Choeung Ek
Kim, Christine, 25
Kim, Jodi, xxvii, 105
Kingston, Maxine Hong, 116, 200n42
Kissinger, Henry, xii, 209n10; Kissinger telecons, 42, 50, 53–56, 95
Kitamura, Keiko, xviii
KK, 98, 101, 103
Kong Sam Oeun, 37
Kong Som Eun, 134
Korea, 73; North, 25, 144; South, 86, 144
Korean Americans, 150
Korean War, 87, 144, 166
Kosal, Ros, xiii, xviii, 191n72
Kulikar, Sotho: *The Last Reel,* 37
Kuy People, 22–23

Lake Huron, 48, 158
landmines, xxiii, 90
Laos, xiii–xiv, 25, 52, 54, 70, 152, 166, 174n22
Lee Kuan Yew, 37
Lê Espiritu, Yến, 16, 24, 148
Lee Xiao Long, 134

neuronovels, 147
New Cold War, 17
New Faces GOP, 20
New Haven, USA, 74
New York Times, 15, 56–57, 115, 144, 153
New Zealand, 170
Ngô, Fiona I. B., 115, 137–38
Ngor Haing S., 26
Nguyen, Mimi Thi, 19, 96–97
Nguyen, Viet Thanh, 24, 40, 119, 167, 179n8; "The Americans," 43, 73–74, 85–93; *The Refugees*, 85
Nguyen, Vinh, 16, 103
9/11, 19
Niven, Douglas, 162
Nixon, Richard, xii, xiv, 53–56, 72, 153, 169, 174n15, 174n21, 209n10
Nixon, Rob, 40, 87–88
nongovernmental organizations (NGOs), xxvi, 57–58, 88–89
Norindr, Panivong, 59
Norway, 110
Nuremburg trials (International Military Tribunal), xxv
Nyers, Peter, 196n100

Ocasio-Cortez, Alexandria, 20
occupation, xx–xxi, 24, 62, 73–74, 76, 87, 93, 115
Oceania studies, 25
Oceanic studies, 25
Oe, Kenzaburo, 86; *Shiiku*, 74–75, 87, 192n15
Ohio, USA, xiv
Ohio National Guard, xiv
Okinawa, Japan, 86
Ong, Aihwa, 12
Ontario, Canada, 48, 69, 135, 139, 158
ontoepistemology, 35, 44, 187n147
ontology, 5, 35, 113–15, 119, 123, 139, 153, 187n147
open secret, xiii, 52, 134
Operation Freedom Deal (1970–73), xii, 174n21
Operation Menu (1969–70), xii, 174n21
orientalism, xix, 42, 62
orphans, xvi
Oscars, xx
Ōshima, Nagisa: *The Catch*, 192n15

Ottawa, Canada, 7
outer wars, 74, 90–91, 167, 195n81
Owen, Taylor, xii, 79, 167

Pacific Century, 24
Pacific Islands, 25
Pacific Ocean, x, xxvii, 22–23, 24–26, 167, 173n2. *See also* transpacific
Pacific region, x
Pacific Rim, 22, 24–25
Pacific studies, 25
Paik, Naomi, 27, 123
Pailin, Cambodia, xiii–**xiv**
Palestine, 36; Gaza, 73, 89; West Bank, 12, 73
Panh Rithy, xvii, xxi, 88–89; *The Elimination*, xi, 42, 49, 119; *The Missing Picture*, xx, 41, 43, 49, 108–9, 118–29, 173n7; *One Evening after the War*, 129–30; *S-21: The Khmer Rouge Killing Machine*, 49, 119; *Shiiku, the Catch*, 43, 73–86, 90, 92, 94, 118–19, 192n14, 193n23
panopticon, 34, 112, 186n142, 199n24
Pan Ron, 129, 134
Papanek, Victor, 80
paper children, 136, 161, 208n170
Parliament Hill, Ottawa, 7, 9
patriarchy, 91, 130, 144
Patterson, Christopher, 185n116
Patterson, William, 73
Peah Hanuman, 134
Pear People, 22
Pentagon, 19, 90, 180n25
permanent war, 9, 44, 56, 130, 166–67. *See also* forever war
Philip, M. NourbeSe, 159
Philippines, 132
Phnom Penh, Cambodia, xvii–xviii, 57, 59, 88, 102, 105, 126, 127, 129, 132–33, 154, 162; bombardment of, 50–**51**; Khmer Rouge in, xv, 58, 165, 168; orphanages in, xvi; pre-war era, 37–38, 126, 134; refugees in, xiii, 72, 94
Phousera, Ing, xvi
Phumi O Pou, Cambodia, 23
Pich Sopheap: "Kapok," 132–**33**
Piepzna-Samarasinha, Leah Lakshmi, 179n8

Y-Dang Troeung is Assistant Professor of English at the University of British Columbia.

Also in the series *Asian American History and Culture*:

Sucheng Chan, ed., *Chinese American Transnationalism: The Flow of People, Resources, and Ideas between China and America during the Exclusion Era*

Rajini Srikanth, *The World Next Door: South Asian American Literature and the Idea of America*

Keith Lawrence and Floyd Cheung, eds., *Recovered Legacies: Authority and Identity in Early Asian American Literature*

Linda Trinh Võ, *Mobilizing an Asian American Community*

Franklin S. Odo, *No Sword to Bury: Japanese Americans in Hawai'i during World War II*

Josephine Lee, Imogene L. Lim, and Yuko Matsukawa, eds., *Re/collecting Early Asian America: Essays in Cultural History*

Linda Trinh Võ and Rick Bonus, eds., *Contemporary Asian American Communities: Intersections and Divergences*

Sunaina Marr Maira, *Desis in the House: Indian American Youth Culture in New York City*

Teresa Williams-León and Cynthia Nakashima, eds., *The Sum of Our Parts: Mixed-Heritage Asian Americans*

Tung Pok Chin with Winifred C. Chin, *Paper Son: One Man's Story*

Amy Ling, ed., *Yellow Light: The Flowering of Asian American Arts*

Rick Bonus, *Locating Filipino Americans: Ethnicity and the Cultural Politics of Space*

Darrell Y. Hamamoto and Sandra Liu, eds., *Countervisions: Asian American Film Criticism*

Martin F. Manalansan IV, ed., *Cultural Compass: Ethnographic Explorations of Asian America*

Ko-lin Chin, *Smuggled Chinese: Clandestine Immigration to the United States*

Evelyn Hu-DeHart, ed., *Across the Pacific: Asian Americans and Globalization*

Soo-Young Chin, *Doing What Had to Be Done: The Life Narrative of Dora Yum Kim*

Robert G. Lee, *Orientals: Asian Americans in Popular Culture*

David L. Eng and Alice Y. Hom, eds., *Q & A: Queer in Asian America*

K. Scott Wong and Sucheng Chan, eds., *Claiming America: Constructing Chinese American Identities during the Exclusion Era*

Lavina Dhingra Shankar and Rajini Srikanth, eds., *A Part, Yet Apart: South Asians in Asian America*

Jere Takahashi, *Nisei/Sansei: Shifting Japanese American Identities and Politics*

Velina Hasu Houston, ed., *But Still, Like Air, I'll Rise: New Asian American Plays*

Josephine Lee, *Performing Asian America: Race and Ethnicity on the Contemporary Stage*

Deepika Bahri and Mary Vasudeva, eds., *Between the Lines: South Asians and Postcoloniality*

E. San Juan Jr., *The Philippine Temptation: Dialectics of Philippines–U.S. Literary Relations*

Carlos Bulosan and E. San Juan Jr., eds., *The Cry and the Dedication*

Carlos Bulosan and E. San Juan Jr., eds., *On Becoming Filipino: Selected Writings of Carlos Bulosan*

Vicente L. Rafael, ed., *Discrepant Histories: Translocal Essays on Filipino Cultures*

Yén Lê Espiritu, *Filipino American Lives*

Paul Ong, Edna Bonacich, and Lucie Cheng, eds., *The New Asian Immigration in Los Angeles and Global Restructuring*

Chris Friday, *Organizing Asian American Labor: The Pacific Coast Canned-Salmon Industry, 1870–1942*

Sucheng Chan, ed., *Hmong Means Free: Life in Laos and America*

Timothy P. Fong, *The First Suburban Chinatown: The Remaking of Monterey Park, California*

William Wei, *The Asian American Movement*

Yến Lê Espiritu, *Asian American Panethnicity*

Velina Hasu Houston, ed., *The Politics of Life*

Renqiu Yu, *To Save China, To Save Ourselves: The Chinese Hand Laundry Alliance of New York*

Shirley Geok-lin Lim and Amy Ling, eds., *Reading the Literatures of Asian America*

Karen Isaksen Leonard, *Making Ethnic Choices: California's Punjabi Mexican Americans*

Gary Y. Okihiro, *Cane Fires: The Anti-Japanese Movement in Hawaii, 1865–1945*

Sucheng Chan, *Entry Denied: Exclusion and the Chinese Community in America, 1882–1943*

www.ingramcontent.com/pod-product-compliance
Lightning Source LLC
Chambersburg PA
CBHW051435270326
41935CB00019B/1829